ROOKWOOD FAMILY PAPERS, 1606–1761

ROOKWOOD FAMILY PAPERS, 1606–1761

Edited by
FRANCIS YOUNG

General Editor
JOY ROWE

The Boydell Press

Suffolk Records Society
VOLUME LIX

A Suffolk Records Society publication
First published 2016
The Boydell Press, Woodbridge

ISBN   978-1-78327-080-4

Issued to subscribing members for the year 2015–2016

The Boydell Press is an imprint of Boydell & Brewer Ltd
PO Box 9, Woodbridge, Suffolk IP12 3DF, UK
and of Boydell & Brewer Inc.
668 Mt Hope Avenue, Rochester, NY 14620–2731, USA
website: www.boydellandbrewer.com

The publisher has no responsibility for the continued existence or accuracy of URLs for
external or third-party internet websites referred to in this book, and does not guarantee that
any content on such websites is, or will remain, accurate or appropriate

A catalogue record for this book is available
from the British Library

This publication is printed on acid-free paper

Printed and bound by CPI Group (UK) Ltd, Croydon, CR0 4YY

CONTENTS

LIST OF ILLUSTRATIONS

PREFACE AND ACKNOWLEDGEMENTS

The Rookwoods of Coldham Hall, in the parish of Stanningfield (five miles south of Bury St Edmunds), were one of Suffolk's most prominent Catholic families – and certainly the most notorious. Two members of the family were executed for high treason, almost exactly a century apart, and for many years at a time the Rookwood patrimony was imperilled by attainders, enforced banishment and crippling recusancy fines. It is nothing short of remarkable, therefore, that the Rookwoods managed to survive all this and, by means of marriage alliances, emerged as the wealthiest of Suffolk's Catholic families in the second half of the eighteenth century. The documents in this volume tell a story of survival, ingenuity and pragmatic self-re-invention by successive generations of the Rookwoods, from the execution of the Gunpowder Plot conspirator Ambrose Rookwood in 1606 to the death of Elizabeth Rookwood, his great-great-granddaughter, in 1759.

This volume complements my book *The Gages of Hengrave and Suffolk Catholicism, 1640–1767*, published by the Catholic Record Society (CRS) in 2015. Both that book and this one are largely based on the Hengrave manuscripts in Cambridge University Library; and my analysis of the Catholic community in Bury St Edmunds and West Suffolk in *The Gages of Hengrave* forms the context for understanding Catholicism in the region in the seventeenth and eighteenth centuries. Having said that, the present volume also stands on its own, since the 'spheres of influence' of the Gages and Rookwoods were geographically separate (north and south of Bury St Edmunds respectively), and the two families were not joined by marriage until 1718. I am grateful to the CRS for allowing me to present my preliminary findings on the Rookwoods in the form of a paper at their annual conference in 2011, 'In the Shadow of Treason: The Rookwood Family, 1606–1760', and for the helpful comments I received from CRS members at that time. Michael Hodgetts's guidance on the hiding places at Coldham Hall was especially useful.

First and foremost, however, I owe a debt of gratitude to Joy Rowe for her helpful comments and editing, as well as for allowing me to draw on her seemingly boundless knowledge of the history of Catholicism in Suffolk. All of my work on East Anglian Catholic history is founded on her pioneering work in the field. I also thank the original readers of the manuscript for their helpful and constructive comments and support for this project, especially Professor Diarmaid MacCulloch, Kt., and Carys Brown who asked me for help with her undergraduate dissertation on Thomas Rookwood in 2012, but ended up helping me just as much as I aided her, since she allowed me to clarify the exact chronology of Thomas Rookwood's career. I have also benefitted from correspondence with Captain Alfred Dillon on the Rookwoods of Euston, and I thank him for sharing his genealogical research.

Dr Simon Johnson of Downside Abbey and the staff of the Manuscripts and Rare Books Rooms at Cambridge University Library, the National Archives at Kew and the Suffolk Record Office, Bury St Edmunds, were unfailingly helpful throughout my research. I acknowledge with thanks the permission of the Syndics of Cambridge University Library to reproduce the dust-jacket image and colour plates I, II, IV, V and VI, and black-and-white Plate 6. I am likewise grateful to Moyse's Hall Museum, Bury St Edmunds, for permission to reproduce the painting of Sir Robert Rookwood in Plate III and to Loyola University Museum of Art, Chicago, for permission to reproduce black-and-white Plate 1. I am grateful to Mike Durrant for contributing his excellent photographs for plates III, 3 and 5 and for laying out the Rookwood family tree. I thank the Bury St Edmunds Past and Present Society for permission to reproduce Plate 4 and the Suffolk Record Office for Plate 2. I owe a special debt of gratitude to Dr Patrick Zutshi, keeper of manuscripts and archives at Cambridge University Library, who in December 2014 arranged for the university to purchase the only known surviving manuscript from the library of Thomas Rookwood, the Rookwood Book of Hours, after I had spotted it for sale at Sotheby's.

This volume is dedicated to my wife, Rachel Hilditch, in gratitude for the love of Suffolk's history that first brought us together.

Ely, Cambridgeshire
February 2015

ABBREVIATIONS

Allison and Rogers	A. F. Allison and D. M. Rogers (eds), *Catalogue of Catholic Books in English Printed Abroad or Secretly in England 1558–1640* (Bognor Regis, 1956), 2 vols
BBKS	F. Blom, J. Blom, F. Korsten and G. Scott (eds), *English Catholic Books 1701–1800: A Bibliography* (Aldershot, 1996)
Bedingfield Papers	*Miscellanea VI: Bedingfield Papers, &c* (London, 1909), CRS 7
Bury Register	Jesuit mission register for Bury St Edmunds, 1756–89
Catalogue	Anon., *A Catalogue of the Whole of the Very Interesting and Historical Contents of Hengrave Hall, Bury St Edmunds* (London, 1897)
Clancy	T. H. Clancy, *English Catholic Books 1641–1700: A Bibliography* (Chicago, Illinois, 1974)
CPCC	M. A. Green (ed.), *Calendar of Proceedings of the Committee of Compounding, 1643–1660* (London, 1889–92), 5 vols
CRS	Catholic Record Society
CSPD	*Calendar of State Papers, Domestic Series*
CUL	Cambridge University Library
Diary	Diary of Alexius Jones OSB, 1732–43, CUL Hengrave MS 69
EANQ	*East Anglian Notes and Queries*
Foley	H. Foley, *Records of the English Province of the Society of Jesus* (London, 1877–83), 8 vols
Hearth Tax	S. H. A. Hervey (ed.), *Suffolk in 1674, being the Hearth Tax Returns* (Woodbridge, 1905)
Hengrave Register	Benedictine mission register for Hengrave and Bury St Edmunds, 1734–51
HMC	Historical Manuscripts Commission
LJ	Journals of the House of Lords
Lords MSS	Various eds, *The Manuscripts of the House of Lords* (London, 1887–1977)
New Grove	*New Grove Dictionary of Music and Musicians* (Oxford, 2001), 29 vols
ODNB	*Oxford Dictionary of National Biography* (Oxford, 2004), 60 vols
OFM	Order of Friars Minor (Franciscans)
OSA	Order of St Augustine (Augustinian Canonesses)

OSB	Order of St Benedict (Benedictines)
OSC	Order of St Clare (Poor Clares)
PCC	Prerogative Court of Canterbury
PSIA(H)	*Proceedings of the Suffolk Institute of Archaeology (and History)*
RFP	Rookwood Family Papers
SJ	Society of Jesus (Jesuit)
SRO(B)	Suffolk Record Office, Bury St Edmunds
SRS	Suffolk Records Society
TNA	The National Archives, Kew

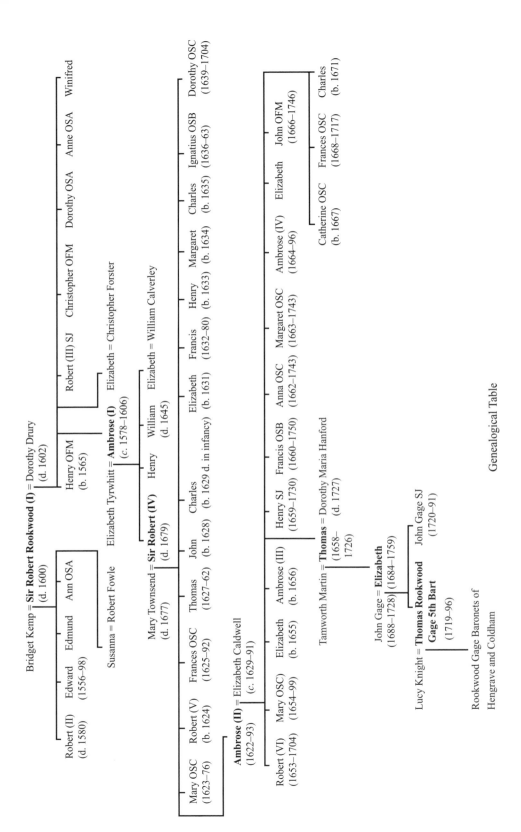

Genealogical Table

INTRODUCTION

In 1619 the compiler of the Rookwood family pedigree remarked that 'there is no famyly of so long a continewance, which hath not often mett w[i]th the turnynge vicissitude of this woorldes revolution; as sometymes to be alofte in the gaze of the woorld, & sometymes to be caste downe so lowe as that it can scarce be p[er]ceyved'.[1] The Rookwoods were acutely aware of the turning wheel of fortune. On account of their passionate adherence to the Roman Catholic faith (and later the Jacobite cause in politics) they found themselves pushed to the margins of seventeenth-century England (or even out of it altogether). The family had endured persecution long before Ambrose Rookwood was hanged, drawn and quartered in Old Palace Yard for his part in the Gunpowder Plot on 31 January 1606. However, Ambrose's death as a traitor was an unprecedented challenge to the Rookwoods' ingenuity and resilience. It also gave the family, quite literally, a bad name. Shakespeare may even have played on it in *Macbeth* (Act 3, Scene 2, lines 55–8):[2]

> Light thickens, and the crow
> Makes wing to th'rooky wood:
> Good things of day begin to droop and drowse,
> Whiles night's black agents to their preys do rouse.

The tragic story of Ambrose's devotion to Robert Catesby, and Ambrose's violent death, have undoubtedly made him the best known member of the Rookwood family. That story is not, however, the subject of these documents, the earliest of which dates from twenty years after Ambrose's death. Their focus is on the survival and recovery of the Rookwood family of Stanningfield, a story no less remarkable than the exploits of the man who put the family's future in jeopardy. The magistrates William Walde-grave and John Heigham, who ransacked Coldham Hall for incriminating writings on 10 November 1605, were probably responsible for the destruction of all family documents predating the Gunpowder Plot, and the somewhat precarious nature of the Rookwoods' existence at Coldham Hall in the years after the plot may explain the absence of any significant documents between 1606 and 1636.

The documents in this volume chronicle the family's struggle to rebuild its fortune

---

[1] CUL Hengrave MS 76/1; J. Gage (ed.), 'Pedigree and Charters of the Family of Rookwood' in *Collectanea Topographica et Genealogica* (London, 1835), vol. 2, pp. 120–47, at p. 121.

[2] C. Asquith, *Shadowplay: The Hidden Beliefs and Coded Politics of William Shakespeare* (New York, 2005), p. 216. Rebecca Lemon, in *Treason by Words: Literature, Law and Rebellion in Shakespeare's England* (Ithaca, NY, 2006), p. 86, has argued that Shakespeare quoted the words of Sir Edward Coke's condemnation of Ambrose Rookwood in his description of the Thane of Cawdor 'as one that had been studied in his death'.

and estates by means of legal ploys to avoid penal legislation, the trials of undeserved exile, the accoutrements of piety and Catholic worship, and one of the largest libraries of Catholic books in mid-eighteenth-century England. The Rookwoods were thrust into the limelight of history again at the end of the seventeenth century, when a second Ambrose Rookwood was executed for high treason for his part in the Barclay conspiracy to assassinate William of Orange. Ambrose's death produced an acrimonious dispute between two of his brothers, and seems to have led the family to abandon overt support for the Jacobite cause. In the early eighteenth century the family finally encountered a greater threat than the hangman's noose when Thomas Rookwood failed to produce a male heir. The last of the Rookwoods, and the woman whose character emerges the most clearly from these documents, was the highly educated and enterprising Elizabeth Rookwood, who died in 1759 (Plate V).

The documents

The majority of the documents included in this volume were originally part of a collection at Coldham Hall (Plate II) organised in the early nineteenth century by Sir Thomas Rookwood Gage, 7th Baronet of Hengrave (d. 1807) and later by his brother, the antiquary John Gage (1786–1842). John inherited Coldham Hall and its documents in 1838;[3] when he died in 1842 Sir Thomas Gage, 8th Baronet (1810–66) rented Coldham to tenants and the Rookwood Family Papers joined the papers of the Kytson and Gage families in the evidence room at Hengrave Hall. When Sir John Wood bought Hengrave Hall and its contents in 1897 the Rookwood manuscripts were included in the auction catalogue as lot 1431, 'Music Book belonging to the Rokewood Family, neatly written with notes, 1600, and other manuscripts: a parcel'.[4]

The Rookwood Family Papers remained at Hengrave until the death of Sir John Wood. In 1952 the entire contents of Hengrave Hall were sold, and Sir John's insurers became the owners of the manuscripts. The Suffolk County Record Office acquired by purchase all of the Kytson, Gage and Rookwood manuscripts relating to land ownership and inheritance (1, 2 and 3 in this volume), including indentures, maps and deeds. The remainder of the manuscripts, including all personal papers, were deposited for safekeeping in Cambridge University Library, but remained the property of the insurers. Cambridge University Library purchased all of the Hengrave manuscripts for £2.5 million in 2005 to ensure that the collection would continue to be available to researchers.[5] Within the Hengrave manuscripts, the Rookwood Family Papers are covered by the series numbers 76 and 77 (although several items have strayed into other series).

In addition to those documents in Cambridge and Bury St Edmunds that once formed part of the family collection at Coldham, I have chosen to include in this volume a number of documents from external collections, since these fill important gaps in the family's history. Although these were not 'Rookwood family papers', in the sense that they were not owned by the Rookwoods, they are documents that are important to the history of the family. They include extracts from printed texts (6, 9),

3   'Obituary: John Gage Rokewode, Esq.', *The Gentleman's Magazine* (December 1842), pp. 660–1.
4   *Catalogue*, pp. 104–7. There were in fact two music books from the mid-seventeenth century; these were the music books reused for the biobibliography (30) and the inventory (31).
5   'Hengrave Hall manuscripts saved', *Cambridge University Library Readers' Newsletter* 34 (October 2006).

cases from the Court of Chancery now held in the National Archives at Kew (**16, 18, 19**) and, in one case, the records of a religious order (**29**).

Hitherto the most important printed source on the Rookwood family has been John Gage's 1835 edition of the first part of the *Vetustissima Prosapia Rookwodorum de Stanningefilde, in Comitatu Suffolciae*, consisting of family trees and transcribed documents to 1619 and a list of family births to 1720.[6] The transcriptions of later family documents added to the *Vetustissima Prosapia* by Sir Thomas Gage, 7th Baronet in the early nineteenth century were ignored by John Gage the antiquary and have remained unpublished until now, although in 1818 John Gage did produce a manuscript genealogical summary focusing on the later Rookwoods (**37**). In 1863 the antiquary Samuel Tymms wrote an article on the Rookwoods that drew heavily on John Gage's published work and skimmed over the later history of the family. There is no evidence that Tymms ever consulted the actual family papers, which were then at Hengrave.[7] Two short articles by John Pickford on Ambrose Rookwood and his family appeared in 1889 and 1903,[8] but the first substantial work on the family was done by Edmund Farrer (1848–1945), vicar of Hinderclay.

Between 1903 and 1906 Farrer paid several visits to Sir John Wood at Hengrave Hall in the course of preparing his book *Portraits in Suffolk Houses (West)* (1908), and took notes on the Rookwood family documents.[9] He also visited Coldham Hall in 1904 when it was owned by Colonel H. T. Trafford-Rawson, in order to photograph the house and its portraits. He visited again in 1918 when the house was sold to a Colonel Hambro. In the 1920s Farrer wrote a fairly extensive article on the Rookwoods and Coldham, based on his notes, for the *East Anglian Miscellany*.[10] The present volume is the first publication since Farrer's article to concentrate specifically on the Rookwood family.

The Rookwood family

The Rookwoods of Stanningfield were the senior branch of an ancient Suffolk family. The anonymous author of the *Vetustissima Prosapia* repeated a family legend in which the ancestor of the family played William the Conqueror at chess and won by outflanking the king with rooks.[11] This fanciful etymology for the surname was probably inspired by the family's coat of arms (Plate I).[12] The first documentary evidence for the name is found in 1301; Alan de Rokewode took his name from the manor of Rokewodes in the parish of Acton (which much later came into the

6   Gage (1835), pp. 120–47. The births of all members of the family were recorded in this book from 1622, together with the saint's day in the Catholic calendar, down to the births of Thomas Rookwood Gage in 1719 and John Gage in 1720. Thomas Rookwood wrote, at some point thereafter, 'I leave th[i]s book to my Hair & desier he, & his Hairs will Continue to sett downe the family as itt increaseth.'

7   S. Tymms, 'Coldham Hall in Stanningfield', *PSIA* 3 (1863), pp. 299–310. The years after 1606 are covered on pp. 305–7.

8   J. Pickford, 'The Rookwood Family of Coldham Hall, Suffolk', *Notes and Queries* 206 (1889), pp. 442–3; J. Pickford, 'Ambrose Rookwood', *Notes and Queries* 267 (1903), pp. 115–16.

9   SRO(B) HD526/123/2 (Farrer's notes).

10 E. Farrer, 'Coldham Hall and the Rookwoods', *East Anglian Miscellany* 6671 (1920s newspaper cutting, now SRO(B) HD526/123/6). A lecture on the Jesuit mission in Bury St Edmunds and West Suffolk by John Ashton, SJ, was published as 'Jesuit Fathers to leave Bury', *The Bury and Norwich Post*, 23 September 1927, p. 10.

11 Gage (1835), p. 122.

12 Argent, six chess rooks sable.

ownership of the Catholic Daniell family, friends of the Rookwoods).[13] The manor of Stanningfield was purchased by Sir John de Rokewode of Stoke-by-Nayland from Richard de Ileigh in 1357, and became the seat of the principal branch of the family.[14] Stanningfield parish church bears much heraldic evidence of Rookwood patronage in the fourteenth and fifteenth centuries. In the mid-fourteenth century a branch of the Rookwoods, descended from the marriage of Robert de Rokewode and Margaret de Buers, settled at Euston.[15] The Euston Rookwoods, who were also Catholic recusants from 1559, could compete with the Stanningfield Rookwoods in the number of sons and daughters they provided for seminaries, monasteries and convents on the Continent. Descendants of the Euston Rookwoods produced further branches of the family in England,[16] Massachusetts and Maryland.[17] However, the genealogical relationship between the Stanningfield and Euston Rookwoods was fairly remote, and it cannot be assumed that the families were close. From the Middle Ages the family name was generally spelt Rokewode, but by the seventeenth century the most common spelling was Rookwood (with variants such as Rookewode, Rookewood, Rockwood and Ruckwood still occasionally occurring). Since the subject of this book is the family in the seventeenth and eighteenth centuries, I follow the most common standard spelling of their surname in that era (Rookwood) in all references to the family, but I have made no attempt to correct variant spellings in quotations or in the documents themselves.

The later Rookwoods defined themselves by their adherence to Catholicism. Their medieval motto, *Tout est en Dieu* ('All is in God'), acquired a new resonance as they risked the loss of all in pursuit of a religious cause. Under the law, the Rookwoods were 'popish recusants', Catholics who absented themselves from divine service in their parish church, and were thus liable to financial penalties.[18] Both the Rookwoods of Stanningfield and their cousins at Euston were among the 116 individuals indicted

---

[13] Gage (1835), p. 124.

[14] Ibid., p. 129; Tymms (1863), pp. 303–4.

[15] The Rookwoods of Euston were probably descended from the marriage of Robert de Rokewode and Margaret de Buers in the mid-fourteenth century (Gage (1835), p. 130).

[16] There were also Protestant Rookwoods; on 6 May 1629 Henry Rookewoode, son of Henry Rookewoode, gentleman of Weston matriculated at Gonville and Caius College, Cambridge (J. Venn, *Biographical History of Gonville and Caius College 1349–1897* (Cambridge, 1897), vol. 1, p. 289); the Weston Rookwoods descended from Firmin Rookwood (d. 1558), third son of Edward Rookwood of Euston (G. H. Ryan and L. J. Redstone, *Timperley of Hintlesham: A Study of a Suffolk Family* (London, 1931), n. p. 57). Edward Rookwood, son of Nicholas Rookwood of Hunston matriculated at Pembroke College on 19 May 1670 (J. Venn, *Alumni Cantabrigienses* (Cambridge, 1924), part 1, vol. 3, p. 485). In 1679 a government agent named Rookwood attempted to induce the secular priest John Sergeant to accuse his fellow Catholics (D. Krook, *John Sergeant and his Circle: A Study of Three Seventeenth-Century Aristotelians* (Leiden, 1993), pp. 134–7).

[17] I am grateful to Alfred Dillon for information on the Massachusetts Rookwoods, descended from Richard Rookwood who converted to Protestantism and emigrated in 1632. On Rookwoods in Maryland see H. W. Newman, *The Flowering of the Maryland Palatinate* (Washington DC, 1961), pp. 298; V. L. Skinner (ed.), *Abstracts of the Testamentary Proceedings of the Prerogative Court of Maryland* (Baltimore, Maryland, 2006), vol. 5, pp. 102, 115, 183; E. G. Jourdan, *Early Families of Southern Maryland* (Westminster, Maryland, 2007), vol. 9, p. 212; E. G. Jourdan (ed.), *Abstracts of Charles County Maryland Court and Land Records* (Westminster, Maryland, 1994), vol. 2, pp. 53, 67, 73.

[18] For an analysis of recusancy and church papistry, drawing on several East Anglian examples, see M. Questier, 'Conformity, Catholicism and the Law' in P. Lake and M. Questier (eds), *Conformity and Orthodoxy in the English Church, c. 1560–1660* (Woodbridge, 2000), pp. 237–61.

as recusants in Suffolk in 1559, the year of Queen Elizabeth I's Act of Uniformity.[19] Robert Rookwood (d. 1566) seems to have made some attempt at a show of conformity, attending Lawshall parish church but not receiving communion, but his wife Elizabeth Heigham does not seem to have done even this. The authorities noted that 'Mr. Rookewood receyveth not, his wif cometh not to churche'.

The Stanningfield Rookwoods were firmly aligned with the conservative religious faction in East Anglia from the start of Elizabeth I's reign, and their ties with other recusants and church papists were strengthened in 1562 when Sir Robert Rookwood (I) (d. 1600) married his second wife, Dorothy Drury.[20] Dorothy was the daughter of Sir William Drury of Hawstead (d. 1589), a well-connected courtier. However, Sir William's father had been a supporter of Queen Mary, along with other leading East Anglian families who cherished conservative views such as the Bedingfields, Cornwallises and Sulyards, and Sir William's second son Henry Drury of Lawshall (Robert Rookwood's brother-in-law) was an early recusant.[21] The Drurys were not alone in being a family divided by religion; Sir Robert Jermyn of Rushbrooke was a Puritan while his brother Ambrose was an 'obstinate papist'.[22]

The parishes of Hawstead and Lawshall were adjacent to Stanningfield,[23] and together these parishes were an early nexus of Catholic missionary activity, even before the arrival of John Gerard in 1589. At least two men associated with the Drurys and Rookwoods became missionary priests. William Hanse, alias Drayton, who was the brother of the martyr Everard Hanse, was reportedly at Coldham Hall in 1586, and was schoolmaster to the Drurys at Lawshall in 1595 (missionary priests frequently masqueraded as schoolmasters). In 1598 he became an assistant to the new Archpriest of England, George Blackwell.[24] Montford Scott, who was born at Hawstead, entered the English College at Douai in 1574. It is reasonable to assume that he enjoyed the patronage of the Drurys. He left before ordination and returned to England in 1576, where he was captured in Essex. Scott was released and returned to Douai in France, where he was ordained priest before coming back to England in June 1577. Scott was captured at Cambridge but released on bonds, but he soon became a wanted man. The authorities finally caught up with him at the house of William Kilbeck in his home village of Hawstead in December 1590. He was convicted of high treason for having received orders abroad from the Bishop of Rome and hanged, drawn and quartered in Fleet Street on 1 July 1591.[25]

Joy Rowe has drawn attention to the preponderance of Catholics in four areas of Suffolk in the late sixteenth and early seventeenth centuries: the western edge of the county (where the Rookwoods of Euston were located), High Suffolk, the town of Bury St Edmunds and 'a solid papist block' running south from Lawshall to Acton

---

[19] C. Talbot (ed.), 'Recusants in the Archdeaconry of Suffolk' in *Miscellanea* (London, 1961), CRS 53, pp. 108–11.

[20] Gage (1835), p. 140.

[21] P. Collinson, *From Cranmer to Sancroft* (London, 2006), p. 35; Gage (1835), p. 142; J. Rowe, 'Drury family' in *ODNB*, vol. 7, pp. 997–9.

[22] J. Rowe, 'Suffolk Sectaries and Papists, 1596–1616' in E. S. Leedham-Green (ed.), *Religious Dissent in East Anglia* (Cambridge, 1991), p. 39.

[23] Collinson (2006), p. 35. Lawshall was a centre of Puritan radicalism that employed its own unlicensed preacher.

[24] G. Anstruther, *The Seminary Priests: A Dictionary of the Secular Clergy of England and Wales, 1558–1850* (Ware, 1969–77), vol. 1, pp. 147–8.

[25] Ibid., p. 303.

and Long Melford.[26] Stanningfield fell, of course, within the 'solid papist block'. Five miles from Bury, it was also within reach of that town's Catholics. However, given the fact that the Rookwoods of Stanningfield owned estates in Essex and originated from Acton, it is not surprising that in their marriage alliances with the families of Drury of Hawstead, Caldwell of Essex and Martin of Long Melford they looked south rather than north. An indenture of 1639 (2) lists seventeen adjacent parishes in which the Rookwoods' trustees held a total of 1,600 acres.[27] If these landholdings still remained just before the Civil War, we can imagine that the extent of the family's lands seventy years previously would have been even more impressive.

The lands that the Rookwood family had built up since the fourteenth century made the family a wealthy one, and in 1574–75 Robert Rookwood (I) built a new house, Coldham Hall, in the parish of Stanningfield. Coldham is an H-shaped house of red brick that served as a headquarters for the Superior of the Jesuits in England, John Gerard, from the summer of 1589 until the winter of 1591.[28] Gerard described Coldham as 'a continual receptacle for priests and a place wherein many other Catholics did often find great spiritual comfort, the house being a very fair great house and [Robert Rookwood's] living very sufficient'.[29] But, by the close of the sixteenth century, Coldham was not the haven of piety and learning that it had once been. In 1606 Robert Forster, who was brought up at Coldham, reported that he 'learnt no other letters apart from what his mother taught him, except when, rarely, a priest used to give him help'.[30] Robert was born at Stanningfield in around 1587, the son of Christopher Forster of Copdock and Elizabeth, the eldest daughter of Sir Robert Rookwood (I) and Dorothy Drury. In 1612 Robert Forster's younger brother reported that he had also been brought up at Coldham.[31]

The chapel at Coldham at this time may be the one alluded to in a short newspaper article announcing the sale of the hall in 1918: 'The remains of another secret chapel are to be seen at the top of the house, wherein Mass was celebrated in private when it was illegal to do so publicly.' The article went on to claim that three hiding places existed in the house, 'two of which have trap-doors, one leading to a secret recess and the other to an apartment below'.[32] Michael Hodgetts visited Coldham Hall on 22 January 1982 and inspected one of these hiding places, which was located over the porch.[33] The existence of two more at Coldham has been widely reported, but has not been confirmed by modern investigation.[34] If these hiding places were built into

[26] Rowe (1991), p. 40.
[27] The parishes were Stanningfield, Whepstead, Hawstead, Brockley, Lawshall, Cockfield, Hartest, Whelnetham, Preston St Mary, Thorpe Morieux, Lavenham, Brettenham, Brent Eleigh, Monks Eleigh, Milden, Stoke-by-Nayland and Polstead.
[28] J. Gerard, *The Autobiography of an Elizabethan* (London, 1951), pp. 24–31.
[29] J. Gerard (ed. J. Morris), *The Condition of Catholics under James I: Father Gerard's Narrative of the Gunpowder Plot* (London, 1871), pp. 85–6.
[30] A. Kenny (ed.), *The Responsa Scholarum of the English College, Rome: Part I, 1598–1621* (London, 1962), CRS 54, pp. 177–8.
[31] Ibid., pp. 252–3.
[32] 'The Coldham Hall Estate', *Bury and Norwich Post*, 27 March 1918 (the newspaper cutting is SRO(B) HD526/123/5).
[33] M. Hodgetts, 'A Topographical Index of Hiding Places', *Recusant History* 16 (1982), p. 189. I am also grateful to Michael Hodgetts for his personal commentary on Coldham Hall.
[34] See A. Fea, *Secret Chambers and Hiding-Places* (London, 1908), pp. 60–1; A. Fea, *Rooms of Mystery and Romance* (London, 1931), p. 107; G. Squiers, *Secret Hiding-Places* (London, 1933), p. 192; J. Errand, *Secret Passages and Hiding-Places* (Newton Abbot, 1974), pp. 61–2.

the house during its construction in the 1570s they would count as early examples.

Patrick Collinson described the year 1578 as 'a watershed in East Anglian history' when the balance of power definitively slipped away from the religious conservatives and towards Protestant gentry.[35] On 9 August of that year Queen Elizabeth arrived at Euston Hall, the home of Robert Rookwood (I)'s distant cousin Edward Rookwood. Edward had been a signatory of the protestation of loyalty signed by several Catholic gentlemen denying the deposing power claimed by Pope Pius V in his Bull *Regnans in Excelsis* against Elizabeth.[36] However, when he kissed the queen's hand he was berated by the Lord Chamberlain for approaching her, since he was excommunicated on the grounds of recusancy. Later, while the queen was watching some country dancing, a statue of the Virgin Mary was found concealed in a hayrick; Elizabeth ordered it to be burned. Edward Rookwood was summoned to appear before the Bishop of Norwich (an unusual measure) and was imprisoned in the gaol in Bury St Edmunds.[37] By October 1588, when he made a protestation of loyalty to the queen before the Dean of Ely, Andrew Perne, Rookwood was one of the Catholic gentlemen imprisoned in the Bishop's Palace in Ely.[38] In 1589 he was obliged to pay a hefty fine of £940.[39] The humiliation of Edward Rookwood marked the beginning of a more aggressive attack on the recusants, which intensified in the aftermath of the Spanish Armada.

In October 1586 Robert Rookwood (I) was convicted of recusancy, the specific charge being that he had not attended church for three years and two months. Rookwood was fined a total of £1,360 and, when he failed to pay it, a commission was appointed to seize half of his lands and goods on 2 July 1587. On 2 November of the same year, half of Robert's lands were given over to the Crown to the yearly value of £102 14s. 5d. A further seizure on 21 September 1589 took land to the yearly value of £4 14s. and goods to the value of £16 16s. 8d. Robert (I) may have been imprisoned at Wisbech Castle in the 1590s, since in 1596 he was moved to the magistrate Sir John Heigham's house in Barrow, along with the widow of Henry Drury and priests transferred from Wisbech on account of an epidemic.[40] Heigham happened to be Robert Rookwood's first cousin (they shared a grandmother in Elizabeth Heigham).[41] On 20 April 1600, following Robert (I)'s death, his remaining lands were seized to the value of £190 a year until the arrears of recusancy fines should be paid (**1**). Ambrose (I) would have inherited little and he was, in effect, a tenant on his own land; this may explain why he took up horse breeding in order to gain an income. In 1603 there were seven male and four female recusants in the parish of Stanningfield, most of them probably members of the Rookwood family.[42]

Such severe financial persecution, combined with the family's early association with the Jesuits, strengthened the Rookwoods' resolve to resist the Elizabethan

---

[35] Collinson (2006), p. 33.

[36] J. Gage, *The History and Antiquities of Hengrave in Suffolk* (Bury St Edmunds, 1822), n. p. 248.

[37] Z. Dovey, *An Elizabethan Progress: The Queen's Journey into East Anglia, 1578* (Stroud, 1996), pp. 53–4.

[38] *Historical Manuscripts Commission 5th Report* (London, 1876), pp. 406–7; F. Young, 'The Bishop's Palace at Ely as a Prison for Recusants, 1577–1597', *Recusant History* 32 (2014), pp. 195–217, at pp. 216–17.

[39] G. Blackwood, *Tudor and Stuart Suffolk* (Lancaster, 2001), p. 115.

[40] Rowe (1991), p. 39.

[41] Gage (1835), p. 138.

[42] 'The Condition of the Archdeaconries of Suffolk and Sudbury in the Year 1603', *PSIA* 11 (1903), p. 7.

regime. Ambrose Rookwood (I) was one of the first pupils at the English Jesuit College at St Omer, in 1592–93, along with his brothers Christopher and Robert (both of whom became priests).[43] The conversion of nostalgic Marian Catholics to militant religion was John Gerard's mission, and by the 1590s the deference to authority shown by Edward Rookwood of Euston had given way to a revolutionary ideology of the pope's temporal supremacy, taught by some Jesuits. The anger, hatred and ideology that motivated the gunpowder plotters first took shape in the reign of Elizabeth. Such ideas would be regarded with horror by loyal Catholics before a few decades were out.

Ambrose Rookwood (I) (c. 1578–1606) and the Gunpowder Plot

As the fifth of Sir Robert Rookwood (I)'s sons it was originally unlikely that Ambrose (I) would inherit Coldham Hall. However, Sir Robert's eldest son by Bridget Kemp, Robert (II), was wounded in battle and died in Flanders in 1580. The second and third sons, Edward and Edmund, also predeceased their father.[44] Next in line to inherit was Henry Rookwood, Sir Robert's eldest son by his second wife, Dorothy Drury. Henry was tutored at Hawstead by a Mr Adams before matriculating at Gonville and Caius College, Cambridge, on 9 February 1579 (following his half-brother Edward).[45]

By the 1570s Cambridge was officially a seedbed of the English Reformation, but the Rookwood brothers' matriculation at Caius was not as surprising as it may seem. John Caius, the Norfolk-born physician who refounded the college as an emblem of Renaissance learning in the reign of Queen Mary, was a lifelong Catholic and the college remained a safe haven for Catholics even after his death in 1573, owing to the tolerance of the president, Richard Swale (Swale stood as surety to Henry Rookwood). Numerous Catholics, including the future Jesuit Provincial Richard Holtby, the martyr John Fingley and Edward Osburne were Henry's contemporaries at the college.[46] However, Henry belonged to the last generation of Catholic students at Cambridge; he was one of a number of students in the college who 'gathered themselves together to consult whether it were lawful to dissemble [their religion] any longer'.[47] In 1582 a small group of fellows brought eighty-eight charges against Swale and, although he was exonerated, the college could no longer be a refuge for Catholics.[48]

Henry Rookwood later became a Franciscan friar and lived at Rouen and Lisbon, naturally taking a vow of poverty.[49] Therefore, by indenture of 20 April 1599, the

---

[43] G. Holt (ed.), *St. Omers and Bruges Colleges, 1593–1773: A Biographical Dictionary* (London, 1979), CRS 69, pp. 224–5.

[44] Edward Rookwood attended Bury Grammar School and was admitted to Gonville and Caius College, Cambridge in 1574 aged eighteen (S. H. A. Hervey (ed.), *Biographical List of Boys educated at King Edward VI Free Grammar School, Bury St Edmunds from 1550 to 1900* (Bury St Edmunds, 1908), pp. 334–5).

[45] Ibid., p. 335. Edward matriculated on 26 April 1574 and was described as 'of Palgrave'. He was 'assigned the fifth lower cubicle in Gonville Court' and he was resident there in September 1575 (Venn (1897), vol. 1, p. 78, with a marginal annotation by Venn in the copy in CUL Rare Books Room, classmark RCS.Ref.Z.97–99).

[46] C. Brooke, *A History of Gonville and Caius College* (Woodbridge, 1985), pp. 88–9.

[47] Venn (1897), vol. 1, p. 100.

[48] Brooke (1985), p. 90.

[49] Another of Ambrose (I)'s brothers, Christopher, was also a Franciscan, described in the *Vetustissima Prosapia* as 'a frier at Madrid in Spaigne' (CUL Hengrave MS 76/1).

Rookwood estates were transferred to Henry's younger brother Ambrose (I).[50] Ambrose's half-sister Ann was the first of several members of the family to join the English Augustinian canonesses at their house of St Monica's, Louvain. In around 1599 Ambrose married Elizabeth, daughter of Sir Robert Tyrwhitt of Kettleby in Lincolnshire (another prominent recusant family). The couple had at least three sons, Robert (IV) (d. 1679), Henry and William, as well as a daughter, Elizabeth, who married a William Calverley (mentioned in Sir Robert Rookwood's will of 1673). Nothing further is known of Henry Rookwood and Elizabeth Calverley; however, Sir Thomas Gage, 7th Baronet thought that a Captain William Rookwood killed at Alresford in Hampshire in the service of King Charles during the Civil War was a younger son of Ambrose Rookwood (I).[51] The 'Mrs Wrookwood' living in a house with seven hearths in the parish of St James, Bury St Edmunds in 1674 may have been his widow.[52]

Although Ambrose (I)'s early encounters with Jesuits and his own Jesuit education imbued him with the radical ideals of the Counter-Reformation, his contact with recusants in London and the Midlands was the proximate cause of his decision to become involved in the Gunpowder Plot. As such, Ambrose's involvement in the plot had little relevance to the local Catholic community in Suffolk, and the plotters came from several counties. The only other individual from Suffolk who became involved, and was executed with Rookwood, was Henry Barrow, a member of the same Barrow family of Bures that produced the Puritan separatist Henry Barrow (*c.* 1550–93).[53] The Henry Barrow who died on the scaffold with Ambrose Rookwood (I) was Rookwood's distant cousin; his great-grandmother Anne Drury was the sister of Rookwood's grandfather, Sir William Drury (d. 1557).[54]

Ambrose Rookwood was apparently recruited to the Gunpowder Plot in the summer of 1604. The Jesuit Oswald Tesimond wrote that Rookwood 'enjoyed a very good income as head of the family, which was both distinguished and of long standing'. Coldham Hall 'was a common refuge for priests, as it had been in the time of his father. Here his catholic neighbours could go to the sacraments, and meet often to hear sermons and talks', in spite of regular 'official visitations'.[55] Tesimond concluded that Rookwood was chosen for inclusion in the plot because 'he kept good stables, his horses being the best in the land'. Horse breeding was an example of the entrepreneurial activity to which Rookwood was forced to turn in the aftermath of the confiscation of much of his father's lands. Tesimond described him as courageous and magnanimous, 'well-built and handsome if somewhat short. His manner was easy and cheerful. His dealings with people were gentlemanly and courteous.' He

50 See M. Nicholls, 'Rookwood, Ambrose' in *ODNB*, vol. 47, pp. 699–700.
51 CUL Hengrave 76/1.
52 *Hearth Tax*, p. 54.
53 P. Collinson, 'Barrow, Henry (*c.*1550–1593)', in *ODNB*, vol. 4, pp. 95–6. Robert Townsend of 'Brawghton Ashe, Suffolk' visited Rookwood at Clopton Park and was arrested, but he appears to have had no involvement in the plot (F. Edwards, *The Enigma of Gunpowder Plot, 1605: The Third Solution* (Dublin, 2008), p. 180).
54 For the relationship between Ambrose Rookwood and Henry Barrow and a family tree, see F. H. S., 'Henry Barrow and Ambrose Rookwood, Conspirators in the Gunpowder Plot', *EANQ* 11 (1906), pp. 145–6.
55 In November 1605 Thomas Rookwood of Clopton and Robert Townsend of Bury St Edmunds were among the priests arrested who were frequent visitors at Coldham Hall (Edwards (2008), p. 177). It seems likely that this Thomas Rookwood was a member of the Euston family.

added that Rookwood was well-educated, and alluded to his time at St Omer.[56]

Rookwood was close to Catesby and a participant in visible Catholic activities such as the pilgrimage to St Winifred's Well.[57] In the summer of 1604 Rookwood brought his horses from their stables at Coldham to Clopton Park near Stratford-upon-Avon, and at Michaelmas 1604 Rookwood purchased the barrels of gunpowder that were later placed in the cellars beneath the Palace of Westminster.[58] Until September, however, Rookwood apparently believed that all of this was part of military preparations for a campaign in Flanders. One evening, after requiring him to swear an oath on a primer, Catesby finally revealed the plot to Rookwood, who was horrified by it, declaring 'It is a matter of conscience to take away so much blood!' Tesimond was surprised that a man of Rookwood's character and learning could become part of the plot, and Francis Edwards has interpreted Rookwood's subsequent adherence to the plot as the only option available to him, having already been party to treason (knowing about treason and not reporting it was misprision of treason, almost as serious a crime as treason itself). Revealing the plot to the authorities might have meant Ambrose's own destruction, and he may have thought that he could moderate the aims of the plotters from within.[59]

On the exposure of the plot, Rookwood was the first of the conspirators to flee London, but he was apprehended in Staffordshire on 8 November 1605 and shot in the leg in the process.[60] Elizabeth Rookwood, his wife, was also arrested.[61] In Suffolk, however, the Justices of the Peace were still looking for Rookwood, unaware of his capture. On 10 November, William Waldegrave and John Heigham reported to the Privy Council that they had visited and ransacked Coldham Hall:

> We got the high constable of the hundred and some of our men to go to Edmund Cosen, a servant of his, where he was likely to go rather than to his own house, but we could not find him, neither have we found any writings or papers mentioning the intended treason, although we did break up cupboards, desks, and other places where writings were kept.[62]

On the scaffold, Ambrose proved the most contrite of the plotters, although he did pray that God would make the king a Catholic.[63] His family was left to suffer the legal and financial consequences of his attainder for high treason.[64] John Gage, writing in 1818 at a time when the campaign for the repeal of the penal laws was still being stalled by Parliament, adduced the mistreatment of the Tyrwhitt family, Ambrose's in-laws, as a mitigating circumstance for his involvement in treason: 'may not the mind of Ambrose Rookwood have been inflamed by the Severity with which the penal laws had been exercised against his Wife's relations? if thei had no operation, the reader shall draw what Conclusions he pleases' (**37**).

---

[56] O. Tesimond (ed. F. Edwards), *The Gunpowder Plot: The Narrative of Oswald Tesimond alias Greenway* (London, 1973), pp. 99–100.

[57] A. Fraser, *The Gunpowder Plot* (London, 1997), p. 145.

[58] Edwards (2008), p. 129. Edwards mistakenly identifies Ambrose Rookwood's mother as a Tyrwhitt when it was in fact his wife Elizabeth who belonged to the family.

[59] Ibid., pp. 130–1.

[60] Ibid., p. 232.

[61] Nicholls (*ODNB*), pp. 699–700.

[62] TNA, Gunpowder Plot Book fol. 78, cited by Edwards (2008), pp. 181–2.

[63] Fraser (1997), p. 233; Edwards (2008), p. 362.

[64] The Act of Attainder against Ambrose Rookwood (I), dated 8 May 1606, is now TNA E 178/4006.

Restoring fortunes: Sir Robert Rookwood (IV) (d. 1679)

All of Ambrose Rookwood (I)'s estates, with the exception of two parcels of land retained by his widow, Elizabeth, were seized by the Crown. In 1612 Elizabeth Rookwood's portion was also seized and granted to William Asshefield.[65] Her appeal against this in the Court of Chancery is one of the earliest documents in the Rookwood Family Papers. Elizabeth drew two large representations of the holy name of Jesus, 'IHS', on the parchment; this was the emblem of the Society of Jesus.[66] At around the same time, a grant of Ambrose's former lands was made to Lord Walden.[67] Coldham Hall remained a place of particular interest to the authorities, and the Jesuit Thomas Garnet may have been arrested on his way there in 1608.[68] Furthermore, the Rookwoods themselves remained under the surveillance of government agents. In 1613 a search was made 'at Mrs Rookwood's house' (presumably Coldham) for Alexander Fairclough (alias Pelsham), an agent in England of Marquis Don Piedro de Cuñiga. When Fairclough was captured and sent to Wisbech Castle, Elizabeth Rookwood sent a bed to him there.[69] The survival of Elizabeth Rookwood's rental book, beginning in 1613, demonstrates that the family's income from its inherited lands at this time was still considerable.[70]

On 23 August 1615 Bishop James of Durham wrote to Archbishop George Abbot, enclosing a report by an informant. Christopher Newkirk claimed that he 'Met in Yorkshire with Winter, Rokewood, and John, William and Tho[ma]s Digby, and Percy &c. After consultation, they agreed to admit him into their confidence, and told him they were authorized by the Pope to take vengeance for the martyrdom of their friends, on pretence of complicity in the Powder Treason.' Newkirk further reported that the conspirators 'had made three engines invented by Signor Alex[ander] Malatesto, who was commended to them by Marquis Spinola, and were going into Cardiganshire to try one of them'.[71] The Rookwood of this report was probably Ambrose (I)'s younger brother, the priest Robert Rookwood (III).[72] This supposed plot by surviving relatives of the gunpowder plotters does not seem to have been taken seriously by the government.

In 1618 the manors of Coldham, Philletts and Lawshall demised to Hugh Floyd and Thomas Wyse and were valued at £500.[73] However, in 1624 the Rookwoods were certainly living at Coldham; Sir Robert (IV)'s second son Robert (V) (b. 1624), on entering the English College in Rome in 1664 stated that he was born at Coldham

---

65 W. A. Copinger, *The Manors of Suffolk* (Manchester, 1910), vol. 6, p. 341.
66 CUL Hengrave MS 76/2/13.
67 *CSPD* 1611–18, p. 243.
68 Foley, vol. 5, p. 541.
69 Foley, vol. 4, p. 596.
70 CUL Hengrave MS 76/2/9.
71 *CSPD* 1611–18, p. 304.
72 Robert Rookwood (III) accompanied his brother Ambrose on pilgrimage to Holywell in August 1605; in 1624 he was described as 'a little black fellow, very compt and gallant, lodging about the midst of Drury-lane, acquainted with collapsed ladies' (P. Marshall and G. Scott (eds), *Catholic Gentry in English Society: The Throckmortons of Coughton from Reformation to Emancipation* (Farnham, 2009), p. 99). Robert Rookwood translated a life of the Scottish Capuchin Friar John Forbes (Angel of Joyeuse) in 1623 (M. Dilworth, 'Forbes, John (1570/71–1606)' in *ODNB*, vol. 20, pp. 294–5). He adopted the surname of his nephew Sir Robert Rookwood's wife Mary Townsend as an alias (Foley, vol. 1, p. 676). Robert died on 12 November 1668 having served for forty-two years as confessor to the Poor Clares at Rouen (CUL Hengrave MS 76/1).
73 *CSPD* 1611–18, p. 550.

and lived there until he was seven or eight years old. Thereafter he lived partly in London and partly at St Omer.[74] Sir Robert Rookwood (IV) was knighted by King James at Royston on 19 January 1624.[75] However, Sir Robert remained under close surveillance, and in around 1630 a report was made that 'Robert Keyes, son to that Keyes that was hanged at the Gunpowder Treason, [was] much in Suffolk at Sir Robert Rookwood's'.[76]

On 15 June 1636 Thomas Hughes, a lawyer acting on behalf of Sir Robert Rookwood, prepared a lengthy defence against 'Information' laid against his client in the Court of Chancery by Sir John Banks, the Attorney General (1). Although the document against which Hughes wrote has not survived, it seems to have made the following accusations:

1. Recusancy fines not paid by Robert Rookwood (I) and Ambrose Rookwood (I) were still owed by Sir Robert Rookwood.
2. Ambrose Rookwood (I) had vested his lands in a feoffment or trust after his first conviction for recusancy.
3. Sir Robert Rookwood concealed the truth that Ambrose's trust dated from after his conviction.
4. Sir Robert Rookwood conspired with Sir Phillip Tyrwhitt to defraud the Crown of recusancy fines due from the Rookwood estates by putting those estates in trust.
5. Sir Robert Rookwood was himself a recusant.

Sir John Banks's 'Information' claimed that when Ambrose (I)'s lands were seized in 1606 they could not be confiscated in entirety because some of them had been conveyed in a trust to Ambrose's brother-in-law, Sir Phillip Tyrwhitt. The point at issue was whether Ambrose created the trust before his first conviction for recusancy on 11 April 1605. If he did, then he had committed no fraud. Neither Sir John Banks nor Thomas Hughes seem to have had access to a report made into the confiscated estates in 1614, although Hughes asserted confidently that the records of Chancery would bear out his belief that the trust had been made before 11 April. Hughes pointed out, quite correctly, that even if a fraud had been committed Sir Robert could hardly be held responsible as he had been less than five years old in 1605.

However, the question of whether a trust existed in 1605 was academic, according to Hughes, because before 1615 Theophilus Howard, 2nd Earl of Suffolk, had persuaded King James to grant him Ambrose's lands. The Rookwoods bought off the Earl of Suffolk 'for a great Some' and, as a consequence, letters patent issued in 1615 granted the estate not to Suffolk but to Sir Phillip Tyrwhitt. The Court of Chancery ruled that the estates were free from the encumbrances of unpaid recusancy fines. Hughes claimed that since then Sir Robert had lived as a farmer on the lands belonging to Sir Phillip, receiving some financial support from his mother and paying an annual rent of £250. Apart from this rent, Sir Robert enjoyed all of the revenues of the estates as his own. On 13 October 1625, as part of a general enquiry into unpaid recusancy fines, the issue of Coldham arose again but Sir Phillip Tyrwhitt pleaded before Chancery that he had been discharged from these past dues. Chancery

74 Foley, vol. 5, p. 542.
75 Gage (1835), p. 143.
76 *CSPD* 1629–31, p. 429.

confirmed this, and did so again when the issue arose in 1627.

We do not have the other side of the argument, so the truth or otherwise of Thomas Hughes's story is hard to determine. Sir Robert Rookwood was certainly not landless in 1636.[77] However, it is clear that Sir Robert had no choice but to exploit the machinery of the law to its fullest extent in order to survive. Hughes claimed that Sir Robert 'had sixteen children and tenn of them living all young and utterly unprovided for. his wife nowe w[i]th childe and by gods blessinge like to have many more.' However, Sir Robert made no attempt to defend himself against a charge of recusancy directed against him personally, pleading simply that he had always submitted to the Crown and pointing out that 'his Ma[jes]t[y']s like graces and clemencye ... is offered and extended to other that are in this distressing like conditon by his Ma[jes]t[y']s most gracious Commission'. This was a pointed reference to the concessions that Charles I's government made to certain favoured recusants in the 1630s.[78] In effect, Sir Robert was requesting special treatment from a government whose enforcement of penalties against recusants had become increasingly lax.

In the same year in which he submitted his plea against the recovery of past recusancy fines Sir Robert served on a royal commission himself, demonstrating the extent to which he enjoyed normal gentry status in Suffolk, in spite of his eccentric financial arrangements. The commission's task was to investigate the feasibility of making the River Lark navigable between Mildenhall and Bury St Edmunds. Henry Lambe's navigation plan, which came to nothing before the Civil War,[79] was intended to reduce the price of overland carriage of goods from Worlington to Bury (then 3s 4d) by transporting goods by barges. The river route between King's Lynn and Mildenhall was already navigable, so the extension of the navigation to Bury raised the possibility that commodities such as coal could be brought directly from King's Lynn to Bury by water. However, Sir Roger North and Thomas Styward brought a suit against Lambe to prevent the work, which led the king to appoint commissioners. The commissioners produced two reports, a majority of five to three opposing Lambe's plan (Nicholas Bacon of Culford abstained).[80] They reported on 27 April 1636 that 'generally the work is much distasted and feared, and not desired by any, either of the county, or of the town of Bury'.[81]

The three commissioners who favoured the plan were Sir Charles Le Gros, Sir Robert Rookwood and William Buckworth. It is difficult to see how the navigation would have benefitted Sir Robert personally, given that his estates lay to the south of Bury St Edmunds, away from the River Lark. However, a project such as this,

---

[77] The will of Robert Hammond of Long Melford of 24 January 1629 refers to lands held by Sir Robert in that village (N. Evans (ed.), *The Wills of the Archdeaconry of Sudbury 1630–1635* (Woodbridge, 1987), SRS 29, p. 117).

[78] In 1623 when Prince of Wales, Charles had sworn an oath to ensure the complete toleration of Catholicism in England in the event of his marriage to the Spanish Infanta; although the Spanish marriage came to nothing, this event raised Catholic hopes (see A. Sánchez Cano, 'Entertainment in Madrid for the Prince of Wales: Political Functions of Festivals' in A. Samson, (ed.), *The Spanish Match* (Aldershot, 2006), p. 66). Some Catholics were elevated to high political office under Charles's rule and in their case de facto toleration was extended, for example Sir Thomas Savage of Long Melford (L. Boothman and R. Hyde Parker (eds), *Savage Fortune: An Aristocratic Family in the Early Seventeenth Century* (Woodbridge, 2006), SRS 49, p. xxxv).

[79] The project was finally accomplished by Henry Ashley in 1694. See Gage (1822), p. 3.

[80] Sir John Hare, Sir Edward Mountford, Isaac Barrow, Walter Cradock and William Coppinger were opposed.

[81] *CSPD* 1635–36, p. 386.

seen against the background of Charles I's vast land grants to the Earl of Bedford in the Fens, could easily have been politicised by those who saw 'new men' (or the king's men) trampling on their rights and lands. However, the commissioners were not divided on confessional grounds: Sir John Hare of Bruisyard, who opposed the project, was also a Catholic.

The immediate outcome of Sir Robert's 1636 plea in Chancery is unknown, but it would seem that his version of earlier events was eventually accepted. On 4 May 1639 the Rookwood manors of Mortimer's, Stanningfield Hall, Coldham Hall and Philletts were vested in Sir Phillip Tyrwhitt, Sir Peter Fresnold of Stalybridge in Derbyshire, Gervase Markham of Retford in Nottinghamshire and Robert Monson of Northurst in Lincolnshire, who thereafter held the land in trust for Sir Robert **(2)**. These or other individuals held the land in trust for the next thirteen years, until by an indenture of 14 February 1652 Sir Robert Crompton conveyed the manor of Coldham Hall to Sir John Cotton, 2nd Baronet of Madingley (*c.* 1647–1713) **(3)**.[82] Both Cotton and Crompton were listed as trustees in the marriage settlement of Ambrose Rookwood (II) and Elizabeth Caldwell on 16 February 1652. The marriage settlement of Thomas Rookwood and Tamworth Martin (dated 17 February 1683) referred to an indenture of 6 September 1682 whereby Adam Felton[83] and William Covell would hold Stanningfield and other manors in trust for Ambrose Rookwood (II) 'under certain ffines & Assurances … levied and referred to executed by Sir J. Cotton & others trustees in the place of … Sir Robert Crompton & others' **(6)**.

The expedient of vesting their property in trustees spared the Rookwoods from compounding their Suffolk estates as 'delinquents' during the Civil War, and the only reference to Sir Robert in the *Calendar of the Proceedings of the Committee of Compounding* is to the manor of Claverings in Essex. On 11 May 1654, Sir Robert and George Gipps petitioned the Committee of Compounding for the discharge of the manor of Claverings and the 'mansion-house' in South Halstead; this meant that they had paid the composition required by the committee.[84]

Sir Robert's household at Coldham may have been a musical one, judging from the survival of two music books dating from the mid-seventeenth century and containing works for harpsichord by Robert Jenkins (1592–1678), Charles Simpson (1602/6–69) and the otherwise unknown composer Simon Clarke. The composing lives of both Jenkins and Simpson spanned the reign of Charles I, the Commonwealth and the Restoration, so it is not easy to establish a date for these books. It is possible that the Rookwoods acquired these manuscript music books by purchase at a later date. However, Jenkins spent his working life in East Anglia and Simpson was a Catholic. Jenkins was patronised by the Catholic Derehams of West Dereham in Norfolk before the Civil War and later by the Royalist L'Estranges of Hunstanton and the Norths of Kirtling in Cambridgeshire. Jenkins's pupil Roger North noted that the composer 'passed his time at gentlemen's houses in the country' during the

---

[82] Sir John Cotton was descended from a strongly Royalist family and his son, Sir John Hynde Cotton, 3rd Baronet (1686–1752), was a prominent Jacobite in the eighteenth century. See D. W. Hayton, 'Cotton, Sir John Hynde' in *ODNB*, vol. 13, p. 618; E. Lord, *The Stuarts' Secret Army* (Harlow, 2004), pp. 170–80.

[83] Sir Adam Felton, Baronet of Playford was the fourth husband of Lady Elizabeth Monson, the grandmother of Thomas Rookwood's wife Tamworth Martin **(37)**.

[84] *CPCC*, vol. 4, p. 2900. The Stanningfield Rookwoods' experience was in contrast to that of their Euston cousins, who were fined heavily (*CPCC* vol. 2, p. 1425) and eventually lost Euston Hall (Blackwood (2001), p. 198).

interregnum, and Coldham could well have been one of them. In the 1660s he was in the Bury St Edmunds area, visiting Elizabeth Burwell at Rougham. He died at Kimberley in Norfolk, the home of Sir Phillip Wodehouse.[85]

Sir Robert spent at least some time abroad during the Civil War, although whether this was a pilgrimage or a self-imposed exile is unknown. The Pilgrims' Book of the English College in Rome recorded that early in February 1644 'Sir Robert Rookwood, Knight, arrived, & stopped with us the first night; he afterwards dined & for some days took his supper in the College.'[86] On 21 March 1645 a certain J. Barker wrote to Sir Henry Bedingfield, 1st Baronet, at Oxford, listing some East Anglian recusants then in exile in France who included Sir Francis Mannock, Sir Edward Sulyard, John Tasburgh and Robert Rookwood as well as members of the Bedingfield family.[87] By absenting himself from the country Sir Robert opened up the possibility that his estates would be confiscated while he was away. On the other hand, the further he placed himself from the conflict the less likely he was to be accused of 'delinquency' and support for the king.

In 1660 Sir Robert's portrait (Plate III) was painted by Joseph Richard Wright. This picture may have been a gift of Sir Robert to his friend Sir John Cotton of Madingley, since it was hanging at Madingley Hall when Sir Thomas Gage, 7th Baronet described it:

> He is seated, the head uncovered, the right hand open and extended, as if in the attitude of discourse, the left hand holds his gloves – He wears a gold tissue doublet with sleeves open at the wrists, fastened by a stud, over his doublet a black cloak; a sword by his side, his collar turned down and fastened by a brooch; a small bronze figure of Mars seen in the back ground.[88]

Sir Robert married Mary, daughter of Sir Robert Townsend of Ludlow, by whom he had nine sons and five daughters between 1622 and 1639, including his eldest son and heir Ambrose (II). John Gage the antiquary thought, on the basis of Hugh Tootell's *Church History*, that Sir Robert's second son, Robert (V) (b. 1624), was killed at Oxford fighting for the Royalist side in the Civil War.[89] If this did happen, it was after Robert (V)'s return from Rome, where he tried to enter the English College to train for the priesthood in 1644.[90] On his entrance to the college Robert (V) declared that his parents were 'each imbued with true Catholic faith and that they partake of the living spirit of it'. He reported that he had one brother studying philosophy and two others doing business in Maryland; the rest were at home with his mother, while one sister was a professed nun and another a pupil of the Poor Clares. It is likely

---

[85] A. Ashbee, 'Jenkins, John' in *New Grove*, vol. 12, pp. 946–8. On Simpson see C. D. S. Field, 'Simpson, Christopher' in *New Grove*, vol. 23, pp. 408–11.

[86] Foley, vol. 5, p. 542.

[87] *Bedingfield Papers*, p. 18. Sir Robert was a knight in 1645 but the letter does not refer to him as such, raising the possibility that it refers to his son.

[88] CUL Hengrave MS 76/1. The portrait was later acquired by the Rookwood Gages since it was included in the contents sale of Hengrave Hall in 1897 as lot 507 (*Catalogue*, p. 43). It was bought by Prince Frederick Duleep Singh and it was hanging at Old Buckenham Hall in 1905 (E. Farrer, *Portraits in Suffolk Houses (West)* (London, 1908), pp. 378–9).

[89] C. Dodd, *The Church History of England* (Brussels, 1742), vol. 3, p. 74; Gage (1822), note on p. 249.

[90] A. Kenny (ed.), *The Responsa Scholarum of the English College, Rome: Part II, 1622–1685* (London, 1963), CRS 55, pp. 482–3; Foley, vol. 5, p. 542.

that Tootell confused Robert (V) with the Captain William Rookwood who died at Alresford; Robert (V) may not have been killed in the Civil War at all.

It is difficult to identify these brothers of Robert (V) with certainty, especially those who went to Maryland. Sir Robert's seventh son, Henry (b. 1633) was educated at St Omer 1652–54 and entered the English College in Rome in November 1655, but was dead by May 1656; the college diary noted that he 'came to the College infirm'.[91] Sir Robert's ninth and youngest son, Ignatius (b. 1636), had a brief career as a Benedictine monk and died on 10 November 1663.[92] Two daughters, Mary (1623–76) and Frances (1625–92), entered the monastery of Poor Clares at Dunkirk; both of them served as abbess of the community at one time.[93] The idea that Sir Robert had two sons who were both killed in the Civil War can be found in two nineteenth-century guides to Suffolk,[94] but this idea is unsupported by any direct evidence in the Rookwood Family Papers themselves. It is more than likely that the story was fabricated for romantic reasons, to give yet more 'tragical ends' to members of the family that produced the two Ambrose Rookwoods.

Sir Robert Rookwood (IV) was indicted for recusancy at the 1664 spring quarter sessions in Bury St Edmunds, presided over by Sir Robert Hyde,[95] and his son Ambrose was indicted ten years later at the January quarter sessions of 1674.[96] Bishop Compton of London's census of religious practice in 1676, which collected only numbers without names, found sixteen papists in the parish of Stanningfield,[97] the second largest concentration of Catholics in Suffolk after the two parishes of Bury St Edmunds. Nevertheless, the number was small enough to account for just the Rookwood family and their immediate servants, without demonstrating the existence of a wider Catholic community in the village sustained by the presence of a Catholic landlord. Curiously, the Rookwoods are missing from *A List of the Names of Papist & reputed Papist in the County of Suffolk* drawn up at the time of the Popish Plot scare and containing thirty-six names,[98] but this is probably because the family was still in self-imposed exile. Francis Rookwood of Egmere, who was probably the sixth son of Sir Robert (IV), did appear in a list of Norfolk Catholics drawn up in the same year.[99]

Sir Robert's will (**4**), drawn up on 4 October 1673, left his estates, together with timber and fishing rights on the manors of Coldham, Philletts and Lawshall, to his eldest son Ambrose (II), together with all of his furniture and linen except what his widow Mary might select for herself. To his widow he bequeathed the manor of Mortimer's as well as Hamlin's Farm in Lavenham. His daughter Margaret Perry was granted an annuity of £80 from the manors of Sheriff's and Claverings in Essex.

---

[91] Holt (1979), p. 225; Foley, vol. 6, p. 394.
[92] A. Allanson (ed. A Cranmer and S. Goodwill), *Biography of the English Benedictines* (Ampleforth, 1999), p. 71.
[93] Mary Collet Rookwood was professed on 12 August 1640; Clare Frances Rookwood was professed on 21 November 1646 (CUL Hengrave MS 21/1/203).
[94] *A Concise Description of Bury Saint Edmund's and its Environs* (London, 1827), p. 301; J. Wodderspoon, *Historic Sites and Other Remarkable and Interesting Places in the County of Suffolk* (London, 1839), pp. 37–8.
[95] 'Convicted Recusants Chas. II' in *Miscellanea V* (London, 1908), CRS 5, p. 302.
[96] SRO(B) 558/1.
[97] A. Whiteman and A. Clapinson (eds), *The Compton Census of 1676: A Critical Edition* (London, 1986), p. 238.
[98] 'Popish Recusants in Suffolk', *EANQ* 1 (1885–86), p. 345.
[99] *Lords MSS* 1678–88, p. 234.

Sir Robert's sons Ambrose (II) and Francis each received £500 in ready money; Ambrose (II)'s son Henry received £150,[100] while Francis's son and daughter Francis and Dorothy received £300 and £200 respectively. Sir Robert's second eldest son Robert (V) received the residue of Claverings after his mother's annuity and a farm purchased from Anthony Howdge at Whepstead. Sir Robert's executors were two prominent East Anglian Catholics, Sir Henry Bedingfield and John Tasburgh of Bodney, while the will was witnessed by Peregrine Short and Dr Richard Short of Bury St Edmunds and John Petre, a younger son either of the Petres of Cranham in Essex or of William, 2nd Baron Petre of Waltham; the Shorts and Petres were likewise staunch Catholic families. Sir Robert was buried in Stanningfield church on 10 January 1680.[101]

Sir Robert Rookwood's will was scarcely that of a man reduced to poverty by recusancy fines and the confiscation of his estates. He expected £1,650 in ready money to be available to his heirs, in addition to the manors of Coldham (presumably including Stanningfield), Philletts, Lawshall, Mortimer's, Hamlin's Farm and Howdge's Farm in Suffolk, as well as Claverings and Sheriff's Farm in Essex. He also owned a house in Bury St Edmunds with seven hearths in the parish of St James.[102] At the end of his life Sir Robert was a wealthy man, albeit the Rookwoods never recovered the magnificence they had known in the sixteenth century. The Acton estates, including the manor of Rokewodes itself, were never regained. Nevertheless, Sir Robert held land in two counties and his assets were impressive given the heavy financial impositions on recusants.

Revival and revolution: Ambrose Rookwood (II) (1622–93)

Sir Robert (IV)'s eldest son and heir, Ambrose Rookwood (II), was the only member of the Rookwood family to experiment briefly with local government. He served as a Justice of the Peace and a member of the Bury St Edmunds Corporation during the reign of James II. He and his wife revived the Rookwoods' patronage of the Jesuits, but they also suffered from the 1688 Revolution; Ambrose (II)'s wife, Elizabeth, died in exile and his two eldest surviving sons were forced to seek a new life in France.

Ambrose (II) was educated at St Omer, following the family tradition, from 1636–43.[103] He entered the English College, Rome, in October 1643 and took the alias Ambrose Gage,[104] although if he had any intention to train for the priesthood he evidently decided otherwise. In around 1655 he married Elizabeth Caldwell (c. 1629–91), daughter of Daniel Caldwell of Canters in the parish of Horndon-on-the-Hill, Essex. On Elizabeth's memorial stone (**6**) the family claimed to trace its ancestry to the Welsh King Cadwallader 'by the most tested genealogical tree'. Whatever the truth of that claim, the family was certainly well-connected; another of Daniel Caldwell's daughters, Anne, married a member of the Petre family.[105] Ambrose and Elizabeth had eight sons and seven daughters.[106] Nine of Ambrose's

[100] Henry Rookwood SJ (1658–1730).
[101] Copinger (1910), p. 341.
[102] *Hearth Tax*, p. 52.
[103] Holt (1979), p. 225.
[104] Kenny (1963), p. 478; Foley, vol. 5, p. 542.
[105] E. E. Estcourt and J. O. Payne, *The English Catholic Nonjurors of 1715* (London, 1885), p. 60.
[106] CUL Hengrave 76/1.

children are mentioned in an indenture of 17 May 1667: Robert (VI), Mary, Thomas, Henry, Francis, Ann, Margaret, Ambrose and John.[107]

At least eight of Ambrose's children chose the religious life and went abroad. His fourth son Henry (1659–1730) trained as a Jesuit on the island of Malta and was professed in 1681 and ordained in 1690.[108] Henry returned to England in 1693 and appears periodically in the accounts of the Jesuit College of the Holy Apostles until 1725.[109] Geoffrey Holt thought that Henry could have been the chaplain at Coldham 1691–1727,[110] although Henry died in Norfolk in 1730.[111] The fifth son, Francis (1660–1750), was professed as a Benedictine monk at St Gregory's, Douai, in 1680. He was sent on the mission in the South Province and held various positions of authority in the English Benedictine Congregation, eventually being appointed titular Prior of Rochester in 1705 and Provincial of Canterbury from 1712–13. For much of this time he was based at Witham Place in Essex,[112] but in 1715 he was at Acton Burnell.[113] In 1737 he gave £100 to the South Province of the English Benedictines in return for a payment of £5 a year; he died in Worcestershire in 1750.[114]

Ambrose's seventh son, John, entered the Franciscans at St Bonaventure's Friary, Douai, and was professed in 1686. He was ordained in 1690 and died in 1746, having served as Guardian and Definitor of the Province on several occasions.[115] Furthermore, five of Ambrose's daughters entered religion. Four of them (Mary, Anna, Margaret and Catherine) became Poor Clares, while Frances (1668–1717) joined the Augustinian canonesses at the English Convent in Bruges.[116] The Rookwoods' contribution to the English religious houses on the Continent was prolific; they produced eight priests and eleven nuns in 150 years.[117] For large Catholic families there was an economic advantage to younger sons entering holy orders, since this diminished the need for the family estate to be divided for their maintenance. In the case of daughters, most convents required the payment of a dowry, but this was often smaller than the marriage settlement expected by a husband in England. Ambrose II's youngest son, Charles (b. 1671), would later become a thorn in the flesh for his brother Thomas through his continual lawsuits. Since the family name Ambrose was given to two of Ambrose (II)'s sons, Ambrose (III) (b. 1656) may well have died in infancy before 1664, when Ambrose (IV) was born.

The Popish Plot scare of 1678–80 threatened all English Catholics. Some sought temporary refuge on the Continent from the royal proclamations reinforcing the

---

[107] SRO(B) 326/52. (NB: It is unclear whether Ambrose (II)'s second son Ambrose (III) or sixth son Ambrose (IV) is meant here.)

[108] D. A. Bellenger, *English and Welsh Priests 1558–1800* (Bath, 1984), p. 103.

[109] A Jesuit jurisdiction covering East Anglia and Essex.

[110] G. Holt, *The English Jesuits 1650–1829: A Biographical Dictionary* (London, 1984), CRS 70, pp. 214–15.

[111] *Miscellanea VIII* (London, 1913), CRS 13, p. 175.

[112] Bellenger (1984), p. 103; H. N. Birt, *Obit Book of the English Benedictines, 1600–1912* (Edinburgh, 1913), pp. 98–9.

[113] Estcourt and Payne (1885), p. 223.

[114] South Province Contract Book, Downside Abbey MS 70, fols 64–5.

[115] R. Trappes Lomax (ed.), *Franciscana* (Exeter, 1923), CRS 24, p. 308.

[116] Two of the daughters of Sir Robert Rookwood (I), Ann and Dorothy, had been canonesses at St Monica's, Louvain, the mother house of the Convent of Nazareth at Bruges, which was founded in 1629. On Frances Rookwood see C. S. Durrant, *A Link between Flemish Mystics and English Martyrs* (London, 1925), p. 311. On Ann and Dorothy see pp. 216, 221, 348.

[117] For details on the Rookwood nuns see 'Who were the Nuns? A Prosopographical Study of the English Convents in Exile 1600–1800', http://wwtn.history.qmul.ac.uk.

severity of the penal laws and the fury of anti-Catholic mobs. Catholics were obliged to obtain passes from the Secretary of State both to leave England and to return. On 25 February 1679 a pass was issued to Ambrose Rookwood, his wife Elizabeth and children John, Catherine, Frances and Charles, together with a male and female servant.[118] However, this pass may not have been used, because on 30 April the government issued a second pass to Ambrose, his wife and children and 'Elizabeth Monson, a kinswoman'. Lady Elizabeth Monson (née Reresby), by her second husband Edward Horner of Melles in Somerset, was the mother of Tamworth, wife of Sir Roger Martin, whose daughter Tamworth was the wife of Thomas Rookwood. She was thus Thomas Rookwood's grandmother-in-law.[119] The Rookwoods returned after a pass was issued for them to do so on 24 August 1679.[120] Most Catholics congregated in the Austrian Netherlands, at Bruges or Brussels, and the Rookwoods joined other Suffolk gentry such as Sir Roger Martin of Long Melford, William Mannock of Stoke-by-Nayland and William Gage of Hengrave.[121]

Catholic fortunes changed dramatically with the accession of James II in 1685, although the new king's plans for religious toleration met with sustained opposition. In July 1688 James's close friend Henry Jermyn, Lord Dover (the younger brother of Henry Jermyn, Earl of St Albans) was instructed by the king to pack the Bury Corporation with Catholics and Protestant dissenters. The aim of this exercise was to secure a Member of Parliament for Bury St Edmunds who would back plans for religious toleration in the next Parliament. Since Bury's corporation and its electoral franchise were one and the same under the town's Royal Charter of 1684, a sympathetic corporation would secure a sympathetic MP.[122] Henry Jermyn was the man for the job, because his family had traditionally influenced the outcome of elections in Bury. Tory loyalists were forced out to make way for the new members, but only five Catholics could be found willing to take their seats: the mercer John Stafford (who became mayor), Dr Richard Short, Dr Thomas Short, Henry Audley and Ambrose Rookwood (II). Dover recommended Rookwood to John Stafford as a possible candidate.[123] Rookwood had already been appointed as a Justice of the Peace, along with fellow Catholics William Mannock of Stoke-by-Nayland, Edward Sulyard of Haughley and Richard Tasburgh of Flixton.[124]

The Shorts were one of the oldest Catholic families in the town of Bury St Edmunds and they had been connected with the Rookwoods of Euston before the Civil War.[125] Peregrine and Richard Short witnessed Sir Robert Rookwood (IV)'s will and the Coldham Hall accounts kept by Benjamin Cussons (a servant at Coldham) recorded £1 'Rec[eive]d of Dr Short for a Load of Hay' on 11 December 1692 as well

---

[118] *CSPD* 1 January 1 1679 to 31 August 1680, p. 333.

[119] On Elizabeth Monson see document **37**.

[120] *CSPD* 1 January 1 1679 to 31 August 1680, p. 333.

[121] Blackwood (2001), p. 235.

[122] On the attempt to pack the Bury Corporation see P. E. Murrell, 'Bury St. Edmunds and the Campaign to Pack Parliament, 1687–8', *Bulletin of the Institute of Historical Research* 54 (1981), pp. 188–206; F. Young, '"An Horrid Popish Plot": The Failure of Catholic Aspirations in Bury St Edmunds, 1685–88', *PSIA(H)* 41 (2006), pp. 209–55.

[123] Henry Jermyn, Lord Dover to John Stafford, 23 August 1688, SRO(B) E2/41/5 fol. 44.

[124] Blackwood (2001), p. 241.

[125] William Short, the grandfather of the Dr Thomas Short who sat on the corporation, was Rector of Euston until 1645. See S. Colman, 'Three Seventeenth-Century Rectors of Euston and a Verse in the Parish Register', *PSIA(H)* 37 (1992), pp. 134–43.

as 7s. spent 'ffor keeping Dr Shorts horse'.[126] Whether the Rookwoods were patients as well as social acquaintances of the Shorts is not known.

The Rookwoods supported the Jesuit College of the Holy Apostles, which acquired permanent premises in 1685 in the old abbot's palace among the abbey ruins in Bury St Edmunds and set up a school and public chapel.[127] Ambrose (II)'s wife Elizabeth was the donor of fifty chalices to the college just before the accession of James II. In the 1940s Fr Owen Hardwicke endeavoured to trace as many of these chalices as he could. One at Bury was a rose chalice imitating pre-Reformation design with the inscription 'Col[legium] Ap[ostolicum] S[ocietatis] J[esu] / Ex dono D[omi]nae Elizabethae Rookwood / 1684' on the foot, and this chalice is now in the Martin D'Arcy collection of Jesuit artefacts at the Loyola University Museum of Art in Chicago (Plate 1). Hardwicke noted the existence of seven more chalices of identical design, but without the inscription, at Catholic churches in Bury St Edmunds, Peterborough, Luton, Great Yarmouth, Beccles and Stafford.[128]

On 17 October 1688 James caved in to the Tory backlash against his Declarations of Indulgence and issued a proclamation restoring the 'Antient Charters, Liberties, Rights, and Franchises' to corporations. This had the effect of reinstating Bury St Edmunds's earlier charter of 1668. On 22 October the Tory members of the corporation met and formally ejected Ambrose Rookwood (II) and the other Catholics *in absentia*.[129] William of Orange landed in England on 5 November and anti-Catholic riots broke out in London on 10 and 11 December.[130] The diarist Narcissus Luttrell noted on 7 December 1688 that 'Some disturbance was lately at Bury in Suffolk upon pulling down the masse house there, and said some mischeif was done.'[131] This 'mischief' involved a man named Prettyman who was killed trying to defend the Jesuit chapel (although he killed three of the rioters). His mother's 'corner tavern' in the marketplace was then pulled down by the mob.[132] On 30 December a sensational pamphlet claimed that Catholics in Bury St Edmunds had made an attempt to blow up the town, and included a rather unconvincing letter supposedly written by John Daniell of Acton to the ex-mayor John Stafford.[133]

A second riot broke out in Bury St Edmunds on 27 December when a mob formed in response to a rumour, already disproved by scouts, that an army of Irish was approaching the town. The mob congregated on Newmarket Heath and sacked Lord Dover's house at Cheveley; on the same day the houses of some Catholics in Bury were searched and looted. The commander of the local militia confronted the rioters on Angel Hill with armed militiamen, who simply lowered their muskets and allowed the shot to fall out, before joining the rioters. It took Sir Robert Davers of Rushbrooke to restore order and return the property that had been taken, as well as confining the looters to the town gaol.[134] Since Dover is the only Catholic mentioned in the

---

[126] CUL Hengrave MS 76/2/15.

[127] On the Jesuits in the old Abbot's Palace see Young (2006), pp. 213–14.

[128] I am grateful to Joy Rowe for access to Fr Owen Hardwicke's MS notes.

[129] Young (2006), p. 213.

[130] J. Callow, *King in Exile* (Stroud, 2004), p. 8.

[131] N. Luttrell, *A Brief Historical Relation of State Affairs from September 1678 to April 1714* (Oxford, 1857), vol. 1, p. 483.

[132] Unknown correspondent to Edmund Bohun, 30 November 1688, CUL Add. MS 4403/27.

[133] For the text of the pamphlet see Young (2006), Appendix II, pp. 223–4.

[134] *The London Mercury or the Orange Intelligencer* (31 December 1688 to 3 January 1689) reprinted as Appendix I in Young (2006), pp. 222–3.

Plate 1. A chalice given to the Jesuit College of the Holy Apostles in 1684 by Elizabeth Rookwood. This is one of eight surviving chalices from a collection of fifty donated by her. Photographed by Mary Ruth Albert and reproduced by kind permission of the Martin D'Arcy S.J. Collection, Loyola University Museum of Art, Chicago

surviving newspaper account we do not know whether the Rookwoods' townhouse in Bury was the object of the mob's attention.

The collapse of James II's regime precipitated Dr Richard Short's flight to Douai by the middle of November 1688.[135] He had more reason to fear the anti-Catholic backlash than most, since James had made use of the controversial royal prerogative to impose him as a fellow on Magdalen College, Oxford, on 14 March 1688.[136] Ambrose (II) seems to have remained in England but his wife and two of his sons, Thomas and Ambrose (IV), left for the Continent. Elizabeth Rookwood took refuge at the English Convent in Bruges, where she died in 1691. The convent annals recorded that 'Mrs Rookwood boarding without in our Confessor's House got the infection of the Small Pox and being with our Lord Bishop's leave brought into our Infirmary to be tended amongst our Religious, she made a Christian pious end on the 23d of March [1691] and is buried in our Vault.'[137] Ambrose erected a memorial to Elizabeth (**6**) in the convent church, which recorded that 'on account of her pure faith in God and King James, having been encouraged to go again into exile by her dearest husband, after the pains of illness piously and bravely borne, she happily reposed this praise in the peace of the Holy Church'. The use of the word *iterum* ('again') to describe the exile was a reference to the family's earlier exile at the time of the Popish Plot.

It is likely that Ambrose (II) remained in England in order to minimise the possibility of the family's estates being seized by the new government of William and Mary. In his will of 10 October 1692 Ambrose left £400 to his Jesuit son Henry, £400 to his Benedictine son Francis, £50 to his Franciscan son John and £400 to his youngest son Charles. Ambrose divided £200 between his four surviving daughters – Elizabeth, Margaret, Elizabeth and Catherine[138] – and left £97 to charity. He bequeathed the manors of Sheriff's and Barrow, together with lands in Colne, to his son Ambrose (IV).[139] Claverings was to be sold and the proceeds used to pay the legacies (**8**). Ambrose (II) was buried on 6 December 1693.[140] The estate should have been inherited by Ambrose (II)'s eldest son, Robert (VI). However, there is no mention of Robert in Ambrose (II)'s will or any subsequent document, and it is therefore likely that he predeceased his father. The estates consequently demised to Ambrose (II)'s eldest remaining son, Thomas.

Ambrose Rookwood (IV) (1664–96) and the Barclay Conspiracy

Ambrose Rookwood (IV), the sixth son of Ambrose (II) and Elizabeth Caldwell, followed James II to France in 1688, perhaps accompanied by his brother Thomas, and entered the royal bodyguard at St Germain-en-Laye. He fought in Ireland for the Jacobite cause and, by 1695, held the rank of brigadier in James's guards. In December 1695 James issued Brigadier Sir George Barclay with a vague commission

---

135 F. Young, 'The Shorts of Bury St. Edmunds: Medicine, Catholicism and Politics in the Seventeenth Century', *Journal of Medical Biography* 16 (2008), p. 192.

136 Dodd (1742), vol. 3, p. 460; Estcourt and Payne (1885), p. 265.

137 CUL Hengrave MS 76/1.

138 These were the only four daughters who did not become nuns – and nuns could not be legatees.

139 Paul Hopkins thought that Sheriff's escaped confiscation in 1696 as Ambrose (IV) never took possession (P. Hopkins, 'Rookwood, Ambrose' in *ODNB* vol. 47, pp. 700–1).

140 Copinger (1910), p. 341 erroneously gives the year of Ambrose's burial as 1692, when he had not yet written his will, but the correct burial date is contained within the Stanningfield parish registers, SRO(B) J552/8.

'to do from time to time such … acts of hostilitie against the P[rin]ce of Orange and his adherents, as may conduce most to our service'.[141] Barclay interpreted this as an invitation to assassinate William of Orange and recruited a group of officers in James's service to carry out the deed. Among them was Ambrose Rookwood (IV).

The Jacobite agent John Bernardi ran into Ambrose by accident in a tavern at Christmas 1695. Bernardi had known Ambrose for seven years, but had not seen him lately, and Ambrose told Bernardi 'that he was quite tir'd out in Foreign Service, that his Brother [Thomas] had a good Estate, and Interest enough to obtain Leave for him to come Home, and that he was come over to that End, but kept himself a little private until his Brother had gain'd him a License to appear'. This was because Ambrose had come back to England without permission.[142]

One of the officers who were part of the Barclay Conspiracy, Thomas Prendergast, was so horrified by the thought of regicide that he revealed the entire plot to Hans Willem Bentinck and William himself in February 1696.[143] A proclamation was accordingly issued, naming Ambrose Rookwood and other conspirators. Ambrose turned up at Bernardi's lodgings in London, 'and his Countenance and Behaviour seem'd to discover him under some Disturbance of Mind':

> Bernardi thereupon ask'd him if any Evil had happened to him? To which he answer'd no, but said that if any Body should be so malicious as to give Information of his being come over at that Time, he should certainly be taken up … his Name was in a Proclamation, which came out upon that very Day, to seize him as one of those, who were concern'd in the said Assassination Plot, tho' Bernardi had not then heard any Thing of the Matter, and Rookwood concealed it from him, intending as appeared by his Behaviour afterwards, to spend that Evening with Bernardi; but Bernardi told him that he was under a Promise and Engagement to sup that Night at a Tavern on Tower-hill.[144]

Ambrose agreed to accompany Bernardi to the tavern, and they spent the whole night there and ended up sharing a room for the night. The next morning, constables accompanied by armed men burst into the room and arrested the two men, who were placed under armed guard until noon. It emerged that a serving maid had become suspicious after one of the men had refused to tell her who they were, and had sent her brother to inform the Recorder of London. Bernardi and Ambrose, who was then going under the name of Felton (an alias probably inspired by Sir Adam Felton, one of the trustees of the Rookwood estates), were taken before the Recorder and questioned.[145] The Recorder sent them to the Poultry Compter rather than Newgate, but their true identities were still unknown.[146] Unfortunately for Ambrose, he placed complete trust in a man named George Harris, to whom he revealed his true identity. As soon as a reward of £1,000 each was offered on 22 March for the apprehension of the conspirators, Harris identified Ambrose and Bernardi and they were taken from the Poultry Compter with a detachment of guards on the night of 24 March, examined

---

[141] Callow (2004), p. 271.
[142] J. Bernardi, *A Short History of the Life of Major John Bernardi* (London, 1729), p. 86.
[143] Callow (2004), p. 273.
[144] Bernardi (1729), pp. 87–8.
[145] *CSPD* 1696, p. 99.
[146] Bernardi (1729), pp. 88–90.

before the Privy Council and committed to Newgate.[147] Here, Ambrose was visited by his brother Thomas (**37**).

At his trial Ambrose's reluctance to participate in the plot emerged. According to the evidence of Harris, Rookwood declared that 'I am afraid we are drawn into some such Business [i.e. assassination]; but if I had known it before I came over, I should have begg'd the King's pardon at St. Germain's, and not have come over hither.' Rookwood 'own'd it was a barbarous Thing'.[148] In spite of the argument of the defence counsel (the first appearance of a defence counsel in English legal history) that Rookwood never explicitly consented to the assassination,[149] he was convicted of high treason.[150] Ambrose Rookwood (IV) was hanged, drawn and quartered at Tyburn on 29 April 1696. Although he made no speech from the scaffold (**9**) he handed a paper to the sheriff, which the government declined to publish. However, Jacobites took the matter into their own hands and Rookwood's last words soon appeared in print, prefaced by a reminder of the inviolability of a man's dying wish.

Ambrose's chief concern in his final statement was evidently to exculpate James II of any knowledge or involvement in the plot, while his defence of his own behaviour rested on the idea that he was obeying the orders of a superior officer and acting as a soldier. The government responded to the Jacobites' pre-emptive publication of the paper with their own version, which claimed that the paper had not been printed before because Ambrose did not specifically instruct this or extract a promise to that effect.[151] A third pamphlet followed, reproducing the text 'with Reflections thereupon' designed to discredit Ambrose's assertions about James's innocence.[152] Whatever the truth that lay behind these political pamphlets, Ambrose's actions had undermined the ideological consistency of a Jacobite position that condemned the killing of kings, and thereby further tarnished the Rookwood family name. Of more pressing concern to the family, however, was the fact that Ambrose's attainder and intestate death opened up the question of who should inherit his Suffolk and Essex manors. In the course of time a dispute over this issue would divide Ambrose's surviving brothers, Thomas and Charles.

The trials of exile: Thomas Rookwood (1658–1726) (Plate IV)

There is some evidence that Ambrose (IV)'s elder brother Thomas entered foreign military service. He was called 'Co[lone]ll Rookwood' by Thomas Marwood in December 1700,[153] and described as a 'knight of the Kingdom of France' at his gaol delivery on 28 August 1696. Evidence for Thomas's early movements after James II's flight to France in 1688 is lacking; it is possible that he joined the Jacobite court at St

---

[147] Ibid., pp. 90–2.

[148] Anon., *A Complete Collection of State-Trials and Proceedings upon High Treason* (London, 1730), vol. 4, pp. 674–5.

[149] Ibid., p. 677.

[150] For the complete trial, ibid., pp. 649–86.

[151] A. Rookwood, *True Copies of the Papers which Brigadier Rookwood, and Major Lowick, delivered to the Sheriffs of London and Middlesex, at Tyburn, April 29. 1696* (London, 1696). A German engraving of the plotters includes the only likeness of Ambrose, reproduced in Lord (2004), plate 8.

[152] A. Rookwood, *A True Copy of the Paper delivered by Brigadier Rookwood, to the Sheriffs of London and Middlesex, at Tyburn, the Place of Execution, April 29 1696. With Reflections thereupon* (London, 1696).

[153] *Bedingfield Papers*, p. 80.

Germain and received his knighthood at around that time. However, the description of the knighthood as French suggests that it was conferred not by James II but by Louis XIV (Thomas is not referred to as 'Sir' in any document). A number of Suffolk Catholics were connected with the Paris court of the queen dowager, Henrietta Maria, before her death in 1669. Henry Jermyn, Earl of St Albans, was Master of the Queen's Horse, and Sir Thomas Bond, whose second son Thomas was a leading Catholic in Bury St Edmunds, was Comptroller of her Household. Sir Thomas's daughter Mary Charlotte became a maid of honour to Henrietta, Duchess of Orléans, the youngest daughter of Charles I, and married Sir William Gage, 2nd Baronet of Hengrave, who was presented at the queen dowager's court when a student in Paris in 1668.[154] The Duchess of Orléans became a focus of English activity in Paris between the old queen's death and the arrival of James II; it is possible that Thomas Rookwood became attached to her court through the influence of his Gage or Bond neighbours. Had he done so, then he could have been knighted by the Duke of Orléans, although this is mere speculation.

It is certain that Thomas was back in England in 1694 and then went abroad without the permission of the Secretary of State; this time not to France (with whom England was then at war) but to Bruges in the Austrian Netherlands. In the summer of 1695, however, the Duke of Bavaria ordered the Intendant of the Province to eject Thomas (perhaps at the instigation of the English government) and send him to France. The justification for this may have been that Thomas was a French knight, although there is no evidence that he became a naturalised French subject, as many Jacobite exiles did. Anxious that his presence in a hostile country might be construed as a sign of involvement in Jacobite conspiracies, Thomas decided to return to England. On arrival he approached Charles Talbot, 1st Duke of Shrewsbury (a former Catholic), who advised him to explain the situation to an unknown government administrator. The letter that Thomas Rookwood sent on 6 July 1695 can be found in the *Calendar of State Papers (Domestic Series)*.[155]

The government was unconvinced by Thomas's plea and he was ordered to appear before the Middlesex quarter sessions at the Old Bailey on 9 July 1695 'to answer what shall be objected against him on his Maj[es]ties Behalfe' (**10**). Thomas was ordered to enter into recognisances for good behaviour amounting to £500, including £200 to the Crown. In the meantime he was confined to Newgate. Just over a year later, on 28 August 1696, Thomas was deemed to have discharged these recognisances and, since the judges 'found nothing evil concerning him', he was released. Shortly thereafter Thomas left England for a second visit to Bruges.[156] It seems that he had an official pass to do so this time, as William Covell suggested in a letter of 7 December 1696 (**11**) that he could get his pass extended. No record survives of a formal banishment, so it may be that Thomas incurred automatic banishment by outstaying the time that his pass permitted. From then on, he was an exile living close to the English Convent, where his daughter Elizabeth was a pupil.

Two letters written to Thomas by his steward William Covell reveal the problems

---

[154] J. Gage, *The History and Antiquities of Suffolk: Thingoe Hundred* (London, 1838), p. 205. On Sir William Gage's visit to the queen's court, see Dr Francis Gage to Sir Edward Gage, 4 March 1668 (CUL Hengrave MS 88/2/181).

[155] *CSPD* 1 July–31 December 1695, p. 6.

[156] On 1 July 1699 William Covell wrote to Thomas Rookwood at 'St Augustins Monistary att Brudge' (document **12**).

created by Thomas's prolonged foreign exile.[157] As he was unable to appear in person at the Prerogative Court of Canterbury, Thomas was unable to prove his father Ambrose (II)'s will, which meant that legacies from it could not be paid. On 12 October 1695 Benjamin Cussons noted that only £1,272 12s of the £1,547 bequeathed to Ambrose (II)'s heirs had been received (**8**). This was insufficient to pay all of the legacies, which gathered interest as the years went by. Thomas's younger brother Charles began to show an interest in managing the Rookwood estates and was keen to buy a farm, which Covell did not think it worth paying for. Covell implored Thomas to release him from his trusteeship of the Rookwood estates on the grounds that he was 'very old & declining'. However, Covell said enough to suggest that the real reason for his reluctance to administer the estates was the possibility that Thomas's brothers and sisters, angry at being denied their share of their father's will, would launch further lawsuits against him (**11**).

Covell reported that a 'complaint' of John Eldred of Great Saxham against the Rookwood estate at Barrow had cost £120, probably in legal fees. It is likely that this was a boundary dispute or an argument about customary rights, as Eldred's estate abutted on that of the Rookwoods. Eldred's complaints were a source of embarrassment to Covell as they risked alienating one of the Protestant trustees of the Barrow estate, Thomas Macro, who was one of Eldred's tenants as well as a tenant of the Rookwoods.[158] On 1 February 1697 Charles Rookwood, together with James Harvey, formally took over the management of the Rookwood estates on behalf of Thomas Rookwood, probably as a response to Covell's request to be free of the task. Charles Rookwood remained in charge until 5 July 1703 and later claimed that he had been promised a bond of £900 to cover his expenses during that period (**16**).

Charles's intervention did not bring an end to the problems. In 1699 Covell wrote to Thomas again, reporting that Thomas's brother Francis (a Benedictine monk) was now threatening a lawsuit in the Court of Chancery, as he had so far received nothing from his father's will. Covell complained that he was 'dayly insolted by some of your family', possibly a reference to Charles, who was then living at Coldham Hall. Thomas's exile had brought matters to a critical point; Covell earnestly wished 'there might bee a way found to bring you home amongst us otherwise I greatly fear ruine will fall uppon your estate & family' (**12**). Covell was also experiencing difficulties selling Barrow, which according to the terms of Ambrose (II)'s will should have been sold along with Claverings in order to pay legacies (**8**).[159] It is likely that this sale and the lack of ready money was a consequence of the Double Land Tax imposed on papists in 1692.

Thomas eventually resorted to a direct petition to Queen Anne on 20 January 1703

---

157 The Covells lived at Horringer House (W. M. Hervey, *Annals of a Suffolk Village: Being Historical Notes on the Parish of Horringer* (Cambridge, 1930), pp. 64, 87) and served the Rookwoods, the Gages and the Herveys. William Covell the elder (d. 1661) was steward at Hengrave in 1659 (Gage (1838), p. 208). William Covell the younger (d. 1707) is mentioned in a letter from the 1670s (CUL Hengrave MS 88/2/175) and in 1695 he testified on the value of timber at Hengrave to a committee of the House of Lords (*LJ*, 1693–95, vol. 1 (New Series), pp. 504–5). William Covell the younger was acting as steward to the Herveys at Ickworth as early as 1695 so he evidently served both them and the Rookwoods at one time; see S. H. A. Hervey, *Horringer Parish Registers: Baptisms, Marriages and Burials, with Appendixes and Biographical Notes 1558 to 1850* (Woodbridge, 1900), pp. 294–6.

158 Thomas Macro paid the Rookwood estate 4s 'Lords Rent' in October 1695 (CUL Hengrave MS 76/2/15).

159 Barrow was evidently a recent acquisition as it was not mentioned in the will of Ambrose's father Sir Robert (IV).

(**13**). Here he protested that he had never consorted with the queen's enemies or willingly entered a hostile nation. Thomas's Protestant friends and neighbours were prepared to testify to his good character and loyalty. The petitioners were Thomas Hanmer,[160] Symonds D'Ewes of Stowlangtoft, Robert Davers of Rushbrooke, John Poley of Boxted, Thomas Robinson, Bartholomew Young, James Harvey, John Risby, George Walgrave, William Rowett and Thomas Macro. Sir Symonds D'Ewes, 2nd Baronet of Stowlangtoft was intimately connected to the Catholic families of Suffolk through the marriage of his daughters Delariviere, Mary, Merelina and Henrietta to Catholic gentlemen,[161] while Thomas Hanmer was distantly related to the Gages of Hengrave by marriage and had long been a trustee of their estates.[162] Understandably, local Catholics did not think it worthwhile to subscribe to the petition in their own right, but the Gages may have urged their Protestant neighbours to do so.

The petitioners insisted that Thomas Rookwood's 'continuance in Exile will Fatally and inevitably involve him in great Debts, inextricable Law Suits, intirely ruine his Estate, and finally disable him from paying his just Debts, and consequently redound to many of yo[u]r good Subjects irrecoverable Loss and Detriment'. It was typical of the Suffolk gentry to close ranks to protect their own. Robert Davers of Rushbrooke, a signatory of the 1703 petition, had opposed the Catholics in their attempt to seize control of the Bury Corporation in 1688, but when the mob attacked the houses of the gentry he led the restoration of law and order in the town. Likewise, John Risby was removed as a Justice of the Peace under James II (presumably for adherence to Tory principles) but evidently bore no ill will to Catholics.[163] The welfare of the Rookwood estates in the interconnected web of land ownership outweighed such abstract issues as Thomas Rookwood's religion and the legality of his presence in this or that foreign country.

Eventually, Thomas seems to have decided that returning to England without permission was worth the risk, since a warrant was issued 'to apprehend Thomas Rookwood for coming from France without leave' on 18 November 1704.[164] However, if any punishment followed this misdemeanour it cannot have been particularly serious, since Thomas was able to prove his father's will (**7**) at last on 10 November 1705, twelve years late. In spite of his long exile, Thomas was welcomed back into the circle of the Catholic gentry of East Anglia. Frances Jerningham of Costessey wrote to Thomas at Coldham in 1706 inviting him and his daughter Elizabeth to visit her in Norfolk (**15**).

Thomas's return to England was not the end of his troubles. On 7 July 1705 John Perry, the widower of Ambrose (II)'s sister Margaret (b. 1634), drew up an account of the money he was due from Claverings to satisfy the £80 annuity bequeathed to

---

[160] The Hanmer family were distant relatives of the Gage family of Hengrave Hall (who as Catholics would not have featured on the petition) and their inclusion may have owed something to the Gages' influence.

[161] Delariviere married Thomas Gage (1684–1716) of Hengrave (Gage (1822), p. 249); Mary married Francis Tasburgh of Flixton (F. Blomefield, *An Essay towards a Topographical History of the County of Norfolk* (London, 1807), vol. 6, pp. 15–19); Merelina married Richard Elwes and later a Mr Holmes in London (Diary, 1 October 1731); Henrietta married Thomas Havers of Thelveton (Diary, 31 December 1736).

[162] Sir Thomas Hanmer (1612–78) took refuge at Hengrave during the Civil War and married Susan Hervey, the stepdaughter of Penelope Gage, who was the mother of Sir Edward Gage, 1st Baronet of Hengrave. See E. Scarisbrick, *The Holy Life of Lady Warner* (London, 1691), p. 4.

[163] Blackwood (2001), p. 241.

[164] *CSPD* May 1704–October 1705, p. 117.

Margaret by her father Sir Robert Rookwood (IV). Perry sent this account to William Covell, congratulating him on his return to Coldham and offering to pay him to advance his cause.[165] On 19 September he wrote to Covell again (**14**), complaining that although Ambrose (II) had kept 'the Essex estate' (Claverings) in good order, 'You know (as all that Country too) that Mr [Thomas] Rookwood never layd out one penny for wages in all the Nyne Yeares tyme my whife Enjoyed it'. As a consequence of Thomas's reluctance to put the estate in 'good & tenantable repayre', John Perry had difficulty finding tenants for the farm.

In 1704 Charles Rookwood began a suit against his brother in Chancery for a bond of £900 (with £50 interest) that he claimed he had been promised in return for his administration of the Rookwood estates in Thomas's absence. Thomas claimed that Charles's accounting was in error, but agreed to pay him £35 in addition to the £950. Charles, however, insisted that he was already owed more than the total of £985, as he had still not been paid the original £400 bequeathed to him by his father Ambrose (II) with eleven years' interest. Charles failed to turn up when Thomas attempted to pay him the money on 23 March 1705, offering to meet his clerk in a tavern the next day. When Thomas's clerk offered goldsmiths' bonds instead of ready money, Charles initially refused to sign the deed of release for the bond, but eventually agreed that a goldsmith could take the bonds and that he would sign the deed as soon as he had the money. When Charles failed to do this, Thomas offered him another £27 to cover interest, and when this failed Thomas launched his own suit in Chancery against Charles on 28 April 1705. The court ordered that Thomas should pay £950 to the goldsmith in possession of the bonds within one month, and that Charles should then sign the deed of release. On 13 July Thomas's clerk agreed to meet Charles at the goldsmith's shop in the Strand, but Charles never turned up; the same thing happened again on 29 October. Finally, on 19 November Thomas's clerk brought the money into the Court of Chancery itself and Charles came to collect it.

However, on 4 March 1709 Charles brought a second suit against Thomas for £1,800, including the original £950 and the interest due on it since 1704. Charles also claimed, for the first time, that he was entitled to the estates bequeathed to Ambrose (IV) and that Thomas had entered into an unlawful 'confederation' against him, presumably with Ambrose (II)'s other children. Charles's case does not survive, but in his reply to the suit on 13 March 1709 (**16**), Thomas set out in detail how he had attempted to pay Charles, and also argued for the first time that '[Ambrose (IV)] being attainted of high Treason his personall Estate if any there was ... cannot anyways belong to the p[lainti]ff nor can the p[lainti]ff claime any title to the same or any part thereof'.

No evidence survives of whether Thomas or Charles won the 1709 case, but on 24 May 1711 Thomas formally recovered his family estates when the trustees (William Covell, Sir Thomas Hanmer, Sir Robert Davers, Phillip Yorke and John Cotton) rented Coldham Hall back to him as a tenement (**17**). However, on 16 July 1711 Charles launched a third suit (**18**) against Thomas, this time claiming that Ambrose (IV), before his execution, promised to make him his heir, which Charles had confirmed by Letters of Administration from the Prerogative Court of Canterbury on 30 July 1707. Charles claimed that he was entitled to half of the value of Ambrose (IV)'s lands of

---

[165] John Perry to William Covell, 7 July 1705 (CUL Hengrave MS 76/2/23).

Sheriff's, Claverings and Barrow, and accused Thomas of pretending that Ambrose (IV) had actually made a will and bequeathed the lands to him. Charles even accused Thomas of stealing 'one Sorell Mare with a Colt and Bay Mare, three holland shirts, one Silke Damask waistcoat, one shag pair of Brieches a Night Gown and cover and several other goods of value and a setting Dog'. Charles admitted that he had no witnesses to the promise made to him by Ambrose (IV), because most of his relatives had gone abroad and he did not know where they were.

Thomas's reply to Charles's last attempt to sue him in Chancery (**19**) was brief, and seems to have put the matter to rest. On 14 May 1712 Thomas reminded the court that 'Ambrose Rookwood … in or about the ninth yeare of the reigne of his late Majesty King William the Third was at a sessions held at the Old Bayly in the said year for the County of Middle[se]x indicted for and convicted or attainted of High Treason for Conspiring the Assassination or death of his said late Majesty King Will[ia]m and dyed thereof convicted or attainted.' Consequently, Ambrose (IV)'s estates were forfeit to the Crown and Charles 'cannot have any lawfull title to the same or any part thereof'. This legal argument was likely to gain the court's sympathy, as it presented Charles as defying the Crown by attempting to regain the estates of an attainted traitor, and it seems to have been decisive. However, there can be no doubt that Thomas Rookwood's relationship with his brother was irreparably damaged by the divisive legacy of Ambrose's treason. It is difficult to see Charles's behaviour as anything other than the product of desperation or greed. As the youngest son, Charles's financial prospects were bleak, but he was evidently able to afford a succession of lawyers, which suggests either some private means or a great deal of confidence that he would win his cases. However, Charles experienced a brief period as effective master of Coldham between 1697 and 1703, and his brother's return and failure (in his eyes) to sufficiently compensate him for his outgoings seem to have been hard to bear.

Thomas Rookwood's estates continued to be held in trust for the remainder of his life. In 1721 the trustees of the estate were George Bate and Francis Harvey (**22**), the latter being the uncle of Thomas's second wife, Dorothy Maria Hurst (née Hanford) (**26**). However, Thomas Rookwood's financial troubles did not altogether disappear. He had to defend himself against claims brought by Richard Babbage in 1715 and Mary Beachcroft in 1718–20,[166] but these suits involved small sums compared to his battle with Charles. Thomas Rookwood married Tamworth,[167] the only daughter of Sir Roger Martin of Long Melford, in 1682, by whom he had one daughter, Elizabeth.[168] Following the death of his first wife he married Dorothy Maria Hurst (née Hanford) at Lawshall on 22 March 1721 (**23**). Sir Thomas Rookwood Gage, 7th Baronet noted that a portrait of Thomas at Coldham painted in 1713 depicted him 'half length … In a flowing wig & holding a book.'[169] In his will of 17 March 1725 (**24**) Thomas bequeathed everything to his second wife and thereafter to Elizabeth, having made provision for annuities of £50 to his sisters Anna (b. 1662) and Margaret

---

[166] TNA E 134/1Geo1/Hil 7 (Babbage vs Rookwood); C 11/34/25 (Rookwood vs Beachcroft).

[167] Tamworth accompanied her husband into exile; Thomas Marwood encountered her in Bruges in November 1700 (*Bedingfield Papers*, p. 77).

[168] In his will (**35**) John Martin of Long Melford bequeathed his entire estate to Thomas Rookwood Gage and Anthony Hatton of Tong in Yorkshire.

[169] This painting was lot 512 in the Hengrave sale of 1897 (*Catalogue*, p. 43) and was acquired by Prince Frederick Duleep Singh. It was hanging at Old Buckenham Hall in 1905 (Farrer (1908), p. 379).

(b. 1663). Thomas died on 21 August 1726, the exhausted survivor of a difficult and chaotic period in the history of the family.[170]

Elizabeth Rookwood (1684–1759) and the Rookwood Gages

Elizabeth Rookwood, the only child of Thomas Rookwood and Tamworth Martin, did more than anyone else to preserve for posterity a record of Coldham Hall, as well as of her own scholarly interests. Elizabeth was sufficiently different from other Catholic ladies to attract the disapproval of her daughter-in-law Lucy Gage, who considered her 'too masculine to be a Beauty', with 'the Air of an Empress but too much of the Hauteur to be agreeable' (20). Elizabeth certainly defied contemporary stereotypes of femininity and undertook tasks that were more usually done by men. In addition to the usual embroidery, she kept an 'Angling Rod' and 'two Guns' in her bedroom. She defied her father's wishes by marrying in secret, and turned out to be a shrewd estate manager after her husband's death. She and her sons founded the Jesuit mission in Bury St Edmunds, and she had an intense interest in books, especially English Catholic authors, that went beyond mere pious reading.

Elizabeth was born on 4 January 1684; her mother, Tamworth Martin, died in childbirth. In February 1689, at the age of five, she was received as a convictress at the English Convent in Bruges, where she remained until 21 June 1695. Sir Thomas Gage, 7th Baronet thought that she was educated in Paris, and it is possible that she 'received all the advantages of the first Masters at Paris' after leaving Bruges, as she seems to have remained on the Continent until her father's final return from exile in 1704. Elizabeth was thus an expatriate Catholic from the age of five to the age of 21. Her prolonged period abroad seems to have left its mark in her taste for European art and piety, and she did not share the reluctance of many eighteenth-century English Catholics to make a display of religious art. She was a woman of 'strong principles, a superior Understanding, and a highly cultivated Mind', as well as being her father's only child and heiress. Thomas Rookwood intended her to marry an unknown Catholic baronet, but the baronet's death prevented this, and thereafter he forbade her to marry without his permission. Thomas seems to have been reluctant to part with his daughter, but at the age of 34, on 7 January 1718, she secretly married John Gage (1688–1728), third son of Sir William Gage, 2nd Baronet of Hengrave, 'an intimate Friend of Mr Rookwood's, and often on hunting parties at Coldham'.

The clandestine marriage was solemnised in a Catholic ceremony conducted by the missionary priest in Bury St Edmunds at the time, Hugh Owen, and witnessed by John's sister Henrietta Gage (d. 1757) and a Catholic labourer, Nicholas Horsman (21).[171] However, in spite of its secrecy (which was only discovered when Elizabeth became pregnant), the marriage was an ideal dynastic match. The Papists' Estates Act of 1716 and the death of Sir William's eldest son and heir Thomas Gage on 1 March 1716 had brought considerable financial pressure to bear on the Gages,

---

[170] Copinger (1910), p. 341. Dorothy Maria Rookwood was buried at Stanningfield on 2 May 1727 (CUL Hengrave 76/1).

[171] Sir Thomas Rookwood Gage, 7th Baronet pasted the original certificate of marriage (21) into the Rookwood family genealogy. A 'James Horsman, labourer' was recorded as a Popish Non-Juror in 1745 (SRO(B) D8/1/3 bundle 2) and numerous members of the Horsman family appear in the Benedictine mission register of 1734–51, the Jesuit mission register (from 1756) and the 1767 Returns of Papists.

who had been forced to sell a number of manors.[172] However, Elizabeth's clandestine marriage initially estranged her from her father and it was not until 1726, shortly before his death, that he finally conferred a marriage settlement on her. As Elizabeth was his heir general in any case, this settlement never came into effect and was soon revoked.[173] However, the marriage was of critical dynastic importance to the Gages, because by John Gage's marriage to Elizabeth Rookwood he acquired the right for his heirs to inherit the Rookwood estates and, eventually, the estates of the Martins of Long Melford. As a consequence of the failure of the senior line of the Gages, it was John Gage and Elizabeth Rookwood's son Thomas who inherited the Hengrave baronetcy in 1767.

In 1726 John and Elizabeth arranged with Sir Thomas Hanmer, trustee of the Rookwood estates, for the continuation of the old arrangement whereby the Rookwoods would raise an income by means of fines that were levied on an estate held by trustees (**25**). In 1728 the trustees were named as Sir Thomas Hanmer, Sir Henry Bunbury and Richard Whitborne. Indentures of release in that year (**27**) specified that John and Elizabeth's eldest son should take the Rookwood surname as a condition of inheritance. This stipulation had probably been arranged much earlier by Thomas Rookwood, who would have been anxious that the family name should not die out with his daughter. In February 1727 Sir William Gage of Hengrave died suddenly when he was thrown from his horse against the gates of Hengrave Park, making his wife his sole executor. Unfortunately, she died so soon afterwards that it was impossible to execute his will. This created a dispute between Delariviere Gage (née D'Ewes), the mother of the new baronet (who was still a minor), and Sir William's other children. However, Elizabeth Rookwood seems to have made common cause with Delariviere rather than opposing her, as both women had apparently suffered at the hands of Edmund Howard, Sir William's former agent, who was championing the cause of the other Gage children. Elizabeth had once entrusted Howard with documents and now, according to Delariviere, she no longer placed any faith in him.[174]

The earliest evidence for a chaplain at Coldham Hall dates from this period. On 23 April 1717 the accounts of the South Province of the English Benedictine Congregation record that a monk named Francis Howard (d. 1755) was given money to travel from Bath, where the Benedictines had a headquarters at 'the Bell-tree house',[175] to 'Whallam Hall in Suffolk'. Gregory Allanson read 'Whallam' as a mistake for Coldham, which is borne out by later evidence, and it is likely that Howard became chaplain at Coldham in 1717. Howard was certainly in Bury St Edmunds in 1720,

---

[172] This Act permitted two Justices of the Peace to tender the Oaths of Allegiance and Supremacy, as well as an Oath of Abjuration of the Pretender, to any Catholic they chose, as well as obliging Catholic landowners to register their estates with all future conveyances and wills (J. Rowe, 'The 1767 Census of Papists in the Diocese of Norwich: the Social Composition of the Roman Catholic Community' in D. Chadd (ed.), *Religious Dissent in East Anglia III* (Norwich, 1996), pp. 188–9). On the Gages' financial situation at this time see Gage (1838), pp. 9, 236, 328.

[173] The original settlement made on John and Elizabeth on 20 November 1726 was revoked by endorsement on 28 June 1729 (SRO(B) 449/4/19).

[174] Ralph Pigot to Delariviere Gage, 6 November 1729 (CUL Hengrave MS 88/4/30).

[175] On the Bell-tree house see G. Scott, *Gothic Rage Undone: English Monks in the Age of Enlightenment* (Bath, 1992), p. 47.

as he testified that John Talbot Stonor, Vicar Apostolic of the Midland District (the bishop with jurisdiction over East Anglia) confirmed the three grandsons of Sir William Gage of Hengrave in that year.[176] By 1734 Howard was no longer at Coldham and was instead based permanently at Hengrave. Later, in 1741, the death of Hugh Owen made him the leading missionary priest in Bury St Edmunds. He remained there until his death in 1755.

John Gage and Elizabeth Rookwood had two sons. Thomas Rookwood Gage, born on 21 June 1719, was the heir to the Rookwood patrimony and, following the failure of either of his Gage cousins to produce an heir, he inherited the Hengrave baronetcy, as 5th Baronet, in 1767. Thomas Rookwood Gage was tutored by James Dennett, later Provincial of the English Jesuits,[177] who accompanied him abroad and later performed the same service for his son. Dennett may have been the chaplain at Coldham from as early as 1734, when the Benedictine Francis Howard moved to Hengrave. One document among the Rookwood Family Papers is a detailed argument prepared by Dennett against a claim by Sir Jasper Cullum of Hawstead that the manor of Philletts lay within his lands, which was based on the fact that Thomas Rookwood was once prosecuted for seizing a gun from a servant of Sir Dudley Cullum. Sir Jasper argued that the successful prosecution established that Thomas was exceeding his rights, but Dennett proceeded in the manner of a scholastic disputation to disprove every possible point that Cullum might raise.[178]

A portrait of Dennett in later life is to be found among the papers of Edmund Farrer in the Suffolk Record Office, Bury St Edmunds (Plate 2).[179] Dennett had the unusual distinction of achieving literary immortality as the model for the austere old ex-Jesuit, Mr Sandford, in Elizabeth Inchbald's novel *A Simple Story* (1791). Inchbald, who was born in Stanningfield in 1753 as Elizabeth Simpson, would have made her first confession when she was around twelve years old and Dennett was in his early sixties. Maria Edgeworth noted that Inchbald claimed to have based Sandford on 'her first confessor', whom Patricia Sigl and Michael Tomko have erroneously identified as John Gage the Jesuit.[180] It is highly unlikely that the younger missionary priest, who was based in Bury St Edmunds and not at Coldham, was the formative spiritual influence in Inchbald's life. Bury and Coldham were separate missions, and furthermore there is evidence that Inchbald was friendly with Dennett later in life; he visited her five times during the three months that she spent with her family in Stanningfield in 1781, a period when she was forming her novel of Catholic gentry life.[181]

John Gage, the father of Thomas and John, died at Winchester on 20 July 1728. Elizabeth was obliged to travel to Winchester in order to retrieve her husband's body

[176] Hengrave Register, 10 June 1720.
[177] Foley, vol. 5, p. 542.
[178] CUL Hengrave MS 76/2/12.
[179] SRO(B) HD526/123/9. The etching is unidentified in the SRO(B) catalogue but Edmund Farrer was told that it represented a Catholic priest called 'Mr Dunnett' when he was given it by Mr Cullum of Hardwick. See SRO(B) HD526/123/6.
[180] Maria Edgeworth to Mrs Ruxton, 2 March 1810, quoted in P. Sigl, 'The Elizabeth Inchbald Papers', *Notes and Queries* 29 (1982), p. 223; M. Tomko, *British Romanticism and the Catholic Question: Religion, History and National Identity, 1778–1829* (Basingstoke, 2011), p. 56.
[181] E. Inchbald (ed. B. P. Robertson), *The Diaries of Elizabeth Inchbald* (London, 2007), pp. 256, 259, 265, 269, 271. I make the argument that Dennett was the model for Sandford in F. Young, 'Elizabeth Inchbald's "Catholic Novel" and its Local Background', *Recusant History* 31 (2013b), pp. 573–92.

Plate 2. A stippled etching of James Dennett, SJ (1702–89), Jesuit Superior and chaplain at Coldham Hall (SRO(B) HD526/123/9), who provided the model for Mr Sandford in Elizabeth Inchbald's novel *A Simple Story* (1791). Reproduced by kind permission of the Suffolk Record Office, Bury St Edmunds

for burial in Stanningfield church, where he was interred in the chancel six days later under a slab (Plate 3) that bore the letters 'O. P. A.', *Ora Pro Animis*, a bold (and indeed illegal) statement of Catholic identity in eighteenth-century England.[182] The trip to Winchester was an expensive one, costing a total of £142 2s, including £39 19s 6d for 'Mr Kerwoods bills for morning & pray[e]rs att the Chaples'.[183] 'Prayers' was normally a euphemism used by Catholics for Mass, but no priest of the name of Kerwood is known; it may be that he was simply the tradesman who provided cloth for mourning purposes. At any rate it would seem that a requiem Mass was said for John Gage in Winchester.

Elizabeth Rookwood proved an astute yet conservative estate manager following her husband's death. In 1730, the farms she owned (excluding woods) were valued at £921 1s 10d, from which tax of £137 10s 2d was owed (**28**). Elizabeth noted that she gave her fields over to the use of her tenants unless she could get a good price for the crops she would otherwise grow: '2 Acres is generally Cut Every yeare to allowe the tenants wheare there is a deficiancy of Cropings – 4 Acres more I usialy Cut if I meet w[i]th a Chap th[a]t will give 5 pounds an Acre at ii years grothe, other ways I Lett them stand'. Elizabeth continued charitable arrangements with regard to tenants that her father had established, such as allowing John Gough to hold a tenement in Stanningfield rent-free 'th[a]t he may Look after the woods & Stope gaps'. She also seems to have acted on occasion as a pawnbroker for her friends and neighbours, lending them money against rings, watches and silver spoons that were left in her safekeeping. Although the majority of her customers were probably local people, the 'mr J[oh]n Taybers' who left her eight spoons, two silver-chased buckets, a piece of gold lace, two gold rings and one silver ring in 1745 was probably John Beaumont Tasburgh of Bodney, a Catholic and Jacobite.[184]

The library at Coldham Hall

Elizabeth Rookwood continued the commonplace books that her father Thomas had begun in a pair of reused seventeenth-century music books. Hints on horticulture and arboriculture copied from popular texts jostle in these pages with Thomas and Elizabeth's attempt at an exhaustive biobibliography of English Catholic authors (**30**). This document is the earliest attempt I am aware of at a complete list of English Catholic authors and their books. The biobibliography is an alphabetical list of 161 separate authors (as well as some repetitions) with a few lines outlining the biography or achievements of each one and a list of their books. The authors range from late medieval theologians to contemporary authors such as 'Charles Dodd' (Hugh Tootell), with a bias towards Marian and early Catholic authors of the 1560s (many of whom were involved in controversy with the Elizabethan Bishop of Salisbury, John Jewel). Among the late sixteenth- and early seventeenth-century authors there is a bias towards Jesuits, who account for 33 of the 161. This is hardly surprising, given Coldham Hall's longstanding association with the Society of Jesus.

---

[182] This was a 'superstitious inscription', illegal under a law of 1643. See J. Spraggon, *Puritan Iconoclasm during the English Civil War* (Woodbridge, 2003), pp. 73–6.

[183] CUL Hengrave MS 76/3.

[184] CUL Hengrave MS 76/2, fol. 20. On this family see F. Young, 'The Tasburghs of Bodney: Catholicism and Politics in South Norfolk', *Norfolk Archaeology* 46 (2011), pp. 190–8.

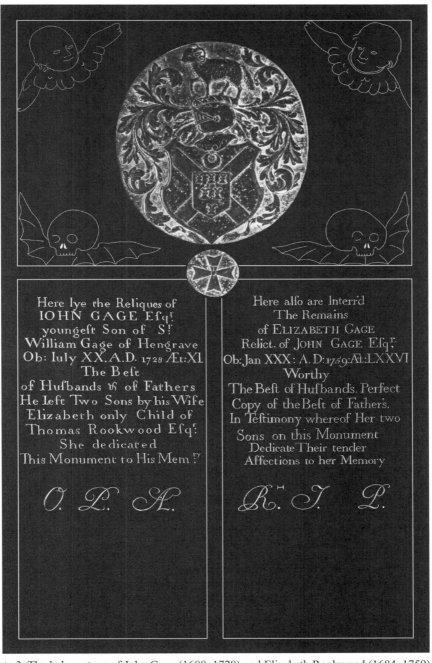

Plate 3. The ledger stone of John Gage (1688–1728) and Elizabeth Rookwood (1684–1759) in the chancel of Stanningfield church, bearing the letters O. P. A. (*Ora pro Animis*) and R. I. P. (*Requiescant in Pace*), which were illegal 'superstitious inscriptions' under an Act of Parliament of 1643. Photograph by Mike Durrant

The biobibliography was composed over a number of years, and was probably begun by Elizabeth Rookwood in her father's lifetime. At one point there is a reference to a manuscript book on the Gospel of Nicodemus 'in mr Rookwoods hands'. Compilers of the time often referred to themselves in the third person, but in the light of Elizabeth's later dedication to the library catalogue it seems likely that she was responsible for the biobibliography as well. Furthermore, the latest entry in the list is the Jesuit Lewis Sabran, who died in 1732, six years after Thomas Rookwood. The biobibliography is not reproduced here in entirety, because it has been surpassed in accuracy and detail by contemporary scholarship. I have therefore reduced the biobibliography to a list of the authors to be found in it, together with their dates of birth and death. The majority of these authors have entries in the *Oxford Dictionary of National Biography*.

The interest of the biobibliography lies in the fact that it was an attempt to tell the story of the English Catholic community through its books and their authors, rather than a mere catalogue of books. Indeed, not every author in the biobibliography featured in Coldham's library, suggesting that Elizabeth drew on other sources as well. The library catalogue (**32**) was a distinct document begun by Elizabeth, like the inventory of the house (**31**), in the summer of 1737. Although the catalogue was continued after her death (probably by her son Thomas Rookwood Gage), Elizabeth was responsible for recording the vast majority of the 1,889 individual volumes. Of these books, 522 (28 per cent of the total) are identifiable as 'English Catholic books', and it is the entries for these books only that are reproduced in this volume. I define 'English Catholic books' as:

1. Books found in the standard lists of English Catholic books (Allison and Rogers (1956), Clancy (1974), and Blom et al. (1996)).
2. Books of significance to the Catholic community that were published before 1559.
3. Latin works by English Catholic authors.
4. Books of Jacobite interest.

All of the manuscripts owned by the Rookwood family, because of their uniqueness and intrinsic historical interest, are also included. Catholic theological and spiritual works in French or Latin works by non-English authors are not included. Also excluded are Catholic books whose subject matter pertained principally to Ireland, but not Irish authors who were read by English Catholics. The numbering of books in the original manuscript is retained, although this was not always consistent. Therefore I have assigned sequential numbers distinct to this volume, with the prefix **RFP**, to each individual item in the collection. Books bound together and listed in the manuscript as one entry are here listed as separate items. Dates of publication were not always accurately recorded by Elizabeth, and I have not corrected these, although I supply them in square brackets where they are lacking entirely. The catalogue should be read in conjunction with the standard lists of Catholic books identified above. However, Coldham's library contained numerous rare and unusual Catholic books and pamphlets, some of which are not recorded in the standard catalogues.

Coldham Hall's collection of English Catholic literature was a rich one for mid-eighteenth-century England. By way of comparison, the library of the Jesuit College of the Immaculate Conception, which was seized by the authorities at Holbeck Hall, Nottinghamshire in 1679 and taken to London, contained 990 books, around 275 of which were works of controversy.[185] The library of the College of St Francis Xavier in Wales and the West Country, at Cwm on the Welsh–Herefordshire border, contained around 350 books.[186] Although there is insufficient evidence to be sure that Coldham Hall's library was the missionary library of the College of the Holy Apostles, the library was undoubtedly both used and added to by Jesuits. A handful (seventeen) of the books at Coldham were printed before 1559 and represent treasured relics of Henrician and Marian Catholicism, although they seem to have had little monetary value at the time the catalogue was compiled. Of the books in the collection 168 were printed before 1641, when only a tiny number of Catholic books were printed on secret presses in England as well as foreign presses in France at Douai, St Omer and Paris; Allison and Rogers (1956) identified only 930 books in total from this period. A smaller but nevertheless significant number of the Catholic books (seventy-four) were printed in the brief period between 1685 and 1688 when Catholic printing enjoyed a brief period of freedom during the reign of James II.

Of those books in the collection printed before 1685, the most common city of origin was Paris, accounting for 20 per cent. Douai followed close behind with 15 per cent, while 13 per cent came from the presses at St Omer. Other locations included Antwerp, Louvain, Rouen, Brussels, Lyon, Mechelin and Amsterdam.[187] Only eighty-six books in the collection were published after 1700 and, of these, the latest was published in 1761. This is a small proportion of the total, given that Catholic printing mushroomed in the eighteenth century, with Blom et al. (1996) listing almost 3,000 books; the Rookwoods were clearly conservative when it came to acquiring new publications. An anomaly in the collection is the appearance of the 1786 edition of Bossuet's *Exposition of the Doctrine of the Catholic Church*. If the catalogue is to be believed, not a single new book was purchased by Thomas Rookwood Gage for sixteen years. It seems highly likely that books were purchased throughout the 1760s, 1770s and 1780s, but that Thomas only made an effort to continue his mother's practice of maintaining a detailed catalogue in the 1750s.

Although Coldham Hall was a centre of Jesuit activity from as early as 1589, there is no evidence to support the idea that the early works present in the library in 1737 were acquired by Ambrose Rookwood (I). Coldham was thoroughly ransacked by magistrates in November 1605, and it is likely that any Catholic books would have been removed and destroyed on that occasion. However, the large number of English Catholic books at Coldham, and the fact that a number of them were in duplicate, suggests that the library's purpose went beyond the personal and domestic. One possibility is that the duplicates arrived in the personal collections of Coldham's chaplains; another is that they were books belonging to the Jesuit College of the Holy Apostles. However, the collection's theological bias was not exclusively Jesuit; it also featured texts by the fiercely anti-Jesuit secular priest John Sergeant, the Dominicans Louis of

---

[185] H. Dijkgraaf, *The Library of a Jesuit Community at Holbeck, Nottinghamshire (1679)* (Tempe, Arizona, 2003), p. 237 (for a graphic breakdown of the collection; for the complete catalogue see pp. 96–227). In contrast to Coldham, the Holbeck library contained a large number of Latin theological works; Hendrik Dijkgraaf considered the library in its European context and made no attempt to analyse the number of books of specific interest to the English Catholic community.

[186] H. Thomas, 'The Society of Jesus in Wales, c.1600–1679: Rediscovering the Cwm Jesuit Library at Hereford Cathedral', *Journal of Jesuit Studies* 1 (2014), pp. 572–88, p. 577.

[187] Hannah Thomas has found that Cologne, Antwerp and Mainz were the most frequently occurring imprints at the Cwm library (Thomas (2014), p. 577).

Granada and William Perin, the Franciscans Francis Loraine and Richard Mason, and the Benedictines Maurus Corker and Serenus Cressy.

After the English Catholic books, the remaining 72 per cent of Coldham's library was made up of foreign Catholic theological and devotional works, a large number of Protestant theological, devotional and liturgical works, political pamphlets (with a preference for the work of Tory propagandists such as Sir Roger L'Estrange) and legal, medical and historical texts. Given Elizabeth Rookwood's continental education, the presence of French works is unsurprising. The library was home to seventeen manuscripts, most of which seem to have been theological or didactic in nature; the only one known to survive today is Cambridge University Library Add. MS 10079, the Rookwood Book of Hours (probably **RFP9** in this catalogue). There were few identifiable works that were Jacobite in sympathy, at first glance a surprising omission given Thomas Rookwood's chequered past. However, the absence of such works may be evidence that Thomas lost interest in the Jacobite cause early on. In light of his brother Ambrose (IV)'s awful fate and his own strenuous efforts to return to England in the 1690s this may not be quite as surprising as it first appears.

There is evidence in the catalogue that Thomas Rookwood Gage lent or gave a small number of books to friends or acquaintances, but not enough to disperse the library. However, an undated library catalogue, which judging from the handwriting dates from the late eighteenth or early nineteenth century, records only 314 books.[188] It is possible that this list is simply incomplete. Alternatively, it may be that Thomas Rookwood Gage sold off much of the library after 1767. It is known that the remaining contents of Coldham Hall were moved to Hengrave in 1843, and an undated 'Catalogue of the Books from Coldham Sold by Auction' may date from this time. However, almost all of the books in this list were published between 1760 and 1830.[189] The catalogue prepared for the auction of Hengrave's contents in 1897 likewise contains no obvious references to the Catholic books from Coldham Hall.[190] However, at some point in the nineteenth century, a large number of books from the library of Hengrave Hall were acquired by the Benyon family for Englefield House in Berkshire. It is possible that some books that were once at Coldham may survive there, but the majority of Elizabeth Rookwood's collection seems to have been dispersed.

Elizabeth Rookwood's domestic inventory

Elizabeth Rookwood began a detailed domestic inventory of the contents of Coldham Hall (**31**) in August 1737. The inventory provides a snapshot of the material wealth of the Rookwoods, and since Elizabeth also added to it after 1737 it gives insight into the extent to which the family purchased and inherited new items over the next decade or so. The list of vestments, rare for this early period, is especially illuminating with regard to the family's religious life. However, Elizabeth's faith would have been immediately evident to any visitor to Coldham, Catholic or Protestant, on account of her preference for religious pictures. On the staircase was a picture of St Ignatius and

---

[188] CUL Hengrave 76/2/30.
[189] CUL Hengrave MS 76/4.
[190] It is possible that the books described in *Catalogue*, lots 1255, 1260, 1326 and 1328 were originally from the library at Coldham, but the catalogue descriptions are too vague to be certain.

Plate 4. The great hall at Coldham Hall in the early twentieth century, showing the portraits of Frances Cary and another Augustinian canoness. These are the only original portraits to remain at Coldham Hall to this day, and their removal is reputedly associated with bad luck. Photograph from the Spanton Jarman Collection, reproduced by kind permission of the Bury St Edmunds Past and Present Society

'Mrs Cary a nun' (Plate 4),[191] as well as twenty prints of 'Our Saviour's Passion' and a crucifixion. Similarly, in 'the chamber over the old kitchen' were prints of Christ, St John the Baptist and St Mary Magdalene, and there was 'one little tabernacle' in the hall along with '4 marble images', 'An Ivory Crucifix & Cross inlaid tortos shell with foot', a brass crucifix, a panel of a medieval triptych depicting the Three Kings, a Madonna and child, a nativity, an 'ecce homo' and another Madonna. In Elizabeth's own room was a diptych of the Visitation, pictures of Ss Catharine and Barbara, Christ carrying the cross, 'One print of a pope' and 'A print of the saints of the dominicans'.

The evidence suggests that Elizabeth Rookwood went out of her way to obtain items for a collection that, whilst capable of masquerading as *objets d'art* in the age of the Grand Tour, was in reality a powerful statement of Catholic identity. Secular items from the Continent were accumulated as well: in 1732 the walls of the dining room at Coldham were lined with 'fine old leather' removed from Castle Borenta near Seville.[192] By way of comparison, the Mannocks at Stoke-by-Nayland decorated the walls of Gifford's Hall with cloth from India and Persia. Gabriel Glickman has observed that in this period 'the pressures of marital advancement served ... to embolden recusant gentlemen towards displays of social ostentation'.[193] Unlike their neighbours, Catholics lacked the financial resources (on account of recusancy fines) to express their cultural sophistication through building, and the Rookwoods and Mannocks seem to have chosen to use the medium of interior design instead.

Vestments were treasured possessions for recusant families, and they were often few in number, with a single chasuble consisting of fabric of every liturgical colour sometimes serving for all occasions. Given the fear of searches and informants, and the need for secrecy, large collections of lavish vestments were impractical even if a family could afford them. Within Elizabeth Rookwood's lifetime an anti-Catholic mob had roamed the Suffolk countryside searching the homes of papists, and popular consciousness of the continued Jacobite threat did not make such extra-legal mob action any less likely as the eighteenth century progressed. In the light of these threats, the sheer size of the Rookwood collection of vestments is surprising, as is Elizabeth's decision to record the entire collection alongside ordinary household items in a domestic inventory.

Elizabeth recorded twelve chasubles in the Rookwood family collection, most

---

[191] This was one of the few portraits belonging to Coldham Hall that was still there when Farrer visited in 1904, although it was no longer identified as Mrs Cary (Farrer (1908), p. 325). The portrait was moved to Hengrave in 1869 and sold in 1897, together with another painting of a nun, as 'a pair of full length portraits "The Rev. Mother" (Mary More) last descendent of Sir Thomas More, and "A Sister"' (*Catalogue*, p. 44). Whoever wrote this description was evidently unaware that the painting came from Coldham; Mother Mary More was the prioress of the English Convent at Bruges who took refuge at Hengrave from 1794–1802. Given that Mrs Cary was wearing an Augustinian habit she was probably Frances Cary (Sister Frances of St Ignatius), one of the foundresses of the Canonesses Regular of the Holy Sepulchre at Liège in 1642 (P. Guilday, *The English Catholic Refugees on the Continent 1558–1795* (London, 1914), p. 392). The two pictures were associated with ghostly apparitions in 1807 and are the only original portraits to remain at Coldham to this day, since their removal is supposed to bring about bad luck (F. Young, *English Catholics and the Supernatural, 1553–1829* (Farnham, 2013), pp. 104–8).

[192] Anon., *A Stanningfield Century 1837–1939: A Portrait of a Suffolk Village* (Bury St Edmunds, 1997), p. 15.

[193] G. Glickman, *The English Catholic Community 1688–1745: Politics, Culture and Ideology* (Woodbridge, 2009), p. 62.

with matching accoutrements, as well as three more bought from Margaret Martin of Long Melford, executor of the will of an aunt of Elizabeth Rookwood. Purchases made after 1737 were also added to the list, including 'A Chalice w[hi]ch was S[i]r Rogers [i.e. Sir Roger Martin's]' and a 'Chalice & patten bought of mrs harrington' in 1741. In addition, Elizabeth seems to have actively added to her collection of Catholic curiosities and relics by purchasing them from other Catholic ladies, noting on 18 November 1741 that she 'bought of mrs Keddington pope Clemens X a silver pi[ece] w[or]n 1674 for w[hi]ch I payd her 18d'. This was probably a medal blessed by the pope.

One of the Rookwood chasubles was 'Blew wrote with Gold', indicating that at least one pre-Reformation tradition survived at Coldham. Blue vestments had no place in the Counter-Reformation liturgy (the Tridentine Mass of Pope Pius V), but they were worn on feasts of the Virgin Mary in the medieval English Sarum usage. The Sarum usage was continued by surviving Marian priests after 1559, and a Sarum manual was published at Douai as late as 1626. However, by the end of the seventeenth century the Sarum usage had largely died out on the English mission.[194] The blue chasuble at Coldham may well have been a treasured relic of the medieval past. The presence of embroidered antependia (altar frontals) in the Rookwood collection suggests that there was a full-size purpose-built altar at Coldham as opposed to a portable consecrated altar stone (usually of slate) that would be laid on top of an ordinary table. Things may well have been different at Melford Place, as there was an 'alter ston' among the effects bought from Margaret Martin. The evidence of the inventory suggests that the Rookwoods were very bold indeed about their practice of the Catholic faith, at a time when it was still a capital offence for a priest to say Mass.

Whereas Elizabeth treated the vestments and altar linen as a distinct category of possessions, when it came to silver she indiscriminately mingled the sacred and profane. Among the chapel silver were 'Two flat Candlesticks with father & mothers arms on th[e]m',[195] and two chalices with patens, one of which had belonged to her aunt ('old Aunts'). Elizabeth's description of these as 'cups' rather than chalices may be an indication that they were tiny recusant chalices as opposed to the full-sized chalices that her grandmother donated to the Jesuits in 1684. Some chalices were designed to contain no more than a thimbleful of wine, so that they could be more easily hidden. Elizabeth mentioned a further chalice that had belonged to her grandmother Lady Monson but which was now 'at Bn.', probably an abbreviation for Beyton, where the home of the Burton family had been a centre of Jesuit activity in the 1690s.[196] Beyton was evidently still a Mass centre in the 1730s. The only other sacred silver identifiable in the inventory consisted of '3 small boxes for oils [and] one pixis'. In all, Coldham was a great deal richer in vestments than it was in altar silver.

Exactly how the Rookwoods managed to obtain so much from the Continent is unclear; one possibility is that visiting priests acted as agents. By the late 1730s it is possible that Elizabeth's eldest son Thomas Rookwood Gage was already on the

---

[194] S. Morison, *English Prayer Books: An Introduction to the Literature of Christian Public Worship*, 4th edn (Cambridge, 2009), pp. 140–2.

[195] These were probably the candlesticks featuring the arms of Thomas Rookwood and Tamworth Martin mentioned in a later inventory, CUL Hengrave MS 76/4.

[196] On the Jesuits at Beyton see T. Hunter, *An English Carmelite: The Life of Catharine Burton* (London, 1876) and Young (2006), pp. 209–55.

Grand Tour with his Jesuit tutor, James Dennett; he would have been eighteen years old when the inventory was made. However, it is noticeable that the Rookwoods collected not only fashionable prints and rococo religious paintings but also medieval artefacts such as diptychs and triptychs painted on wood. The fifteenth-century Rookwood Book of Hours,[197] produced in the Low Countries in the 1460s, was in Thomas Rookwood's possession by 1726 and was probably purchased or inherited from the Martin family of Long Melford, perhaps through his wife Tamworth Martin who died in childbirth in 1684. The Rookwoods were not alone in treasuring the remnants of a real or imagined Catholic past; in 1730 the Benedictines removed from Hengrave 'an old valuable vestment supposed to be given by St Edward ye Confessor, w[i]th a silver guilt Chalice', presumably for safekeeping.[198]

In spite of her interest in the past, Elizabeth Rookwood was very much involved in the present-day life of the Catholic community in Bury St Edmunds. In 1746 her son Thomas Rookwood Gage married Lucy Knight, the heiress of William Knight of Kingerby in Lincolnshire.[199] Elizabeth Rookwood marked the occasion by giving her son a diamond-studded buckle, earrings and a cross from her collection (valued at £422 14s 18d) for his new wife (**31**). The entailment of Kingerby stipulated that it could not be sold and a private Act of Parliament was required in 1766 to vest the estate in trustees so that the proceeds of its sale could be used to purchase or release from mortgages the manor of Harleston in Suffolk, an ancient property of the Gages. Thomas Rookwood Gage and Lucy Knight had a son, Thomas Rookwood Gage, 6th Baronet, and three daughters. It is likely that Elizabeth Rookwood left Coldham Hall in 1746 and settled in her house in Bury St Edmunds until her death; it was here that she became a key figure in the refoundation of the Jesuit mission to the town.

Elizabeth Rookwood's second son, John Gage (he was not obliged, like his brother, to use the Rookwood surname), was educated at the Jesuit College at St Omer and trained for the priesthood; he was ordained at Watten near Calais in 1740 and studied philosophy at Liège before returning to England.[200] Unlike most Jesuits, who were received into the Society of Jesus as brothers and later ordained, John Gage was not professed as a Jesuit until 2 February 1756.[201] Gage's first and only mission was to Catholics in Bury St Edmunds; it was not uncommon for relatives of influential Catholic families in a locality to be sent there, thus preserving and strengthening existing bonds of trust within and outside the Catholic community. John Gage was in Bury as early as December 1753, when the secular priest Alban Butler complained that Gage was one of the clergy who refused to accept a brief of Pope Benedict XIV.[202] Francis Howard, the Benedictine monk who had been chaplain at Coldham in 1717 and had served Bury since 1741, died on 12 December 1755,[203] allowing John Gage to step into the role of running the main mission for the town. Many years later, in 1793, Sir Thomas Rookwood Gage, 6th Baronet wrote that his uncle 'knew Father

---

[197] **RFP9**. The Rookwood Book of Hours was acquired at auction by Cambridge University Library in December 2014 and is now CUL Add. MS 10079. See Plate VI
[198] On Catholic medievalism in the eighteenth century see Glickman (2009), p. 68.
[199] The couple's marriage indenture was dated 28 February 1746 (**33**).
[200] Foley, vol. 7:1, p. 283.
[201] Foley, vol. 5, p. 539.
[202] Alban Butler to Bishop John Hornyold, 23 December 1753 (Archives of the Archbishops of Westminster, A 40/97).
[203] Downside Abbey, South Province Book R, 1717–1826, p. 82.

Howard, the last Benedictine'.[204] On 1 January 1756 John Gage began his mission register (the Bury Register).[205]

The Benedictine mission in Bury St Edmunds was not based in a single place, and the monks made use of the Bond family's chapel in Eastgate Street (now demolished), the Gages' townhouse in Northgate Street (now numbers 9, 10 and 11) and the house owned by Delariviere Gage, the mother of Sir William Gage, 4th Baronet. Elizabeth Rookwood's house in Southgate Street (Plate 5) may also have been used, and it was certainly the centre of John Gage's missionary activity, except when he occasionally made use of the Bond family's chapel. In the years 1758–61 John Gage was not the only Catholic priest in Bury St Edmunds, as the Dominican Ambrose Gage was chaplain to the Short family (whose home was in Risbygate Street) during this period.[206] Ambrose Gage was a cousin of the Hengrave Gages, being descended from a younger son of Sir Edward Gage, 1st Baronet.[207]

At John Gage's mother's house in Southgate Street he ministered in a chapel that was able to accommodate a congregation of fifty, 'in which divine service was performed in secret, and which was afterwards tenanted by a Mrs White who was a friend of the Gages though a Protestant and from whom the lane which there branches off from the street is still called Madam White's Lane'.[208] A separate external staircase from Madam White's Lane led directly to the chapel and permitted discreet access for local Catholics. Madam White's Lane is now known as St Botolph's Lane and Elizabeth Rookwood's house still stands, although the brickwork reveals that an extra storey was added to the house in the late eighteenth century.

In her will of 16 November 1758 (**34**) Elizabeth Rookwood left her entire estate to her eldest son Thomas Rookwood Gage, leaving aside legacies of £100 to John Gage the Jesuit and £50 to her goddaughter Elizabeth Gage. John Gage already had his own income from land, since in 1735 his mother had bought him the manor of Fresels in Westley, which he used to cover the costs of the mission.[209] Elizabeth died at her house in Southgate Street on 30 January 1759 and was buried in Stanningfield parish church; John Gage paid tribute to her in a note in his mission register that described her as *paene fundatrix* ('almost the foundress') of the Bury mission, and decreed that the *De Profundis* should be said every day for the repose of her soul after the Liturgy of the Blessed Virgin Mary.[210] Within three years John Gage had exchanged the chapel in his mother's house for a handsome purpose-built chapel funded jointly by his brother Thomas Rookwood Gage, Sir William Gage of Hengrave and the Jesuit Province in the form of the Superior, James Dennett, who remained the chaplain at Coldham.[211]

The deaths of John Martin of Long Melford in 1761 and Sir William Gage in 1767 rendered the Rookwood Gage family the inheritors of both Melford Place and Hengrave Hall. These estates were not merely an addition to the family's material

---

[204] Foley, vol. 5, p. 538.
[205] I am grateful to Joy Rowe for giving me access to John Gage's mission register, 1756–89 (Bury Register).
[206] W. Gumbley, *Obituary Notices of the English Dominicans from 1555 to 1952* (London, 1955), p. 78.
[207] Gage (1838), p. 209.
[208] J. Rowe, '"The lopped tree": The Re-formation of the Suffolk Catholic Community' in N. Tyacke (ed.), *England's Long Reformation 1500–1800* (Abingdon, 1998), pp. 167–94, at p. 186.
[209] Gage (1838), p. 93.
[210] Bury Register, p. 101.
[211] Bury Register, p. 102.

Plate 5. Elizabeth Rookwood's townhouse in Southgate Street, Bury St Edmunds, which was the base of John Gage SJ's mission chapel 1753–61. The lane running beside the house is St Botolph's Lane, formerly Madam White's Lane, which provided discreet access for worshippers to the chapel at the back of the house. Photograph by Mike Durrant

wealth; both the Martins and the Gages were Catholic families of long standing whose local influence was assumed by the Rookwood Gages. The family became the undisputed leaders of Suffolk's Catholic community. However, Sir Thomas Rookwood Gage, 5th Baronet chose to honour the Rookwood inheritance above all. Melford Place was sold shortly after John Martin's death (**36**), and Hengrave became the residence of Sir Thomas's eldest son. Coldham Hall remained the seat of the family for many decades, and a repository of the treasures of three of Suffolk's Catholic families.

The Rookwood Gages continued to live at Coldham Hall until 1843 when, on the death of John Gage the antiquary, Sir Thomas Gage Rokewode, 8th Baronet (1810–66), made Hengrave Hall his main home. In 1843 the family name was changed to Gage Rokewode, reviving the medieval spelling of the name. Coldham Hall continued to be let to tenants until it was finally sold in 1869, three years before the death of the last baronet. It has been in private hands ever since.[212] Following the death of the last Gage Rokewode baronet in 1872 the Rookwood surname was picked up by a remote relative, Robert Darell of Calehill in Kent, who was the great-grandson of Elizabeth, the second daughter of Sir Thomas Rookwood Gage, 5th Baronet.[213]

The Rookwood family left a lasting legacy in the parish of Stanningfield, in the form of the survival of Catholicism there as a significant element of village life. Although it cannot be demonstrated that a continuous Catholic community existed in the village outside of Coldham Hall itself throughout the sixteenth and seventeenth centuries, by the eighteenth century the presence of a chaplain at Coldham, and the fact that it was one of relatively few centres where Mass could be heard regularly, meant that Stanningfield sustained a small number of Catholics beyond the immediate household of the Rookwoods and Rookwood Gages. In the 1767 Returns of Papists, thirty-two Catholics were recorded in Stanningfield, more than in any other parish in the county outside Bury St Edmunds.[214] These included two widows farming their husbands' former lands, two labourers and two widows described as mantua makers.[215] The Catholic farmer John Simpson was apparently, until his death in 1761, 'greatly esteemed by the gentry of the neighbourhood' and possessed 'a moderate farm', suggesting that Stanningfield was a place where it was possible for Catholics to prosper.[216] In the second half of the eighteenth century, Coldham became the centre of a 'riding mission' extending into south Suffolk, with another centre at Withermarsh Green next to Stoke-by-Nayland. This was increasingly distinct from John Gage's town mission in Bury St Edmunds, although Gage continued to baptise children from further afield from time to time.

There seems to have been a public chapel in Stanningfield, distinct from the

---

[212] Anon., *A Stanningfield Century* (1997), p. 12.

[213] Robert Darell took the surname Rokewode-Darell in accordance with the provisions of the 9th Baronet's will. His great-grandmother Elizabeth Gage had married Henry Darell at Stanningfield on 18 November 1767 (CUL Hengrave MS 76/1; see also *The London Gazette*, 23858 (17 May 1872), p. 2361). The Darell family later assumed the surname Darell-Blount; the last descendant of this family was Agnes Mary Darell-Blount (d. 1918), whose present-day heir is John Joseph Eyston of Mapledurham (b. 1934).

[214] E. S. Worrall (ed.), *Returns of Papists Volume 2: Dioceses of England and Wales, except Chester* (London, 1989), p. 128.

[215] Rowe (1996), pp. 213–14.

[216] J. Boaden (ed.), *Memoirs of Mrs Inchbald* (London, 1833), vol. 1, pp. 3–4.

Rookwoods' family chapel inside Coldham Hall, at least as early as 1781. In that year Elizabeth Inchbald, on a visit home to her family, recorded that she 'went to prayers [i.e. Mass] by home field'.[217] In 1792 Sir Thomas Rookwood Gage, 5th Baronet appointed trustees to administer Barfords, a moated farmhouse on Stanningfield's Donkey Lane, 'as a mission or funds'. Barfords was buried deep in woodland at the time and the farm consisted of sixty-nine acres, straddling the parish boundary of Stanningfield and Lawshall.[218] A list of manors owned by the Rookwood Gages in 1804 included 'Barfords ffarm, belong[ing] to the priest'.[219] Barfords was succeeded by the church known as 'Coldham Cottage' in 1858. This building remains a mission church within the parish of St Edmund, King and Martyr, Bury St Edmunds, and Mass is celebrated there regularly, two and a half centuries after the death of the last Rookwood.

The involvement of family members in treason exposed the Rookwoods to the threat of persecution to a greater extent than other Catholic families, and their survival as a landed family with at least some of their ancestral lands intact was a considerable achievement. The sympathetic attitude of their Protestant neighbours undoubtedly did more than a little to ensure that the Rookwoods were not extirpated or expropriated during the penal years. By way of comparison, the Rookwoods of Euston were destroyed by recusancy fines and composition for their estates in the 1640s. They were forced to sell Euston Hall and their descendants emigrated to America. However, the Stanningfield Rookwoods did more than survive, and the household documents of Elizabeth Rookwood testify to the religious, cultural and intellectual vitality and richness of Coldham Hall in the eighteenth century. Foreign exile and Jesuit influence ensured that the Rookwoods were at home in the expatriate English Catholic community abroad, although they avoided being absorbed into it altogether (in contrast to the Mannocks and Timperleys) and their ancient bond with Suffolk was strengthened as they acquired the lands of the Martins of Long Melford and the Gages of Hengrave in the 1760s. The Rookwoods eventually forged an identity for themselves that, whilst quietly at odds with the mainstream of Hanoverian England, was nevertheless recognised as harmless by their friends and neighbours.

---

[217] Inchbald (2007), p. 256.
[218] Anon., *A Stanningfield Century* (1997), p. 32.
[219] CUL Hengrave MS 76/2/34.

EDITORIAL METHODS

The documents are numbered chronologically, with their identifying number in the relevant manuscript collection given in square brackets after the number assigned to them in this edition. Folio and piece numbers are given where available. However, CUL Hengrave MS 76/1, from which several of the documents are taken, has no numbered folios. Insertions in the original MS are shown between oblique lines thus \.../. Readable deleted sections are shown within angled brackets <...> while illegible words are marked [*illeg.*] and sections that cannot be read owing to damage are marked [*damaged*]. Numbering of original folios has been retained, although this was not always done consistently by the original compilers.

Dates quoted in original documents have been retained, but in all editorial references to those same documents (including document titles), Julian dates are given with the year taken to begin on 1 January (so 1 January 1690 or 1 January 1690/1 becomes 1 January 1691). Naturally, all dates after September 1752 are Gregorian. All dates before 1752 are given according to the Julian Calendar (OS). Dates in the body of the documents themselves have been left in their original form.

Original spelling has been retained, with the exception of the archaic letter thorn (þ, later written as y), which is expanded to 'th' in all cases. Capitalisation has also been retained, as in the original documents. Punctuation has been inserted in square brackets where it aids understanding of the text.

Documents in languages other than English are provided with a full translation; Latin sections of documents that are partly in English and partly in Latin have also been translated. Brief Latin insertions in other documents, such as 'anno' for 'in the year' and Latinisations of regnal dates are not translated. Likewise, Latin entries in the library catalogue (**32**) are left untranslated, since the information given (author, edition and place of publication) is conventional and easily understood. All translations from the Latin are my own unless otherwise stated. Naturally, I take responsibility for any errors or omissions in the texts.

Forenames and surnames have not been modernised (except in the list of authors in the Rookwood library, **30**), and abbreviated Christian names have been extended. Place names have not been modernised.

Suspensions and contractions used in the original documents have been extended in square brackets, apart from those that are readily understood (such as 'Dr' and 'Mr'). Ampersand (&) has not been expanded to 'and'. No attempt has been made to retain superscript minimalisations in the text such as '8th' for '8th', with the exception of '8°' to mean 'octavo' or 'on the eighth day'.

Numbers, weights and measures used in the original documents are retained here, and no attempt has been made to correct arithmetical errors in the accounts and inventories.

Numbering of books in the library catalogue has been retained, as in the original.

These numbers are not in a single sequence and begin anew for each book type (quartos, octavos, duodecimos, and books in different languages). However, all of the books listed in this volume have also been assigned a new number with the prefix **RFP**. This number is given in bold, and is assigned so that these books can be referred to with ease in any subsequent scholarship on the Rookwood library. Where the publication date of a book is not given in the original MS I have supplied it in square brackets. Where several books were assigned a single value, they were bound together in a single volume. Elizabeth Rookwood estimated the value of volumes, not individual works.

ROOKWOOD FAMILY PAPERS

1. [SRO(B) 326/48] *Sir Robert Rookwood's plea to the Attorney General against recusancy fines due from his father and grandfather, 15 June 1636*

The severall Plea and Assurance of S[i]r Robert Rookwood K[nigh]t one [*damaged*] defendants to the informaton of Sir John Banks knight his Ma[jes]t[y]s Attorney gen[er]all

Term[in]o s[anc[t]issim]i Trin[ita]te Anno ximo R[egi]S Carolj[1]

This defendant savinge to himselfe both nowe and att all tymes hereafter all advantages of Exception to the [*illeg.*] and insufficiencie in Lawe of the said Informaton, for answere unto Soo many thereof and doth confine this defendannt to make likewise unto saith That Robert Rookwood Esquier this defendants grandfather in the said Informaton named was seised in his demeasne here or there or of some other estate of inheritance of land in all or some of the mannors Lands and Tenements in the said Informaton mentoned. And the said Robert Rookwood the grandfather being seised as beforesaid was convicted of Recusancie for not cominge to church by the space of threescore and eight moniths [*illeg.*] about October in the eight and twentieth yeare of the late Queene Elizabeth[2] upon the statute of the three and twentieth yeare of her rayne [*illeg.*] after twenty poundes a monith [*illeg.*] (and this defendant [*illeg.*] to about one thousand three hundred and sixtye poundes. And this defendant further saith that upon or aboute the second day of July in the nine and twentieth yeare of the rayne of the said late Queene[3] a commission issued out of this honorable Court to enquire of and seise the goods and twoo parts of the lands of the said Robert Rookwood the grandfather for not paying \payment/ of the said arriars of one thousand three hundred and sixty pounds and about the second of November in the nyne and twentieth yeare of the said Queene Elizabeth[4] an Inquisicion was formed of the said Roberts Lands and two parts thereof were seised into her Ma[jes]t[y]s hands att one hundred twoo pounds fowerteene shillinge five pence p[er] Ann[um]. And afterward vicesimo primo September Anno trigisimo uno Elizabeth[ae][5] other lands of the said Robert the grandfather not formerly [*illeg.*] were seised att fower pounds fowerteene shillings p[er] Ann[um]. And his goods weere seised to the value of sixteen pounds

---

[1] 'In Trinity Term in the eleventh year of King Charles'.
[2] October 1586.
[3] 2 July 1587.
[4] 2 November 1587.
[5] 21 September 1589.

1

sixteen shillinges and eight pence. And afterwards about the three and thirtieth yeare of the said late Queene Elizabeth[6] the said Robert the grandfather dyed. After whose death a [*illeg.*] [*illeg.*] was awarded. And about vicesimo Aprilio quadragesimo tertio Elizabethae[7] and Inquisiton was formed. And the said Roberts Lands weere seised thereby att one hundred and nynetie pounds p[er] Ann[um] for satisfaction of the arriars of twentye pounds a month for the said Roberts recusancye th[a]t any such arriars weere. And this defendant further saith that the said Commissions and Inquisitions and other the like Inquisitions concerning ever the said Robert the grandfather remayne upon recorde in this hon[ora]ble courte: By meanes whereof this defendant to contendeth that the Crowne hath beene answered out of the value of the said Roberts Landes and goods more than the \sayd/ arriars came unto, and (as this defendant is informed by his Counsell) the said payements and land ought to bee in full satisfaction of the said arriars. And this defendant further saith that after the decease of the said Robert the grandfather Mannors Lands and p[re]misses descended and came to Ambrose Rookwood his sonne and heire in the said informaton named beinge after a Recusant, who enterd in and upon the p[re]misses and being thereof possessed seised in his demeasne and of such or of some other estate of inheritance was convicted of Recusancye about the tyme and for the moniths in the said Informaton mentioned. And by vertue of a Commission founded to enquire of his Lands an Inquisition was taken undecimo Aprilio Anno tertio Regis Jac[o]bi[8] By w[hi]ch the lands of the said Ambrose were found att one hundred and twenty pounds p[er] Ann[um]. And aboute the third yeare of King James the said Ambrose Rookwood was attainted of high Trieson and did suffer death for the same. By reason of w[hi]ch his attainder all his estate both in lands and parks became forfeited to the Crowne [*illeg.*]. this defendant saith that [*illeg.*] there were arriers of twentye pounds were due by the said Robert the grandfather (wh[ereo]f this defendant expect to prove there are none) or by the said Ambrose Rookwood this defendants father. yett that estate of and in the said Lands w[hi]ch by the means aforesaid came to the Crowne, is not subject to any of those arriars and as for the faffament mentoned in the said Informaton to be made by the said Ambrose Rookwood after his conviction of Recusancye it was made befor his conviction. This defendante contesteth it (under favor) to be a foul suggestion that hee this defendant should conciall it if by such weere. for by that deed of foffament this defendant should had ought to enioy the said Lands in his own right by [*illeg.*] of the Intail suggested to be made thereby. And (as this defendant is informed by his Counsell) free from debts to his Majesty by reason of the Recusancy of this defendants said grandfather or father, yf any such weere. Whereas now the defendant is forced for his have livelyhood to bee a ffarmor of the said Lands in such sorte as after is hereby sett forth. And this defendant further saith that he was an infant att the tyme of the death of the said Ambrose his father and therefore was nott capable nor proved to be guilty of any conspiracy or combynaton with Sir Phillipp Tirwhitt or any other. and in the said Informaton is supposed not did practise or conspirate howe to difeat his late Majesty of the said debts wherewith the said Mannors and Lands were chargeable by any deceiptfull intitulinge the said late king to the inheritance of the said Mannors and Lands w[i]th any intent thereby to merge or extinguish the said debts, or free and discharge the said Mannors and lands

---

6   1591. Robert Rookwood (I) actually died in 1600.
7   20 April 1600.
8   11 April 1606.

from payement thereof in such manner and forme as in the said informaton it is supposed. Butt for manifestation of the truth concerning the intitlinge of his said late Majesty to the said Lands. This defendant saith that (as he hath heard) about the eleaventh yeare of his said late Majesties rayne[9] his Majesties Commission was awarded out of this honorable Courte under the siele of the same Courte [*illeg.*] to contayne Commissioner to inquire what Mannors Lands and tenements the said Ambrose was seised of att the tyme of his attainder But whether any evidence made by the said Ambrose Rookwood were concealed or noe or whether the Intrest upon any feyned evydence found That the said Ambrose was seised in fee of the said Mannors and p[re]misses att the tyme of his Attaynder, this defendant saith he knoweth nott nor [*illeg.*] knowe by reason of that he was then an Infant[10] neither did this defendant ever intend to defraude his Ma[jes]ty of th[a]t w[hi]ch rightly might belonge unto to hym in this case. nor did this defendant by any combynaton unto the said Sir Phillipp Tirwhitt or unto any other p[er]son or p[er]sons in the said Informaton named or mentioned to be knowen or unknowen to obteyne from his said late Majesty in the twelfth yeare of his rayne[11] a graunt by his Majesties Letters Patents of the said Mannors unto the said Sir Phillipp Tirwhitt and others in the said Informaton named and their heirs to the use of them and their heirs in such manner and forme or to such intent or purpose as in the said Informaton it is supposed. But this defendant saith that (as he hath heard) the right honorable Theophilus nowe Earle of Suffolke[12] did beg of the said late kinge James the benefitt of this defendants said fathers estate in Landes and goodes due to his Majesty by <the> \his/ said Attaynder. And for a greate Some of money paid to the said Earle hee procured a graunt to bee made by his said late Majesty of this defendants said fathers Lands and estate by letters patents under the greate Seale of England to the said Sir Phillipp Tirwhitt and others named in the said Graunt. And this defendant hath heard and verily believeth that afterwards the said Patentes in the said Graunt findinge thuise [*illeg.*] afterward to hand or foote and in chardges for the recusancie of this defendants said grandfather and father did in or about hillarie Terme in the twelfth yeare of Kinge James[13] by Plea in this Courte w[hi]ch confession and Judgement of this Courte procured a discharge of all [*illeg.*] and extents upon the lands graunted unto them by the said letters Patents as aforesaid for or in respect of the recusancie of the said Robert and Ambrose. And this defendante further saith that duringe this defendants mothers life (who had a [*illeg.*] in some of his saide fathers Lands) hee this defendant had such maintenance from her as she could afforde him. And this defend[an]t afterwards comm[in]ge to some [*illeg.*] of grant and chardge comm[in]ge upon him, hee this defendant made [*damaged*] to the said Patentees to be a ffarmor unto them of the lands late his said fathers and procured a lease from them to bee made unto him this defendant for some terme of yeares w[i]th ytt [*illeg.*] att the yearely rent of twoo hundrede and fifty pounds and besides payeinge threescore pounds p[er] Ann[um] in Annuytie and bearing all charges goinge out of the same. By vertue of w[hi]ch lease this defendant [*illeg.*] and was and is thereof possessed accordingly, and hath and doth take to his owne use the rents issue and profitts of the said Mannors lands and premises as he h[o]peth under the

---

[9]   1614.
[10]   Sir Robert cannot have been more than five years old when his father was executed for high treason.
[11]   1615.
[12]   Theophilus Howard, 2nd Earl of Suffolk (1584–1640).
[13]   1615.

good favor of this honourable Courte it is and shall bee lawfull for him to doe. And this defendant further saith that as he hath heard and verily believeth afterwards a gen[er]all Commission issued out of this Court to inquire of the goodes and Lands of thuise Recusants within the said County of Suff[olk] amongst whom the said Robert Rookwood the grandfather was one, and that aboute the thirteenth of october in the two and twentieth yeare of Kinge James,[14] the said Robert Rookwoods lands were found att three hundred seventy nyne pounds p[er] Ann[um] w[hi]ch beinge putt in chardge the same Patentees came in [*illeg.*] and pleaded to that Inquisition as they did to the former and obteyned the like discharges of it as of the former as aforesaid in hillary Terme in the second yeare of the kinges Majesties rayne that nowe is.[15] All and ev[er]y w[hi]ch sev[er]all Commissions Inquisitions and the said Pleas w[hi]ch Confessions and Judgm[en]ts thereupon abovementioned (as this defendant hath heard and verily believeth) doe remaine of record in this honorable Courte whereunto this defendant for more certainty regarding [*illeg.*]. And as for any other Inquisition or Plea hereunto made conserninge the said lands and premisses or any p[ar]te or p[er]rill thereof this defendant saith hee knoweth nott other than those above herein sett forth by this defend[an]t as beforesaid. And this defendant also saith that he hath noe other estate or benefitt in the said lands or any p[ar]te thereof than the said leasee and under her rents and paiements before mentioned [*illeg.*] [*illeg.*] bee (w[hi]ch this defendant knoweth not) such a feoffment as mentoned in the said Informaton w[hi]ch may cast some other estate proceeding by lawe upon him and w[hi]ch would bee an unexpected good fortune unto him and hee also saith that the whole estate of his said father was never found to be above fower hundred pounds p[er] Ann[um] by the depositions of the tenants that held the same, much of the said lands beinge sould awaye by the said Patentee, and that land w[hi]ch is lefte this defendant hath the possession thereof under the rents and paiements before mentioned. And this defendant denyeth all <combinaton> \maner/ of combynaton, confounding practises, fraud double dealing or <dealing> deceipt in the said Informaton [*damaged*] against him. And as for this defendants owne recusancy in the said Informaton mentoned This defendant thereunto saith that hee beinge convicted thereof most humbly submitted himselfe and implored [*illeg.*] his Ma[jes]t[y']s like graces and clemencye as is offered and extended to other that are in this distressing like conditon by his Ma[jes]t[y']s most gracious Commission under the greate siele of England And most humbly deposes that hee may be admitted to compound for [*illeg.*] [*illeg.*] estate as hee hath, hee havinge had sixteen children and tenn of them living all young and utterly unprovided for. his wife nowe w[i]th childe and by gods blessinge like to have many more w[hi]ch he humbly referreth to the consideration of this honorable Courte w[i]thout that that any other matter cause thing or circumstance in the said Judgment conteyned materyall or effectuall in the cause of this defendant to be answered unto and hereby not sufficiently confessed and avoyded [*illeg.*] and denyed is here in such manner and forme as in the said Informaton. All w[hi]ch matters this defendant is ready to avowe and prove as this honorable Courte shall awarde him humbly praying to be dismissed.

Tho[mas] hughes
Prestitit [*illeg.*] in Can[cellario] xvo die Junii Anno undecimo R[egi]s Carolj[16]

---

[14] 13 October 1625.
[15] Spring 1627.
[16] In a later hand on the outside of the document is the following inscription: 'S[i]r Rob[ert] Rookwood's

4

2. [SRO(B) 326/49] *Indenture appointing trustees of the Rookwood estates, 4 May 1639*

This Indenture made the ffourth day of May in the ffourteenth yeare of the raigne of our sovraigne Lorde Charles by the grace of God Kinge of England Scotland ffrance and Ireland defender of the ffaith & Betweene Robert Monnson of Rowthorpe in the County of Lincolne esq[ui]re on thone parte and \the right honorable/ S[i]r Thomas Jermyn of Rushbrooke in the county of Suffolk knight and vicechamberlaine to his Maj[esty] Edmond Pooley of Badley in the said county esq[ui]re and Robert Crompton of fakenham in the said county esq[ui]re on thother parte Witnesseth that whereas our late sovraigne Lorde Kinge James by the grace of God kinge of England Scotland ffrance and Ireland defender of the ffaith & by his letters pattents under the greate seale of England and bearinge date the eleveanth day of December in the yeare of his raigne of England ffrance and Ireland the Twelvth and of Scotland the eight and ffortieth did for the considerations therein expressed give and grant unto S[i]r Phillip Tyrwhitt of Stanefeild in the County of Lincolne knight and baronett S[i]r Peter ffreshnold of Staley in the county of Derby knight Gervase Markham of Retford in the county of Nottingham and Robert Monnson of Northurst in the aforesaid county of Lincolne esq[ui]re and their heires for ever. All those the Mannors of Mortimers & Staningfeild hall Coldham hall Philletts <and [*illeg.*] hall> w[i]th th[e] appurt[enance]s in the County of Suffolk. And alsoe Twenty Messuages Three [*illeg.*] fforty gardens ffivehundred acres of land Three hundred acres of meadowe ffivehundred acres of pasture Two hundred acres of wood and One hundred acres of heath and Gorse w[i]th th[e] appurt[enance]s in Staningfeild al[ia]s Stanfeild Whepsteed hawsteed Brockly Lawsall Cockfeild hartest Wel[ne]tham Preston Thorpe Marieux Lavenham Bretenham Brent Ely monkes Ely Milden <Stoke iuxta Nailand> and Polsteed in the said County of Suffolke w[i]th all and singular their appurtenances beeinge late prolls of the poss[ess]ions of Ambrose Rookewood Esq together w[i]th all and singular Messuages Mills houses edifices buildings barnes stables dovehouses Orchards gardens lands tenem[en]ts meadows feedings pastures waist waste lands demeasne lands Comons heath Cowst ffurse moores marshes woods lu[m]berwoods and trees and all the soile whereon the said woods underwoods or wood were growing and all waters water courses fishinges crevices mines quarries vents cordrons and [*illeg.*] rents charge [*illeg.*] sacke and rents and services as well of ffree as customary tenants farmes ffee farmes Advowsons and patronage of churches Annuities knights fee wards marriages Escheates releised heriotts fines and [*damaged*] Courts leets Courts barron Court of ffrankpledge profits and of quests of Court of [*illeg.*] Comon of [*illeg.*] faires m[ar]ketts tolles waifes strayes goods of ffelons and fugitives [*illeg.*] [*illeg.*] liberties ffranchises priviledges effitts comodities advantages emolum[en]ts and hereditam[en]ts whatsoever of what kinde or natur soever the same bee, by what name soever the same bee or shall happen to bee called or known scituate lying and beeing ariseinge growinge renewinge or cominge in the aforesaide county Townes fields places parishes or hamletts aforesaid or in any of them or elsewhere as the

---

plea against the Atturney General, th[a]t nothing was due from his Estates for the recusancy of his ancestors. By th[i]s it appears Two thirds of the Estate was seizd by the Crown for recusancy from the 29th of Eliz[abeth] to the 3d of James. XI of Charles the 1st'. The inscription probably dates from the reign of Charles II as Charles I is referred to as such but James I is not given a regnal number, as he would have been after 1685.

aforesaid Mannors messuages lands tenem[en]ts and p[re]misses or any of them any way belonginge incident or appendant or as any parte or p[ar]cell of them or any of them knowne accepted reputed or taken or to be w[i]th the same or any parte of them usually occupyed poss[ess]ed or inioyed in as full and large a manner as Ambrose Rookwood esq[uire] heretofore seized of the same or any other soever p[er]sons heretofore seized of the same or any parte thereof have used and inioyed the same or in any parte or p[ar]cell thereof To have and to holde all the aforesaid Mannors messuages lands tenem[en]ts meadowes pastures feedings woods underwoods advowsons Courteleets Courts barron views of ffrankpledge proffitts comodities emolum[en]ts and hereditam[en]ts and all and singular the p[re]misses unto the said S[i]r Phillipp Tirwhit S[i]r Peter ffreshnold Gervase Markeham and Robert Monnson their heires and assignes for ever to the onely sole and proper use and behoof of them their heires and assignes for ever. As in and by the said letters pattents move at large appare[n]tly: And whereas the said S[i]r Peter ffreshnold one of the said pattentees by his deed bearinge date the ffowerteenth day of July in the Sixeteenth yeare of the raigne of our said late sovraigne Lord Kinge James of England ffrance and Ireland the sixteenth and of Scotland the one and and ffiftieth did for the consideratons therein exp[re]ssed for himselfe and his heires demise release and quite claime unto the said S[i]r Phillip Tirwhit Jervase Markeham and Robert Monnson in full and peaceable possession and seisen beeinge all the estate right title interest claime and demand whatsoever w[hi]ch he the said S[i]r Peter ffreshnold then had or w[hi]ch his heires or assignes thereafter might have or p[re]tend to have of in to or out of the said Lordships Mannors messuages lands tenements meadows pastures woods comon of pasture Courtes proffits of Courtes [*illeg.*] [*illeg.*] advowsons and patronages of Churches and of in and to all and any the hereditam[en]ts and thinges comprised in the said lettres pattents by vertue of them or otherwise howsoever As by the said deed of release relaton beeinge thereunto had more att large appeareth And whereas also the said Jervase Markham and Robert Monnson after the decease of S[i]r Phillip Tyrwhit knight beeing seized to them and their heires for ever of all the before mentioned p[re]misses w[i]th appurt[enan]ces and of any p[ar]te and p[ar]cell of them by survivorship by their Indenture bearinge date the Two and Twentieth day of September in the Ninth yeare of the raigne of our sovraine Lord Kinge Charles did for the consideratons therein exp[re]ssed devise grante and confirme [*illeg.*] S[i]r Robert Rookwood of Coldham hall in Stanningfeild in the county of Suffolke knight and esquier the said Lordsh[i]ps Mannors Messuages lands tenem[en]ts medowes pastures woods underwoods Comon of pastures Courtes rents [*illeg.*] services Advowsons and patronages of churches and all and any the hereditam[en]ts and things comprised in the said Letters patents together w[i]th [*illegible line*] To have and to the holde all and singuler the said Mann[o]rs Messuages lands tenem[en]ts hereditam[en]ts and p[re]misses w[i]th their and every of their appurtenances [*illegible line*] on and after the ffeast day of St Michaell the Archangell next endinge the date there unto the full end and [*illeg.*] of Twenty and one [*illegible line*] marriages escheates releises herriotts fines amercem[en]ts Courts leet Courts barron Court of ffrankpledge profits and of quests of Court of [*illeg.*] Comon of [*illeg.*] faires m[ar]ketts tolles waifes strayes goods of ffelons and fugitives [*illeg.*] [*illeg.*] liberties ffranchises privilidges effitts comodities advantages and emolum[en]ts and hereditam[en]ts whatsoever of wh[a]t kinde or nature soever the same bee by whatsoever [*damaged*] shall happen to bee called or knowne scituate lyeinge and beeinge ariseinge growinge renewinge or cominge in the foresaid [*illeg.*] feilds parrishes and places or any of them or elsewhere the foresaid Mannors messuages lands tenem[en]ts and p[re]misses or any of them any now belonginge apperteyninge incident or appendant or as p[ar]te and p[ar]cell of them or any of them knowne reputed accepted or taken or w[i]th the same or any parte of them usually occupied poss[ess]ions and inioyed And all other lands tenem[en]ts and hereditam[en]ts whatsoever w[i]th their and every of their appurt[enance]s before in and by the said lettres pattents given and granted or mentoned or intended to bee given and granted unto the said S[i]r Phillip Tirwhit & Peter ffreshnold Jervase Markeham and Robert Monnson their heires forever together alsoe w[i]th the said L[ett]res pattents and all other deeds evidences and writ[s] made conc[ern]inge the p[re]misses or any parte of them in as full and ample manner and w[i]th such priviledges liberties and advantages as the same were by the said l[ett]res pattents or by any other meanes whatsoever given and granted or conveyed unto the said S[i]r Phillip Tirwhit S[i]r Peter ffreshnold Jervase Markham and Robert Monnson their heires or any of them To have and to holde all and singuler the before recited Mann[or]s Messuages lands tenements meadowes pastures woods underwoods advowsons tithes Courtes view of franke pledge proffitts comodities emoluments hereditam[en]ts and all other the p[re]misses before granted or mentoned or intended to bee granted and any parte and p[ar]cell of them w[i]th their and any of their rights members and appurten[an]ces whatsoever unto the said S[i]r Thomas Jermyn Edmond Pooley and Robert Crompton their heires and assignes for ever to the only sole p[ro]per use and behoofe of them the said S[i]r Thomas Jermyn Edmond Pooley & Robert Crompton their heires and assignes for ever. And the said Robert Munson for himself his heires and assignes doth by these p[re]sents Covenante to p[re]mise and grant to and w[i]th the said S[i]r Thomas Jermyn Edmond Pooley and Robert Crompton their heires and assignes and w[i]th every of them that hee the said Robert Munson shall from time to tume and att all times hereafter duringe the space of seaven yeares next endinge the date of these p[re]sents upon lawfull and reasonable request to him the said Robert Munson and his heires or to any of them to bee [*damaged*] the said S[i]r Thomas Jermyn Edmond Pooley and Robert Crompton their heires or assignes or any of them make doe acknowledge execute and suffer or cause to be made donne knowledged executed and suffered all and every sure farther lawfull and reasonable act and acted thinge and thinges device and devices in the lawe whatsoever for the p[er]fecter assuringe conteyninge and sure makeinge of all and singuler the p[re]misses before by these p[re]sents mentoned or intended to bee granted bargained and solde and of every p[ar]te and p[ar]cell of them or by theire or any of their counsell learned in the lawe shall be reasonably devised or required as by them the said S[i]r Thomas Jermyn Edmond Pooley and Robert Crompton their heires or assignes or any of them or by theire or any of them that are to make the said assurance bee thereby or for the doinge or sufferinge thereof compelled to travaile above tenne miles from the place of his or their abiding or residence att the time of such reques to be made. In witness whereof the parties first above named to these p[re]sent Indentures interchangeable have sett to theire hands and seales the day and yeare first above written: An[n]o D[omi]ni 1638

Ad ass[izes] apud [*illeg.*] Gippe[swic]i xxmo die Julij Anno Regni Caroli [*illegible line*]

Roger North
Lionell Tollemache

Justic[iarii] Regis ad pacem in Commitate conferamus necnon ad assizes ac Aliis par[t]i[bu]s eiusdem Com[itatis] Suff[olciensis]

7

3. [SRO(B) 326/50] *Marriage settlement of Ambrose Rookwood and Elizabeth Caldwell, 16 February 1652*

Articles of agreement Indented tripartite made the sixteenth day of february in the yeare of our Lord one thousand six hundred fifty and two Betweene Robert Rookewood of Coldham hall in the County of Suffolke knight Ambrose Rookewood Esqr: Sonne and heire apparant of the said Sir Robert Rookewood And Sir Robert Crompton of Covent garden in the County of Middlesex knight on the first part Alice Caldwall of Hornden uppon the hill in the County of Essex Widdow And Elizabeth Caldwall Spinster one of the daughters of the said Alice and the Coheiress of Daniel Caldwall late of hornden on the hill in the said County of Essex Esq: [*illeg.*] on the second part and S[i]r John Cotton of Lanwade in the County of Cambridge knight and Betweene Raynes Lowe of Clifton Raynes in the County of Buckingham Esq: Richard Grimes of London Esqr: and William Caldwall of London gentleman on the third part

Imprimis Whereas A marriage by the permission of almighty god is shortly to be had and solemnised betweene the said Ambrose Rookewood and the said Elizabeth Caldwall daughter of the said Alice Caldwall widow It is concluded and agreed by and betweene all the said parties And the said Alice Caldwall the widdow doth for her selfe her Executors and Administratores and every of them covenant grant and agree to and with the said S[i]r John Cotton and S[i]r Robert Crompton their heires Executors and Administrators and to and with every of them by these presents that she the s[ai]d Alice Caldwall the widdow upon resonable request assoone as the lands of the said Elizabeth Caldwall are convayed and assured unto them their heires and assignes by the said Elizabeth her daughter according to the purport and true meaning of these presents shall and will accepte of A lease from the said S[i]r John Cotton and S[i]r Robert Crompton and the [*illeg.*] of them of all the lands Tenements \two pound rent by year/ and hereditaments allotted unto the said Elizabeth Caldwall her daughter by one Indenture of partition formerly made for and duringe the terme of twenty and one yeares if she the s[ai]d Alice Caldwall the widow shall soe longe live att and under the yearly rent of threescore and seaventeene pounds of Lawfull mony of England to be yearly payd for the said lands on the five and twentieth day of march and nine and twentieth day of September or w[i]thin twenty days after any of the said feasts by even and equall portions with this farther covenant to be therein inserted on the behalfe of the said Alice Caldwall and her assignes during her life That Whereas itt is [*illeg.*] that George Evelin the heire of Mary Evelin deceased one other of the daughters and Coheires of the said Daniell Caldwall hath or may pretend A title unto some part of the s[ai]d lands of the yearly value of five pounds thirteene shillings and foure pence peranam or thereabouts that if part of the said lands should happen to be evicted duringe the said terme by the said heire or any other person clayming from or under him or the title of the said Mary Evelin his mother whereby the said yearly rent should come to be apportioned that then she the said Alice Caldwall shall and will demand or also noe apportionment of the said rent of threescore and seaventeene pounds but only for soe much of the s[ai]d lands as shall be evicted over and above the said somme of six pounds thirteene shillings and foure pence \which said six pound thirteene shillings and foure pence or less if less/ upon the recovrey of any part of any part of the said lands she the said Alice Caldwall hath undertaken and doth hereby undertake to pay unto the said S[i]r John Cotton and S[i]r Robert Crompton and their heires and assignes every yeare duringe the said terme if the [*illeg.*] longe [*illeg.*] and after the said eviction if any such be the rest of the value of the lands to be evicted to be borne abated and allowed by the said S[i]r John Cotton and S[i]r Robert Crompton and their heires and assignes and the heires and assignes of the survivor of them.

Item it is further covenanted concluded and agreed by and between all the said parties that whereas the said S[i]r Robert Crompton and S[i]r Robert Rookewood an Indenture bearinge date w[i]th these presents [*illeg.*] unto the said Alice Caldwall Richard Grimes and William Caldwall or some of them their executors administrators and assignes two severall Anuities of twoo hundred pounds by the year and fifty pounds by [*illeg.*] and duringe the terme of foure score and tenne yeares if the said Ambrose Rookewood and the said Elizabeth his w[ife] or either of them shall soe longe live to beginne according to the severall and respective limitations within these Indentures mentioned It is therefore hereby covenanted concluded agreed and declared by and betweene all the said parties that the true intent and meaning of the makinge of the said severall grants

Sealed and delevered by the within named
Alice Caldwall in the presents of
Edward Carpenter
William Brent
Jo[hn] Conyers
J Blount
John Bryan
Mi Chel: Thomas Burton
    Jesson

4. [CUL Hengrave 76/2/1] *Will of Sir Robert Rookwood, 4 October 1673*

In the name of God Amen. Sir Robert Rookwood of Coldham hall in the County of Suff[olk] Kn[igh]t being of p[er]fect & sound memory: Doe move constitute & ordaine this my Last Will & Testam[en]t in Manor & forme following That is to say ffirst I give & bequeath my soule unto Allm[igh]ty God My body to the earth to be buried in decent Christian Manor: And for My Wordly Estate & goods I give & dispose of them as followeth. Item I give & bequeath Unto my oldest sonn Ambrose Rookwood his heires & Executors All the timber of What sort soever standing or growing or that shall stand or growe att the time of my decease moreover all my Lands or grounds In the p[ar]ish of Staningfield In the manor of Coldham In the manor of Philletts In the p[ar]ish of Lawshall Whepstead hasted & in all other p[ar]ishes or places Whatsoever In the County of Suff[olk] afores[ai]d: W[hi]ch I did Reserve to my selfe ffor the Raising of portions for my younger Children: When I settled the Inheritance of my s[ai]d Lands Upon my oldest sonn: Allso I give & bequeath unto him my s[ai]d sonn: Ambrose his heires or: Executors: All Woods & Underwoods w[hi]ch shall be standing or growing Upon any of the p[re]mises att the time of my decease: Allso I give & bequeath Unto my s[ai]d sonn Ambrose & to his heires after decease of his mother my deare Wife: All those Manors Lands & Estates: W[hi]ch are: hereafter given to my s[ai]d deare Wife: for & in Lieu of her Jointure on Condition that the Rents profitts thereof May goe & be Imployed towards the breeding Maintenance & allowance of Robert Rookwood My oldest Grandchilde: sonn & heire of the s[ai]d Ambrose: or soo much of the s[ai]d Rents & profitts as my s[ai]d sonn Ambrose shall Judg fitt or necessary during the nonage of Robert my

9

s[ai]d Granchilde: Butt when the s[ai]d Robert shall attaine the full age of twenty one yeares: My Will & Meaning is that then he shall Receive & enjoye after my deare Wifes decease: The whole profitts of the Lands afores[ai]d: in Jointures to my Wife: To the use of him the s[ai]d Robert his heires & Assigns: for ever: Item I will that my s[ai]d sonn Ambrose doe sattisfie & pay all my Just debts w[hi]ch I shall owe att the time of my decease And shall allso defray & sattisfie the charge of my funerall expenses: Item I give bequeath Unto my s[ai]d sonn Ambrose all my household stuffe & furniture in Coldham hall Excepting only one roome soo furnished w[hi]ch his mother my s[ai]d deare Wife is to take att her own choise W[i]th Linnen necessary & convenient for the same roome to be Used by her: during her naturall Life or any other Linnen for her own use during her Life. Item I give & bequeath Unto my s[ai]d deare Wife Dame Mary Rookwood during her naturall Life for & in Leiue of her Jointure: The Manor of Mortimer in Preston: In the County of Suff[olk] W[i]th all the Rents rightes & appurtenances thereunto belonging: as allso my farme of hamlins Inn: Lying in Lavenham: In the s[ai]d county of suff[olk]: Allso I give & bequeath Unto my s[ai]d deare Wife the use & interest onely of all such sums of money as shall be owing me and not disposed of by me before my decease. Item I give and bequeath Unto my s[ai]d deare Wife all my stocke of cattle sheepe horses corne hay or grasse or any other other rents or profits W[hi]ch shall be due or payable to me from or by any of my tennants or otherwise Upon Condition: that she my s[ai]d Wife doe Leave att the time of her Death Unto my s[ai]d sonn Ambrose tenn Milch cowes One bull four cart \horse/ & thirty breeding ewes: Item I give and bequeath Unto my daughter Margaret One annuity or Rent charge for and during her Naturall Life of ffower-score pounds p[er] ann[um]: of Lawfull money of England W[i]thout any deduction defaltation for This or [illeg.] or Otherwise: to be paid Unto her quarterly att Twenty pounds p[er] quarter Issuing & goeing out of the manor & farme of Sheriffs in the county of Essex & out of the farme of Claverings In the County of Essex, With full power & Authority for her to seize and distraine ffrom time to time for the s[ai]d annuity or the [damaged] thereof Item Whereas: I have already given Unto my sonn Rookwood The sume of five hundred pounds I doe hereby give & bequeath Unto him my s[ai]d sonn: ffrancis the sume: of five hundred pounds more of Lawfull English to be paid unto him his Execut[o]rs: or Assigns: within the space of one yeare from the time of my decease: by my s[ai]d sonn Ambrose or his heirs or Executors: my will & indowing being that my s[ai]d sonn ffrancis shall have & enjoye the use and interest: onely of the s[ai]d first hundred pounds during his naturall Life. And afterward the s[ai]d principall of five hundred pounds to be devised by my s[ai]d sonn Ambrose or his heires or Executors: Between my two Grandchildren the sonn and Daughter of my s[ai]d sonn ffrancis In manor ffollowing: That is to say three hundred pounds sterl\ing/ p[ar]cell of the s[ai]d five hundred pounds To: Dorothy the daughter of my s[ai]d sonn ffrancis And if either of my afores[ai]d Grandchildren shall happen to die before their respective ages of eighteen years: Then the survivor to have & enjoye the Whole five hundred pounds afores[ai]d: Item I give and bequeath unto all my actuall servants att the time of my decease: One whole yeares Wages to be paid to them respectively within one years time after my death: Item I give & bequeath unto my s[ai]d Grandchilde Rob[er]t Rokewood for his p[re]sent maintenance from the time of my death to his being Off the age of one and twenty yeares the residue or overplus of all the rents & profitts w[hi]ch shall remaine due out my s[ai]d farme of Claverings: and the house of hornden after that the fourscore pounds annuity hereby given unto my daughter Margaret be paid unto her according to my Will herein before mentoned: And allso I give unto my Grandchilde Rob[er]t ffor his maintenance as afores[ai]d

The Rent of other Tenem[en]t: w[hi]ch I purchased of Rob[er]t Inhold In the p[ar]ish of Staningfield aforenamed Rented att the sume of eighte pounds paid. Allso I give for his maintenance afores[ai]d: One Other Tenem[en]t W[hi]ch I purchased of John Brooke and now All those aforementioned Rents surplusages & p[re]misses hereby given to my s[ai]d Grand childe Rob[er]t: ffor his p[re]sent maintenance: until his age of one and twenty yeares & no Longer to be enjoyed by him,: my s[ai]d sonn Ambrose from the time that my s[ai]d Granchilde: shall attayne unto the age of one and twenty yeares during the naturall Life of my s[ai]d sonn: Ambrose: And afterwards To the use of Rob[er]t my s[ai]d Granchilde his heires for ever: Item I give unto my Grandchilde henry sonn to my s[ai]d sonn Ambrose The sume of one hundred and fiffty pounds. Item I do here by intreate my s[ai]d Deare Wife to pay unto my sister Mrs Calverly the sume off Ten: pounds p[er] ann[um]: during her naturall Life,: Lastly I doe hereby make constitute and ordaine: Dame mary my s[ai]d deare Wife: And my s[ai]d sonn: Ambrose the Executors of this my Last Will and Testam[en]t: And I doe ffurther appointe as overseers thereof s[i]r henry Bedingfield the elder of Bergholt in the County of norfolke Baronet: And John Tasburgh: of Bodney in the County of norfolke: hopeing and desiring that they Will be aideing and Assisting to my s[ai]d Executors in the p[er]formance of this my Last Will and Testam[en]t: sealed and signed With my own hand this fourth day of October In the five and twentieth yeare Of the Raigne of our soveraigne Lord King Charles the second: And In the yeare of Our Lord God 1673: Ro[bert] Rokewood: sealed signed and published in the p[re]sence of Peregrine shorte Richard Shorte: John: Peter

5. [CUL Hengrave MS 76/1] *Marriage Settlement of Thomas Rookwood and Tamworth Martin, 17 February 1683 (summary by John Gage)*

Articles of Agreement dated 17 February 1682/3 made between Ambrose Rookewood Esq[uire] & Elizabeth his wife and Thomas Rookewood Esq[ui]re therein described as eldest son and heir apparent of the s[ai]d Ambrose and Elizabeth of the 1st part, Sir Roger Martyn of Melford in the County of Suffolk Bar[one]t & Thamworth Martyn Spinster eldest daughter of the said Sir Roger of the 2d part and Adam Felton Esq[ui]r[e][17] & William Covell Gent[leman] of the 3d part. Being articles in contemplation of the Marriage of the said Thomas Rookewood with the s[ai]d Thamworth Martyn Reciting among things an Indenture dated 6th Sept[embe]r 1682 made between the said Adam Felton and William Covel of the one part and the said Ambrose Rookewood of the other part whereby the said Adam Felton and William Covel did declare that under certain Fines & Assurances therein referred to levied and executed by Sir John Cotton & other trustees in the place of the before mentioned Sir Robert Crompton & others they the said Adam Felton and William Covel held & would stand seized of the Manor of Stanningfield and other estates in Suffolk In trust for the said Ambrose Rookewood his heirs appointees and Assigns.

---

[17] Adam Felton became Sir Adam Felton, 3rd Baronet of Playford on the death of his father, Sir Henry Felton, 2nd Baronet, in 1690. Although he was not a Catholic, his grandmother Dorothy was the daughter of the Catholic Sir Bassingbourne Gawdy of Crow's Hall, West Harling, Norfolk. Sir Adam was related to the Rookwood family by marriage since he was the fourth husband of Lady Elizabeth Monson, the grandmother of Tamworth Martin. He died in February 1696. See W. Courthope, *Synopsis of the Extinct Baronetage of England* (London, 1835), p. 76.

It was agreed that in consideration of the said Marriage & of £3000 the portion of the s[ai]d Thamworth Martyn that the s[ai]d Adam Felton & William Covel should convey The Manor of Mortimers, the farm in Lavenham called Lavenham Park, the farm called Little Rookwoods in Stanningfield & certain lands in Lawshall, Stanningfield, To the use of the said Thomas Rookwood & Thamworth afterward his wife for their lives, the same to be for her jointure. Remainder to the said Thamworth in special tail male-remainder over.

And that the s[ai]d trustee should convey the Manors of Coldham Hall, Stanningfield Hall and Phillets and all other the lands of which they were so seized as aforesaid not limited in jointure to the s[ai]d Thamworth To the use of the s[ai]d Ambrose Rookwood for life—remainder to the s[ai]d Thomas Rookewood in special tail male subject to the annuities of £200 and £50 payable to Elizabeth the wife of the s[ai]d Ambrose Rookewood after his decease.

The Articles are executed by all parties excepting Sir Roger Martyn—among the Witnesses is Robert Townshend.

6. [A. Sanderius, A. *Flandria Illustrata* (Hague, 1732), vol. 2, p. 134]
Monumental inscription commemorating Elizabeth Rookwood from the Church of the English Convent, Bruges, 1691

D. O. M.
Lectissimae Matronae Elizabethae
Rookwood quae Cadwalonum de Cantys
in Provincia Angliae Essexiam generi
Paterno oriundo ab antiquis Britanniae
principibus Cadwalladeris exploratissimo
stemmate, originem duxit.
Deinde
Ambrosio Rookwood de Coldham Hall in
Provincia Suffolciensi Armigeri nupta octo
filiorum et sex filiarum Parens felici
faecundicitate facta, pietate in Deum,
dilectione et obsequio in Maritum, sedula
in Liberos, Domesticos proximos ac
Pauperes Beneficentia omnes Matris
familias partes cumulatissime explevit.
Denique
Ob fidem erga Deum, & Regem
Jacobum intemeratam, dilectissimo
Conjugi iterum exulare coacta, post
aegritudinis doloribus, pie et fortiter
perfuncta, hic laudem in Sanctae Ecclesiae
pace feliciter requiescit, Amen.
Anno aetatis suae 60 salutis nostrae 1691
Mens. Mart. 23. optimae Conjugis maerens
posuit Ambrosius Rookwood ipse
octogenarius ac aegre superstes.

Translation

To God best and greatest; to the most beloved woman Elizabeth Rookwood who took her origin from the family of the Caldwells of Cantys in the English province of Essex, having its origin on the paternal side from the ancient British princes of Cadwallader by the most tested genealogical tree. Then, having been married to Ambrose Rookwood, gentleman, of Coldham Hall in the country of Suffolk and having been made the parent of eight sons and six daughters with fortunate fertility, by her piety towards God, by her love and obedience to her husband, by her attentiveness to her children and her generosity towards servants, neighbours and the poor she fulfilled to the utmost all the parts of the mother of a family. Finally on account of her pure faith in God and King James, having been encouraged to go again into exile by her dearest husband, after the pains of illness piously and bravely borne, she happily reposed this praise in the peace of the Holy Church, Amen. In the sixtieth year of her age and the year of our salvation 1691 on 23 March. The mourning of her excellent husband Ambrose Rookwood placed [this monument], himself an octogenarian and with difficulty surviving.

7. [CUL Hengrave MS 76/1] *Will of Ambrose Rookwood, 18 February 1692 (summary by John Gage)*

18th February 1692—Will of Ambrose Rookwood of Coldham Hall Esq[ui]re—He leaves his body to be buried at the discretion of his executors, giving one hundred pounds to be disposed of among the poor. The testator devised to his son Ambrose Rookwood and his heirs the manor of Sheriffes, together with his lands in Colne in Essex. And he devised to his executors his farm of Claverings in Essex to be sold and the money to be applied for the performance of his will—He gave to his son Henry Rookewood £400; to his son Francis Rookwood £200, the remainder of his portion, and likewise the sum of £400; to his son Charles Rookwood £400; to his son John Rookwood, and to the testators daughter Mary, Anne, Margaret and Frances Rookwood £50 a piece; to his servants therein mentioned the sums therein specified. And he appointed his sons Thomas Rookwood and Ambrose Rookwood and his friend Mr William Covell executors of his will. And he gave his sons the said Thomas Rookwood and Ambrose Rookwood the residue of his personal estate for the purposes of his will.

Proved in the Prerogative Court 6th March 1693/4 by William Covell and 10th November 1705 by Thomas Rookwood.

13

8. [CUL Hengrave MS 76/2/16] *Account of legacies from the will of Ambrose Rookwood, 1695*[18]

An Account of what Legasies are Due out of Ambrose Rookwood Esq[ui]r[e] deceased Estate this 10th day of October 1695

	£	s.	d.
To mr Henry Rookewood	400		
To mr Francis Rookewood	400		
To mr Charles Rookewood	400		
To mr John Rookewood	50		
To his ffoure Daughters	200		
His Charity	97		

An Account of what money mr Thomas Rookwood have Rec[eive]d of his ffathers Estate to the 10th day of October 1695:

	£	s.	d.
Stocke within Doores and without	376	7	
Of mr William Covell by Thorpe	200		
Of mr Stephen Gallaway	100		
Of mr Bass[ingbourne] Gaudy	150		
Of mr Kempe in Decemb[e]r 1695	606	5	
Barrow Estate to be Sold	650		
Clavering Estate to be Sold	400		
Rec[eive]d of mr John Cooke by mr Covells order	171	3	
Arreares from the Tennants	168	12	3
From Barrow about	60		
Arreares for Lords Rent	10		
	2912	7	3

An Accompt of what moneys mr William Covell have Received out Ambrose Rookwoods Esq[ui]r[e] Estate since his Death to the 12th day of October: 1695

	£	s.	d.
Ready money in Gold and Silver	236	18	6
Rec[eive]d of Ben: Cossins for Goods Sold by him for Interest and for Rent Rec[eive]d by him	165	16	8
Rec[eive]d of John Cooke for principall & Interest	105		
Rec[eive]d of George Brooke	658		
Rec[eive]d for the Sorrell Colt	2		
Rec[eive]d for Barebones	1	1	6

---

[18] This note of legacies and payments received was part of Benjamin Cussons's accounts of the Coldham estate.

	£	s.	d.
Rec[eive]d of mrs Dassett for a Load of Hay	1	5	
Rec[eive]d of the Widd[ow] Adams p[aymen]te of Arreares	22		
Rec[eive]d of John Adams in p[aymen]te of Arreares	30		
Rec[eive]d of Pansie in p[aymen]te of Arreares	10		
Rec[eive]d at Barrow as doth appeare	40	10	4
	1272	12	

Moneys paid to the 10th of October 1695

	£	s.	d.
Payd ffunerall Expences	101	15	6
p[ai]d for Probate of the Will	25	18	4
Housekeeping to the 12th of May 1694	12	14	6
Debts Paid	70	4	5
paid mrs Peters her Legasie	300		
p[ai]d Benjamin Cossins his Legasie	20		
p[ai]d Susan Day her Legasie	20		
ffor my Owne Legasie	80		
p[ai]d mr Stafford for Thorpe by mr Rookwood ord[e]r	200		
p[ai]d mr Francis Rookewood his Interest to the 4th June 95	20		
p[ai]d mr Francis his Interest to the 4th of June 1695	27		
p[ai]d mr Charles his Interest to the 4th of June 1695	20		
p[ai]d mr Rookewood by mr Cooke att Severall times	171	3	
	1269	5	9
Rest Due to the Estate the 10th day of October 1695 in mr Covells hands	3	6	3

9. *Ambrose Rookwood's final statement before his execution for high treason,* ***1696***[19]

Having committed the Justice of my Cause and recommended my Soul to God, on whose Mercies, through the Merits of Jesus Christ, I wholly Cast my self; I had once resolv'd to die in Silence; But second Thoughts of my Duty to others, chiefly to my True and Liege Sovereign K. James, moved me to leave this behind me.

I do therefore, with all Truth and Sincerity, Declare and Avow, I never Knew, Saw, or Heard, of any Order or Commission from K. James for the Assassinating of the Prince of Orange, and Attacking his Guards; But I am Certainly inform'd, he had rejected Proposals of That Nature, when made unto him.

Nor do I think He Knew the least of the Particular Design of Attacking the Guards at his Landing, in which I was engag'd as a Soldier, by my Immediate Commander, (much against my Judgment,) But his Soldier I was, and as such I was to Obey and Act.

Near twelve years, I have serv'd my True King and Master K. James, and freely now lay down my Life in his Cause. I ever Abhor'd a Treacherous Action even to an Enemy. If it be a Guilt to have Complied with what I thought, and still think to have been my Duty, I am Guilty. No other Guilt to I Owne.

As I beg all to forgive me, so I forgive All from my Heart, even the Prince of Orange, who as a Soldier ought to have consider'd my Case, before he Sign'd the Warrant for my Death. I pray God to open his Eyes and render him Sensible of the Much Blood from all Parts Crying out against him, so the prevent a Heavier Execution Hanging over his Head; than what he Inflicts on me.

10. [CUL Hengrave MS 76/2/20] *Gaol delivery of Thomas Rookwood, 28 August 1696*

Midd[le]sex S[essione]s Memorandu[m] Q[uo]d ad Delibatonem Gaolae D[omi]ni Regis de Newgate tent[ato] pro Com[itate] Midd[lese]x apud Justice Hall in Old Bayly in Suburb[ia] Civitat[is] London die mercur[ii] scil[ic]et vicesimo octavo die Augusti Regni D[omi]ni n[ost]ri Guilelmi tertii Dei Gra[tia] nunc Regiae Angliae et Septimo coram Thoma Lane Milite Majore Civitat[is] London Joh[ann]e Holt mi[lite] & Capita ad Justit[iam] d[ic]ti D[omi]ni Regis. ad pl[ac]ita coram ip[s]o Rege tenend[o] Assign[atis] Joh[ann]e Moor milit[e] Will[elm]o Ashurst mi[lite] & Ald[e]r[man]o dict[i] Civitat[is] London Salathiell Lovell mi[lite] & serviend[ore] ad Legem ac Recordator[e] dict[i] Civitat[is] London & ad suis Justic[iariis] d[ic]ti D[omi]ni Regis ad Gaolam suam de Newgate de Prisonar[io] in eadem existend[o] deliban[do] & assign[ando] ffranciae Regno Armiger unus. Justic[iarius] d[ic]ti D[omi]ni Regis ad pacem in Com[itate] p[raedicti] & Conservan[dum] & Assign[andum] deliberavit hic in Cur[a] quandam Recogn[an]d[o] coram eo & ad capt[andum] de Record[atore] & in forma Juris Terminand[um] & honor[e] Cujus quidem Recogn[an]d[o] sequitur S[essione]s Midd[lese]x S[essione]s. Mem[oran]d[u]m quod nono die Julij 1695 Annoq[ue] R[egis] Gulielmi tertii nunc Angliae et septimo Thomas Rookwood de Coldham in Com[itate] Suffolk Ad Recog[na]nd[um] se debere D[omi]no Regi

---

[19]   The text is taken from A. Rookwood, *A True Copy of the Paper Delivered By Brigadier Rookwood, to the Sheriff at Tyburn, the Place of Execution* (London, 1696).

200 G[uineas] Will[el]mo Alexander de paroch[iae] S[anc]ti Pauli Covent Garden in Com[itate] Midd[lese]x Silkman Recog[na]nd[um] se debere et 100 G[uineas] Samuell Phillipo de eadem in Com[itate] p[raedicto] & Mercer Recog[na]nd[um] se debere et 100 G[uineas] Will[el]mo Russell de eadem in Com[itate] p[raedicto] et Coquus Recog[na]nd[um] se debere 100 G[uineas] Upon Condicon That the said Thomas Rookwood doe personally appeare att the next Sessions of the peace held for the said County of Midd[lese]x at Justice Hall in the Old Bayly there to Answer what shall be on his Maj[es]ties Behalfe Objected against him and in the meantime to keep the Peace towards Our Soveraigne Lord the King and all his Leige People and not to depart the Court without Lycence That then et Super quo ad jstam eandem Delibaton[em] Gaolae dict[i] D[omi]ni Regis de Newgate tent[ato] pro Com[itate] Die Anno horoq[u]e supradict[o] Coram p[ra]efat[is] Justic[iariis] d[ic]ti D[omi]ni Regis & dict[us] Thomas Rookwood solempniter ap[p]ar[ui]t in propria persona sua Comparuit et super inde publica Proclamatio fact[um] fuit Quod si aliquis sit qui p[ra]efat[i] Justic[iarii] [*damaged*] Thomam Rookwood Inform[aret] ut vellet veniret [sic.] et Audire sua. Et quia p[ra]efat[i] Justic[iarii] hic nil Mali de eo Invenie[runt] Ideo Considereat[um] est [sic.] per Cur[a] quod Thomas Rookwood Exoneratur de Recogn[itionibus] p[raedictis] & ea inde s[i]m[il]e die etc.

Translation

Middlesex Sessions memorandum at the delivery of our Lord the King's gaol of Newgate held for the County of Middlesex at Justice Hall in the Old Bailey outside the City of London on Tuesday 28 August [1696] in the seventh year of our Lord William III by the Grace of God King of the Realm of England before Sir Thomas Lane, Lord Mayor of London, Sir John Holt, Lord Chief Justice of our aforesaid Lord the King. Sir John Moor, Sir William Ashurst, Alderman of the aforesaid City of London, Sir Salathiel Lovell, Sergeant at Law and Recorder of the said City of London having been assigned to the pleas being held before the king himself; and to the Justices of our aforesaid Lord the King at his gaol of Newgate concerning a prisoner, one knight of the kingdom of France, being delivered and assigned to the same. The Justice of our aforesaid Lord the King decided this in the court, that having entered into recognisances before him he should be bound over to keep the peace from the Recorder in form of law. With the honour of this man being recognised, the ending of the Middlesex Sessions followed. Memorandum that on 9 July 1695 in the seventh year of King William III of England Thomas Rookwood of Coldham in the County of Suffolk entered into recognisance that he owed 200 guineas to our Lord the King, 100 guineas to William Alexander, Silkman of the parish of St Paul Covent Garden in the County of Middlesex, 100 guineas to Samuel Phillip of the same parish in the same county and 100 guineas to William Russell, cook, of the same parish in the same county. Upon condition that the said Thomas Rookwood do personally appear at the next sessions of the peace held for the said County of Middlesex at Justice Hall in the Old Bailey, there to answer what shall be on His Majesty's behalf objected against him, and in the meantime to keep the peace towards Our Sovereign Lord the King and all his liege people, and not to depart the court without licence. That then and upon which, at that same delivery of the gaol of our Lord the King at Newgate held for the County of Middlesex in the year, on the day and at the hour aforesaid before the aforesaid judges of our aforesaid Lord the King the aforesaid Thomas Rookwood solemnly appeared in his own person and upon the same a public proclamation had been made that if there should be anyone who [*damaged*] let him inform Thomas Rookwood that he should like to come and hear his words. And since the aforesaid Justices find nothing evil concerning him, it was decided by the court that Thomas Rookwood may be exonerated concerning the aforesaid recognisances and that he may go from here on the same day.

11. [CUL Hengrave MS 88/4/25] *William Covell to Thomas Rookwood, 7 December 1696*

7 December 1696

S[i]r

Ben Cossens was this day w[i]t[h] me to lett me know that you have sent for Mrs Kennys money, Mr Charles have beene often portuning me to lett him have itt for he have an opportunity of laying itt out upon Sayers ffarme. I went oute w[i]t[h] him to view itt & in my Judg[me]nt (except by convenience) itt is a Hard [*illeg.*] [*illeg.*] I am very old & declining & would bee gladd to be quit of this trust for you & your family And in order thereunto desier to send a [*illeg.*] from your selfe & your Brothers & Sisters attested by a publique notary & other wittnesse of good creditt (I have sealed away the great conveyance but it by vagrant and in great danger for any man much more for you) And I shalbee ready & willing to suffer the trust to pass as you shall direct for in your Offer to mee you mention to sett y[ou]r sadel on the right horse & to bee a good horseman, I know noe reason for those expressions And doe not well understand y[ou]r meaning otherwise than going into a suit w[hi]ch after the pains & expense I have been att I did better expect from you or your family, for some of them by word of mouth or by writing tell mee they expect the[i]r portions from mee soe that before I p[ar]t[e]d with anymore of the trust I think I have reason to demand a release.

your great ffrend Mr Eldredd and his complaint have since you left England runn Barrowe estat at above 120t into debt for there [*illeg.*] Buryd and I have noe profynt of and ends w[i]t[h] out a Chancery suit & that very chargable & dangerous for Macro who is the [*illeg.*] trustee & in whose name soe many disturbances are taken or \be taken/ for his Landlord Eldredd have since [*illeg.*] last [*illeg.*]yed on all hee have that there is better hope of making him able to rest and I was forced to take upp 40tt uppon bonds to you the execution money for the J[u]d[ge]ment & w[ha]t was received & before your departure by mr J Mich he whose estate wilbee aloud at J[u]d[ge]ment for all last haradst the Baylifs & hay in the field as soone as any J[u]d[ge]ment & at any corne they [*illeg.*] itt for Macro soe that not only the yeares rent but there whole cropp was [*illeg.*] and he [*illeg.*] and forced to buy there owne corne. I have runn through many [*illeg.*] in my life but never mett w[i]th the like nor know not how to gett an end of itt. I feare your whole affayre stands upp in loose [*illeg.*] for except you cann gett from IC w[i]t[h] you to extend your pass your [*illeg.*] att home will doe you better service for I feare you begann at the wrong end. I wish I could see you but my family might not be excused to trouble after my dayly [*illeg.*], I hope I shall dye a iust an honest man all the affronte and comb[in]at[i]ons I have [*illeg.*] w[hi]c[h] in relation to you and yours bolded and I am

your most humble and faithfull servant Will[iam] Covell

12. [CUL Hengrave 76/2/18] *William Covell to Thomas Rookwood, 1 July 1699*

S[i]r

I rec[eive]d yours of the 14th June 99 and would bee gladd to compl[y] w[i]th your desier but 2 or 3 [*illeg.*] from Mr ffrancis and world affronte from your boy, Brother Charles, he p[ro]mised mee a generall release from all the legates before I pled as ms Kemps security. But mr ffrancis is of a contrary opinion and have threatened mee w[i]th a chanc[er]y suit w[hi]ch is the only thing I desier ffor if your circumstance would have given him leave I should before this have exhibited a Bill in Chancery and dilivered & upp[on] your ffathers Will & Inventory as y[ou]r securities and attorny into the Court & take any [*illeg.*] from the Court as is practised every day in that Court.

you know your Brother Adney & ffrancis lefft, knowing that their legaties were given but conditionary to secure the Interest for them. att the making of the will I told your ffather that as itt is worded itt might ind[ic]ate a fact he told mee hee hadd not other security for paym[en]t of the Interest, for the whole estate being entailed hee would make noe other p[ro]vision & doubted not in the least of the legatis complaints for hee said the [*illeg.*] would not admitt E[v]en to see in England. And thearfor gave mee great [*illeg.*] to see his will p[er]formed w[hi]ch I pr[o]missed him to doe for as long as I hadd life and power to act. Mr Adney says nothing to mee but desiers mee to p[er]form the will, But I am sorry Mr ffrancis have such cause of complaynt for hee say[s] hee [*illeg.*] not any benefitt of his ffathers will since his death, If soe itt is my duty to see his Interest paid. And if ms Kemp pay in h[e]r money I will secure itt so well as I am for th[ere]to I benefitt you & your family. I am [*illeg.*] by p[er]sons I must not name for y[a]t p[er]formance of that P[ar]te of your ffathers Will w[hi]c[h] [*illeg.*] his Charity, for w[hi]ch I desier your compliance and direction. Barrow Estate from the beginning & servantkind have given mee much trouble—In all [*illeg.*] of your consent And how to end itt I know not. Indeed hadd any estate of your ffathers in my hande longer than I had opportunity to pay itt. I [*illeg.*] hadd for such the trouble I have hadd and am like to have, I would put appointed to trust for townhouse by edwards I doe have or am like to have, Hawsted Lass and your [*illeg.*]. I will dy a iust an honest man Man[a]g[e]d all y[ou]r affaire I have rec[eive]d, & dayly insolted by some of your family who I fear will ever [*illeg.*] Stuard and your ffriend though I pray God his new ffriende & Counsellor serve him noe worse than the old have done. I know not what measures are taken for your return But am sure that if due mean reward applye & there might bee a way found to bring you home amongst us otherwise I greatly fear ruine will fall uppon your estate & family. I hope this will come to your hands & desier your answer by the first opportunity. beleeve mee that I am & ever will bee

1st July 99

> your most faithfull
> & humble serv[an]t
> W M Covell

Since I wrot this letter mr Arantil have [*illeg.*] [*illeg.*] (but came not to Coldham) & was distressed y[a]t matter about his legate, hee will not owne the Interest was only Intend[ed] him but the principall & say[s] he have taken a Coppy of the will & Shewen itt the great Lawyers who say, th[a]t [*illeg.*] noe question to bee made but the legaties must have [*illeg.*] legaties. I told him by the letter of the will it is soe, And told him what I have mentioned before in this letter that they was only in trust & soe descarded often to and by your father hee did not posetivly deny or confess by [*illeg.*] but was content [*illeg.*] to some to attonyt for the Interest when I have promised to pay him out of Ms Kemps Mortgage

W C

13. [CUL Hengrave 76/2/19, 21] *Petitions for the revocation of Thomas Rookwood's Act of Banishment, 1703*

To the Queen's most Excellent Maj[es]tie

The humble Peticon of Thomas Rookwood of Coldham in the County of Suffolk Esq[ui]r[e]

Sheweth

That for 4 or 5 years before the late Act of Banishment, your Pet[itione]r lived peaceably and quietly at his own house, and during that time never fell into the displeasure of any of the Magistrates of his own Country, Nor in all that time was ever taken up by any Messenger or any other Authority whatsoever.

But in Obedience to the Act of Parliament Intituled an Act against Correspondence with the late King James and his Adherents, Your Pet[itione]r retired to fflanders, and from that time to this day hath never been out of fflanders, or gone into any parts of ffrance, or held any (the least) Correspondence with any of the Enemies of this Kingdom.

And thô it appears by the annexed Certificate that his affaires at home, very much required his personal Presence; ffor want of which he hath very considerably Sufferd, Yet (that he might not give the Government any Jealousy, or occasion any Complaint of his behaviour) your Pet[itione]r hath kept himself close to the Place he retired to upon his Banishment, and from that time to this day hath never returned unto or sett footing in England, as many others have done.

In consideration whereof, and forasmuch his continuance longer in Exile will (not only) inevitably and intirely ruine his Estate and family, but also disable him from paying his just debts, and consequently redound to the irrecoverable loss and Detriment of many of your good Subjects, as by the annexed is Certified.

Your Pet[itione]r most humbly Implores Your Ma[jes]ties Royall Clemency & Goodness may be Mercyfully extended to him; by Graciously Granting him Lycence to return home to his ffamily (after his so long absence) to preserve himself and them from their otherwise impending ruine: He promiseing to behave himself inoffensively & with all dutyfull Obedience to Ma[jes]tie, and to your Lawes & Government.

And as in duty bound will ever pray &c.

To the Queen's most excellent Majesty.

May it please yo[u[r Ma[jes]tie

Wee the Neighbour's and Acquaintance of Thomas Rookwood of Coldham in the County of Suffolk Esq[ui]r[e] (whose hands are hereto subscribed) Doe most humbly certify & declare That hee did for severall yeares live & reside amongst us in the time of his Ma[jes]ties Reigne; During all w[hi]ch time (to our certaine knowledge) hee demeaned himselfe inoffensively, and with respect to the Lawes. And wee are strongly induced to beleeve That he would still constantly manifest a due

Observance of them, and a just and dutifull regard and obedience to yo[u]r Ma[jes]ties Government. Should yo[u]r Ma[jes]tie be graciously pleased of your Royall and accustomed Clemency and goodness to revoake his Exile and permitt his return to his native Country, and residence with us as formerly Which w[i]th profound submission we doe on his behalf implore. In all humility asserting unto yo[u]r Ma[jes]tie That his continuance in Exile will Fatally and inevitably involve him in great Debts, inextricable Law Suits, intirely ruine his Estate, and finally disable him from paying his just Debts, and consequently redound to many of yo[u]r good subjects irrecoverable Loss and Detriment. All w[hi]ch wee most humbly recomend to yo[u]r Ma[jes]ties most gracious consideracion. And for his quiet and peaceable behaviour towards yo[u]r Ma[jes]ties Royall person and Government, wee presume (in all Sincerity) to beleeve, with assured confidence, That wee may be his Guarranties. Witnesse our hands this 20th day of January in ye 3d Year of our Soveraigne Lady Anne by the Grace of God of England Scotland ffrance & Ireland Queen Defender of the ffaith or Annoq[ue] D[omi]ni 1702

Tho[mas] Hanmer. member of parliament.   Simonds D'Ewes
                                          Robert Davers
                                          John Poley
                                          Tho[mas] Robinson
                                          Bartho[lomew] Young
                                          Ja[mes] Harvey
                                          J[oh]n Risby
                                          Geo[rge] Wrayson
                                          Will[iam] Rowett
                                          Tho[mas] Macro

14. [CUL Hengrave MS 76/2/22] *John Perry (widower of Margaret Rookwood) to William Covell, 19 September 1705*

mr Covell

I know You are sole Execut[o]r of mr Ambrose Rookwoods Will who assigned the Essex Estat[e]s to My whife in Satisfaction of the 80tt Annuity Given her by S[i]r Rob[er]t Rookewood her ffather for Life, & Charged upon that Estate to pay, in which assignm[e]nt You know very well that mr Rokewood did Coven[a]nt for himselfe his heires Ex[ecutor]s Admini[strat]ors & Assignes to putt all that Estate in good & tenantable repayre within one Yeare after Executeing thereof, & to allow sufficient Tymber to keepe the same in sure repayre dureing my whifes Life,

And alsoe You know (as all that Countrey doe) that mr Rookewood Never layd out one penny for wages in all the Nyne Yeares tyme my whife Enjoyed it, whereby I lost in that tyme for want of Tennants, & by [*illeg.*] Letteing thereof more than 130tt, So You likewise know that this Matter was Consented with mr Rokewood & yo[u]r selfe long before my whife dyed, (immediately after whose death) I Gave Mr Rokewood quiett possession of all that Estate (upon Mr Thorpes assureing Me on his Master Rookwoods behalf) that I should have reasonable satisfaction for want of those wages & alsoe for the growth of Claverings Wood, & for such arrears of farme Rents, & Quitt Rents as were payable to Me att the death of my whife, which mr Rokwood said,

And since mr Rokewoods death I did in a most friendly Manner by Letters acquaynt mr Thomas Rokewood (before he lefte England, & since his retorne) with my very hard usage from his father, But Never rec[eive]d a word from him in Answere, For that I Now make Application to You herein, who is apply Courteous to answer Me so faste, as being both Ex[ecuto]r to mr Rokewood & Trustee to all his Estate, & doubt Not in yo[u]r honesty to doe me right in the P[re]misses, without a Push att Law, (which indeed May be saied if you please) for I will readily referr my Cause to the result of any Counsell of mr Rokewoods or yo[u]r own Choosing, & will acquiess therein, or rather than Quarrell will freely accept what mr Rokewood will gen[er] ously pay me which I beseech you to lett mr Rokewood know, & with all to forgive this troublesome diversion

Yo[u]r very Obliged ffriend & serv[an]t
Jo[h]n Perry

Bury 19° Sept[ember] 1705

15. [CUL Hengrave MS 76/2/24] *Frances and John Jerningham to Thomas Rookwood, 24 August 1706*

S[i]r

I should be as ready to doe you any service that lies in my power, as I am, to owne my hand wittnes to the writing you sent me, which I doe affirme to be my owne hand writing, I doe not wonder mr Sergeant Wells should not know my hand, for I doe not Remember ever to have writt to him. though he is my verry good Councell and Friend. this I hope will be sufficient to comply with y[ou]r commands From

y[ou]r most Humble Servant
Fran[ces] Jernegan

our whole family send you and y[ou]r Fair Daughter theare Services, and often wish to see you and the young Lady heere.

Cossey August the 24 1706

I doe own (as my Father has don[e] that to be my hand wittness to the writing you sent: so remain

Y[ou]r humble servant
John Jernegan

16. [TNA C 6/470/4] *Thomas Rookwood's reply to Charles Rookwood's Bill of*
Complaint against him in the Court of Chancery, 13 March 1709

The Plea of Thomas Rookwood Esq[ui]r[e] one of the Def[endan]ts to part i this his
Answer to the residue of the Bill of Complaint Charles Rookwood Gent Complainant.

This Defendant by Protestation not confessing or acknowledging all or any of the
matters or things in the Comp[lainan]ts Bill of Comp[lain]t claimed to be true in such
manner and forme as the same are therein and thereby sett forth as to so much of the
said Bill as seeks to call this Debt to an account touching and concerning the su[m]
me of Nine hundred pounds principall money upon Bond or for any interest or
damages relating thereto. This Def[endan]t doth plead in Barr and for plea saith that
the said Comp[lainan]t in the year of Our Lord One thousand seaven hunded and four
Did Com[m]ence an Action against this Def[endan]t upon the said Nine hundred
pounds Bond and held this Depon[en]t to Baile thereon and on the first of January in
the said year of Our Lord One thousand seaven hundred and four the now p[lainti]ff
did Exhibit a Bill into this Hon[oura]ble Court against this Def[endan]t and James
Harvey touching Severall receipts and disbursements of the now P[lainti]ffs in relat[i]
on to the management of the Def[endan]ts Estate by the now p[lainti]ff from the first
day of ffebruary One thousand six hundred ninety seaven untill Midsum[m]er One
thousand seaven hundred and three. to which Bill this Def[endan]t did putt in his
answer on or about the first of March in the said year of Our Lord One thousand
seaven hundred and four and therein Assigned several Errors in the P[lainti]ffs said
Accounts and after sum time as this Def[endan]ts was putt in The now P[lainti]ff and
Mr Benjamin Rawlins his Clerke in Court for and on behalfe of the p[lainti]ff. and
this Def[endan]t and his Counsell and J[oh]n Muchall his Clarke in Court did on the
Eighteenth day of March One thousand seaven hundred and four meet together at the
Castle Tavern in Drury Lane and then and there all matters and Things then depending
between the said partyes the accounts relating to the same lying upon a table before
the said parties were fairly and deliberately Examined stated and agreed to allow the
new P[lainti]ff thirty five pounds which was no part of the said Nine hundred pounds
bond nor no where ment[i]oned in the said accounts nor in this Bill then brought
against the Def[endan]t. but the P[lainti]ff pr[e]tended it was for Interest due before
the said Nine hundred pounds was entred into. And this Def[endan]t for further Plea
saith that after sum time as all matters and things were fairly stated and agreed upon
by Benjamin Rawlins the P[lainti]ffs Clerke in Court in the p[re]sence of the now
p[lainti]ff and def[endan]t and of the aforesaid persons did draw up an agreement in
writing in these words vi[delicet]: Memorandum it is concluded and agreed upon
Between Thomas Rookwood Esq[ui]r[e] and Charles Rookwood Gent[leman] upon
Stating accounts between them concerning the interest due upon a Bond for Nine
hundred pounds entred into by the said Thomas Rookwood to the said Charles
Rookwood and touching the receipt and disbursements of the said Charles in relation
to the management of the said Thomas Rookwoods estate by the said Charles from
the first day of ffebruary One thousand six hundred and ninety seaven untill
Midsum[m]er One thousand seaven hundred and three. And also for the said sum[m]e
of Thirty five pounds due to the said Charles for interest due before the said Bond
was entred into That there is due to the said Charles Rookwood Nine hundred and
ffifty pounds which is to be paid the said Charles Rookwood by the said Thomas
Rookwood. Charles Rookwood witness Edward Bedingfield Benjamin Rawlines
Benjamin Muchall. And after the said Im[plead]er Benjamin Rawlins had drawn the

said Agreement he read the same over to the said Charles Rookwood and this Def[endan]t and the said Charles Rookwood Signed the said paper writing or Memorandum after such time as the same was read over to the new p[lainti]ff as aforesaid as in and by the said Agreement now remaining in the hands of the said Benjamin Muchall may appeare. And this def[endan]t saith for further plea that pursuant to the Agreement this Def[endan]t procured the said Nine hundred and fifty pounds at Six pounds p[er] Cent within the time for payment of the same. And the said p[lainti]ff and Im[plead]er Rawlins his Clerke in Court being acquainted that this def[endan]t would pay the nine hundred and fifty pounds pursuant to the said Agreement upon the Twenty third day of the said Month of March between the hours of three and four in the afternoon at the Chambers of Edward Bedingfield Esq[ui]r[e] in Greys Inn and at the same time [*illeg.*] Seale and grant a generall Release but the new p[lainti]ff refused to come to the said place to receive the said nine hundred and ffifty pounds but insisted that the def[endan]t should meet him next day at the Castle Tavern in Drury Lane at Twelve of the Clock in the forenoone and accordingly the Def[endan]t and the said Edward Bedingfield and one John Rookwood went to the Castle Tavern in Drury Lane and there found the said Charles Rookwood and Benjamin Rawlins his Clerke in Court [*illeg.*] this def[endan]ts Clerke in Court. And this Def[endan]t told then the now p[lainti]ff that this defend[an]t had brought the nine hundred and fifty pounds to [*illeg.*] and was then willing to Signe his Accounts and execute a Generall Release [*illeg.*] afterwards laid upon the table and openly read over in the p[re]sence and hearing of all the Company and afterwards by the said Charles Rookwood himselfe the said Charles [*illeg.*] who refused to execute the same till the money was paid. And thereupon this Def[endan]t did produce two Goldsmiths Bills to the new p[lainti]ff Charles Rookwood or bearer the one Bill was for Six hundred pounds from Mr Coggs Goldsmith and the other for Three hundred and ffifty pounds from Mr Simpson Goldsmith but the said Charles Rookwood objected against the said Bills and said he would not seale till the money was paid [*illeg.*] thereupon the Def[endan]t offered to fetch ready money and thereupon one Mr Thornicroft the p[lainti]ffs Goldsmith took both the said Bills into his hands and declared that both the Bills were as good as so much money and offered to take them and be accountable to the said Charles for so much money. And then the said Charles seemed satisfied with the Bills and thereupon the said bills for nine hundred and ffifty pounds were delivered to the said Thornicroft for the p[lainti]ff notwithstanding the said Charles refused to Seale a Release till such time as this def[endan]t had executed his Release. And this Def[endan]t further for plea saith that pursuant to the said Agreement of the Eighteenth of March One thousand seaven hundred and four he this def[endan]t by the name of Thomas Rookwood of Stanningfield in the County of Suffolke Esq[ui]r[e] Did Signe Seale and [*illeg.*] deliver to the said Charles Rookwood a Generall Release bearing date the ffour and Twentieth day of March One thousand seaven hundred and four as in and by the said Release now [*illeg.*] of the said Benjamin Muchall may appear. And no sooner had yo[u]r Orator executed the said Release but the new p[lainti]ff stood up and declared that he would not accept the money and Seale a Release [*illeg.*] Def[endan]t would pay him Twenty Seaven pounds over and above the said nine hundred and fifty pounds upon which the now p[lainti]ffs Attorney and Goldsmith took up the said Agreement and read over the same then perswaded the p[lainti]ff to receive the said money who refused to accept of the same. And this Def[endan]t for further plea saith that pursuant to the said Agreement the def[endan]t having took up the said Nine hundred and ffifty pounds at Interest and the p[lainti]ff refusing to receive the same this def[endan]t on or about the Eight and Twentieth day of Aprill One thousand Seaven hundred and ffive Exhibited his Bill into this Court against the now p[lainti]ff to compell him to receive the said Nine hundred and ffifty pounds and to deliver up the said Bond to be Cancelled and to Seale a Release according to the said Agreement of the Eighteenth of March One thousand Seaven hundred and ffour to which bill the said def[endan]t putt in his Answer as by the said Bill and Answer now remaining duly filed may appeare. And this def[endan]t further saith for plea that by an order of the Court of the Twenty first of June in the fourth year of the p[re]sent Queen by the then Lord Keeper wherein this def[endan]t was then p[lainti]ff against the now p[lainti]ff then def[endan]t writing that whereas upon an order of the nineteenth instant for the reasons therein contained it was ordered that the Injunction granted in this Cause for stay of the def[endan]ts proceedings at Law should stand dissolved unless the p[lainti]ff should on that day should give this Court good Cause to the contrary. And upon moc[i]on that day made unto this Court by J[oh]n Williams this def[endan]ts Counsell who came to shew cause against the said Order in the p[re]sence of th[i]s Hon[ourable] Court or for [*illeg.*] Rookwood This Def[endan]ts Counsell alledged that this def[endan]t having given the now p[lainti]ff a Bond for Nine hundred pounds and about ffebruary One thousand Six hundred Ninety Seaven going beyond sea he by Letter of Brief did Authorize Charles Rookwood and one Harvey to manage his Estate in Suffolke which they not performing according to the p[lainti]ffs satisfact[i]on discharged them therefrom. And the said Charles Rookwood having vested the def[endan]t on the said Bond he the said Charles Rookwood on the Eighteenth of March then last having had a meeting in order to settle the matters in difference an Agreement was drawn up between them and signed by the p[lainti]ff and def[endan]t which Agreement was that upon stating amounts and interest due on the said nine hundred pounds Bond between them there was due to the now p[lainti]ff nine hundred and ffifty pounds which was to be paid before the ffive and Twentieth day of March and thereupon Generall Releases were to be given to each other pursuant to which Agreement this Def[endan]t promised the said Nine hundred and ffifty pounds at Six pounds p[er] Cent and was obliged to pay so much for the same And sent the said Charles Rookwood word that he would pay the same on the Three and Twentieth day of March last but the said Charles refused to receive the said nine hundred and ffifty pounds or to Seale the Release. And in regard this Def[endan]t was always ready to pay the said nine hundred and ffifty pounds according to the said agreement. And thereupon the said Charles said injunction might be continued untill the hearing of this Cause. And the said Charles Rookwoods Counsell insisting that the said Charles is and always was willing to receive the Nine hundred and ffifty pounds due on the said Bond And that if this Def[endan]t would pay the same together with his further interest due on the said Bond and his Costs at Law and in this Court and pay his amounts he is willing to deliver up the said Bond to the p[lainti]ff but hopes that untill the p[lainti]ff so does he shall be left at Liberty to proceed at Law as he shall be advised. and that upon reading the said Agreement and what was alledged on both sides This Court did then order that this def[endan]t should within a month next pay unto the said def[endan]t at J[oh]n Cogge Goldsmith in the Strand the said Sum[m]e of nine hundred and ffifty pounds according to the Agreement and thereupon the said Charles Rookwood was to deliver up the said Bond to this defend[an]t to be Cancelled and acknowledge satisfaction on Record of the Judgement obtained thereon at this def[endan]ts charge but in default of this def[endan]t paying unto the said Charles Rookwood the said Nine hundred and ffifty pounds by the time aforesaid the said Injunction was to stand dissolved which in the mean time was thereby continued as in and by the said Order [*illeg.*] duly entered with one of the Deputies Registers of this Court and now remaining in Mr Muchalls hands may appeare. And this Defend[an]t further for plea saith that this Def[endan]ts then Clerke in Court upon the Twelfth of July Seaven hundred and ffive did cause the said Charles Rookwood to be personally served and th[en] Benjamin Rawlins his Clerke in Court. And also the Clerke or agent of the [*illeg.*] the said Charles Rookwoods attorney with three severall Notices in Writing in the words or to the effect following Inter Thomam Rookwood etc Quod Carolum Rookwood gen[erosum] Def[endan]t [*illeg.*] pray take [*illeg.*] that I do intend God willing to pay you nine hundred and ffifty pounds pursuant to an Order made in this Cause the One and twentieth day of June last upon ffriday next at four of the Clock in the Afternoon at J[oh]n Cogges Goldsmith in the Strand from yo[u]r loving friends Edward Bedingfield and Benjamin Muchall Clerke for the p[lainti]ff which said Mr Charles Rookwood then lodged in Cecill Court near St Martins Lane London as by an Affidavit of the said service now remaining filed in this Hon[oura]ble Court may appear. And this Def[endan]t further for plea saith that he doubts not \but/ to prove that Mr Benjamin Muchall this Def[endan]ts then Clerke in Court did on the Thirteenth of the said Month of July go to Mr Coggs Shop a Goldsmith in the Strand before four of the Clock the same day and was then and there ready to have paid the said Charles Rookwood Nine hundred and fifty pounds pursuant to an Order made in the Court of Chancery the One and Twentieth day of June last and stayed there till after the hour of five of the Clock the same day in order to have paid the said sume of Nine hundred and ffifty pounds. But neither the said Charles Rookwood nor any other person or persons whatsoever came to receive the same or any part thereof altho[ugh] the said Mr Benjamin Muchall was ready and willing to have paid the same to the said Charles Rookwood upon the termes of the said Order as in and by an Affidavitt of the said Mr Muchall now remaining filed in this Hon[oura]ble Court shall appear. And this Def[endan]t further for plea saith that he doubts not but to make appear that the said Mr Muchall on the Twentieth of October One thousand Seaven hundred and ffive did serve the said Mr Benjamin Rawlins the said Charles Rookwoods then Clerke in Court with a notice in writing by leaving it at Mr Rawlins Seat with his agent there purporting that this Def[endan]t did intend to move this Court on Tuesday then or so soon after as Counsell could be heard That the said Charles Rookwood might receive the Nine hundred and ffifty pounds that then was in Mr Coggs the Golsmiths hands in two days or in default thereof that the same might be paid into Court and thereupon the said Bond might be delivered up to the p[lainti]ff to be Cancelled and satisfa[c]tion acknowledged on record of the Judgement obtained thereon at this Def[endan]ts Charge pursuant to an Order made in this Cause the One and twentieth day of June last. And this Def[endan]t further for plea saith that upon Tuesday the said three and twentieth day of the said Month of October and in the ffourth year of the p[re]sent Queen upon opening of the matter that p[re]sent day unto the right Hon[oura]ble the Lord Keeper of the Great Seale of England by Mr Peter Williams being this Def[endan]ts Counsell in the p[re]sence of Mr How being of Counsell for the said Charles Rookwood alledging That this Def[endan]t was ready and willing to have paid the said Nine hundred and ffifty pounds to the Def[endan]t according to the direction as by Affidavit appeared and upon hearing the said Charles Rookwoods Counsell It was ordered that the said Order of the one and twentieth of June should stand with this addition That in case the said Charles Rookwood should not think fitt to accept of the said Nine hundred and ffifty pounds within a week next the same should be brought into this Court as in and by the said Order being duly entred now resting in the hands of Mr Muchall may appear.

And this Def[endan]t for plea further saith that he doubts not but to prove that upon the Seaven and twentieth day of the said month of October this [*illeg.*] said Clerke in Court did cause the said Charles Rookwood to be Served with a notice in writing signed by the said Edward Bedingfield and Benjamin Muchall that they did intend (God willing) to pay to the said Charles Rookwood the said nine hundred and ffifty pounds pursuant to two Severall Orders made in the Cause wherein this Def[endan]t was then p[lainti]ff and the now p[lainti]ff then Def[endan]t the one bearing date the one and twentieth day of June last and the other the Three and twentieth of that Instant October upon Munday next at three of the Clock in the afternoon at Mr Coggs Goldsmith in the Strand. And this Def[endan]t further for plea saith that this Defend[an]t doubts not but to prove that on Monday the Nine and twentieth day of October One thousand Seaven hundred and five the said Mr Benjamin Muchall went to the house and Shopp of Mr Coggs Goldsmith in the Strand before three of the Clock the same day and stayed there till after the hour of ffour of the Clock and was then and there ready and willing to have paid the Def[endan]t Charles Rookwood the whole and intire sume of Nine hundred and ffifty pounds pursuant to an Order made in this Cause the three and twentieth of the said month of October but neither the said Charles Rookwood nor any other persons for and on his behalfe came to receive the same or any part thereof. And this Def[endan]t further for plea saith that this Def[endan]t obtaining the said Order and giving the Severall Notices to the said Charles Rookwood of paying the said nine hundred and ffifty pounds to him as aforesaid and he not attending at any of the times aforesaid to receive the same he this Def[endan]t pursuant to the said Order of the Twenty Third of October in the fourth year of p[re]sent Queen Did on the Nineteenth of November One thousand Seaven hundred and five bring the said sume of nine hundred and fifty pounds into this Court. And this Def[endan]t further for plea saith that the said Nine hundred and ffifty pounds being brought into this Court One Mr William Grimes gave a receit on the said Order of the said Three and Twentieth of October for the said Nine hundred and ffifty pounds which receit in the words following (vi[delice]t) Received this Nineteenth day of November One thousand Seaven hundred and five for the use of John [*damaged*] Esq[uire] tisher the sume of nine hundred and ffifty pounds brought into Court by virtue of this Order I say rec[eive]d W[illia]m Grimes as by the said receit here remaining in the hands of the said Mr William Grimes. And this Def[endan]t further for plea saith that [*damaged*] Counsell and Clerke in Court pretending that a Second and Third Notice of a mot[i]on to move this Court the first and Second seat after the [*damaged*] Charles Rookwood was not then Capable either to Manage himselfe or the moneys Did by Mr Pe[t]er Williams of Counsell for this Def[endan]t as this Def[endan]t doubts not but to prove severall times for the reasons aforementioned and Oppose in the Open Court the said Charles Rookwood taking the said Nine hundred and ffifty pounds out of Court and insisted that the same might be placed out att interest by A Master of this Court for the benefitt of the said Charles Rookwood. And this Def[endan]t further for plea saith that by an Order of this Court made the fourth day of March in the fifth year of the p[re]sent Queen before the Right Hon[oura]ble the Lord Keeper and now Lord Chancellor of Great Britaine in a Cause wherein this Def[endant] Thomas Rookwood Esq[uire] was then p[lainti]ff and the now p[lainti]ff Charles Rookwood Gent[leman] Def[endan]t upon the mot[i]on of Mr Serjeant [*damaged*] Mr Painefort being Counsell for the said Charles Rookwood in the p[re]sence of Mr Pe[t]er Williams being of Counsell for this Def[endan]t upon the said Charles Rookwoods Counsell alledging that he had brought [*damaged*] at Law against this Def[endan]t upon a Bond of One thousand Eight hundred pounds penalty

27

Condit[i]oned for the payment of Nine hundred pounds with interest and obtained Judgement thereon. the p[lainti]ff Thomas Rookwood had brought his Bill to be releived against the same Setting forth inter al[ia] that he and the Def[endan]t on the Eighteenth of March one thousand Seaven hundred and four Did come to an agreement which there appeared to be due to the Def[endan]t for Principall and Interest in the said Bond the sume of Nine hundred and ffifty pounds which he offering to pay thereupon obtained an Injunction and [*damaged*] of the Twenty first of June quarto Ann[a]e Regin[a]e It was Ordered that the p[lainti]ff should within a month then next pay unto the said Def[endan]t at Mr Coggs Goldsmith in the Strand the said Nine hundred and ffifty pounds And that thereupon the said Def[endan]t should deliver up the said Bond to the then p[lainti]ff to be Cancelled and acknowledge satisfa[c]tion on Record of the Judgement obtained thereon at this Def[endan]ts Charge and at this the p[lainti]ffs paying the said money as aforesaid the said Injunction was to be dissolved And that the said Def[endan]t refusing to receive the same the said sume of nine hundred and ffifty pounds was afterwards by Order of [*damaged*] and twentieth of October brought into this Court. And the said Charles Rookwood being willing to accept the said money on the terms of the said Order of the One and twentieth of June and give up the Bond and [*damaged*] satisfa[c]tion it was then prayed that the said Money might be paid out of Court to the Def[endan]t whereupon and upon hearing the said Order of the One and twentieth of June read and what was alledged or [*damaged*] Court did order that the said Charles Rookwood should deliver up the said Bond to his p[lainti]ff to be cancelled and acknowledge satisfa[c]tion on Record of the Judgement obtained thereon at this Def[endan]ts Charge and that there the said sume of nine hundred and ffifty pounds be paid out of Court to the then Def[endan]t Charles Rookwood. And this Def[endan]t then the p[lainti]ff to be indempnified in so doing as would by the said Order duly [*damaged*] [*illeg.*] belonging to this hon[oura]ble Court may appear. And this Def[endan]t further for plea saith that by one other Order in the said Cause on the one and twentieth of the said month of March in the Sixth year of her p[re]sent majesty made upon the Def[endan]ts petit[i]on to the Right hon[oura]ble the then and now Master of the Rolls therein writing the former orders of the fourth of March then instant and also writing the Def[endan]t therein assigned the said Bond and Judgement and money whatsoever accruing thereby with absolute power to receive recover or Compound the same to one Hugh Molly of the parish of St James in the County of Middlesex Gent but in regard that by the said Order of the fourth Instant the said sume of nine hundred and ffifty pounds was ordered to be paid to the Def[endan]t without adding the words his Order or Assignes the [*illeg.*] of this Court to pay the same to the said Mr Molly. It was before prayed that the said nine hundred and ffifty pounds then in Court should be paid out to the said Mr Molley according to the said Assignement and [*damaged*] him by the Def[endan]t which was ordered accordingly unless cause was shewne to the contrary on this day a Counsell on both sides that day attending and the Assignement of the said Bond and Judgement And [*damaged*] Attorney to receive the moneys due thereon being produced and read and witnesses being Examined viva voce to prove the said Assignement his Honour thereupon and upon hearing the \said/ petit[i]on and what was alledged on either side Did Order that the said nine hundred and ffifty pounds then in Court should be paid out to the said Mr Molley but the Bond and warrant of Attorney were to be left with the Court in case the then p[lainti]ff and now Def[endan]t or his agent did not attend at the time of payment of the said money to be by him delivered to this Def[endan]t or his Agent as in and by the said Order [*damaged*] his hon[oura]ble Court it doth appear. And this

Def[endan]t further for plea saith that the said nine hundred and ffifty pounds was afterwards rec[eive]d out of Court by the said p[lainti]ff or his Assignee And thereupon [*damaged*] hundred pounds was delivered up to this Def[endan]t to be Cancelled as well as the said warrant of Attorney and now resting in this Def[endan]ts Custody or power may appear. All which matters and things are true and doth plead the same in Barr to remain of the said Bill as aforesaid and doth humbly demand the Judgement of this hon[oura]ble Court whether this Def[endan]t shall be compelled to make any further or other [*damaged*] unto the said Bill and the matters and things therein contained save as herein after is answered unto. And this Def[endan]t saving and reserving to himselfe all advantage of Exception to the [*illeg.*] of the said Bill this Def[endan]t not waving his said plea but relying thereon doth for Answer say that he is an utter Stranger to the said Hugh Molly And that he doth not know or have heard [*illeg.*] How does or lately or last did reside or dwell or where he is now or ever was in his life time to be spoken with or found and denyes that the p[lainti]ffs acquaintance with the said Hugh Molly was occasioned [*damaged*] this Def[endan]t for this Def[endan]t was then and now is an utter stranger to the said Molly and of his Executing the Letter of Attorney ment[i]oned in the Bill otherwise than by pleading in the Cause. And this Def[endan]t [*damaged*] time of the said Ambrose Rookwood this Def[endan]ts late Brother and long before his Attainder of High Treason this Def[endan]t had really satisfyed and payed him his full share of what belonged to him [*illeg.*] his late [*damaged*] And as to the personall Estate of the said Ambrose Rookwood this Def[endan]ts late brother this Def[endan]t says that he being attainted of high Treason his personall Estate if any there was (which this Def[endan]t [*damaged*] cannot anyways belong to the p[lainti]ff nor can the p[lainti]ff claime any title to the same or any part thereof. And this Def[endan]t denyes all and all manner of unlawfull Combinat[i]on and Confederation used against [*damaged*] and without that any other matter or thing said in the Comp[lainan]tts said Bill of Comp[lain]tt contained materiall or effectuall in Law for him this Def[endan]t to make answer unto and not herein and hereby [*damaged*] \pleaded or/ answered unto confessed or avoided traversed or denyed is true to this Def[endan]ts knowledge all which matters and things this Def[endan]t is and will be ready to averr maintain and prove as [*damaged*] award and humbly prays to be hence dismissed with his reasonable Costs and Charges in this behalfe most wrongfully sustained.

[*illeg.*] such hoc Pub[licu]m e[t] Generoso responsio apud Bury st Ed[mund]s in Com[ita]t[e] Suff[olciensis] & p[rae]sens Thomas Rookwood [*illeg.*] sive ad delibat[o] exs[eque]ndum Tricesimo Anno die iiiij Annoque Suae Regnae immo Octavo Annoq[ue] D[omi]ni 1709 coram nobis[20]

Rodney Hane
Joane Hargees
John Heights

R[ichar]d Muchall

Thomas Rookwood

---

[20] 'This public and genteel answer [given] at Bury St Edmunds in the County of Suffolk, Thomas Rookwood being present ... or for the carrying out of the delivery on the thirteenth day of March and indeed in the eighth year of her reign and in the year of our Lord 1709 before us ...'

17. [CUL Hengrave MS 76/1] *Indenture allowing Thomas Rookwood to recover his estates, 24 May 1711 (summary by John Gage)*

24th May 1711 Ind[entu]re inrolled in Chancery made between the s[ai]d Thomas Rookwood, William Covell Gent[leman], Sir Thomas Hanmer Bar[one]t and Sir Robert Davers Bar[one]t of the 1st part—Philip Yorke Gent[leman] of the 2d part and John Cotton Gent[leman] of the 3d p[ar]t being a bargain and sale to make a tenemant to the praecipe to a recovery to be suffered by the said Thomas Rookwood of his family estates in Suffolk, which recovery was to ensure to such uses as he should appoint.

18. [TNA C 6/469/70] *Charles Rookwood's appeal to the Lord Keeper of the Great Seal against Thomas Rookwood, 16 July 1711*

16°: die Julij 1711

To the Right Hon[oura]ble S[i]r Simon Harcourt Lord Keeper of the Great Seale of Great Brittaine.

Humbly Complaining sheweth unto your Lordshipp your Orator Charles Rookwood of the Parish of Saint Pauls Covent Garden in the County of Middlesex Gent[leman] that your Orators late ffather Ambrose Rookwood Esq[ui]r[e] being seized and possessed of a very great reall and personall Estate did on the Eighteenth day of February One Thousand Six Hundred Ninety and two duely make and publish his last Will and Testament in writeing and did thereby (inter al[ia]) Give and devise unto his Son Ambrose Rookwood and his heires All that Mannor of Shriefes situate in Calne in the County of Essex together with the woods and Copices thereto belonging And gave his ffarme called C[l]averings in South Hamsted in the said County of Essex to his Executors therein after named to be sold by them and the Ariseing to be for and towards the performance of his Will, and therein gave severall Legacies and particularly ffour Hundred pounds to your Orator and made his Sons Thomas Rookwood and Ambrose Rookwood and William Covill Executors. and the residue of his Estate not therein bequeathed He gave to his said Sons Thomas and Ambrose as by the said Will when produced will more fully appeare. And your Orator thought that the said Ambrose Rookwood the Elder soon after dyed without annulling or weake[n]ing the same and the said Thomas Rookwood and William Covill proved the proved the said Will and took upon them the burthen of the Execution thereof and possessed themselves of the personall Estate of Ambrose Rookwood the Elder sufficient to pay all his Debts Legacies and ffunerall Expences with a Surplus of above ffourteen Hundred pounds besides the said Estate at Claverings devised as aforesaid and a Lease hold est[ate] called Barrows ffarme of the value of ffifty pounds \per annum/. And your Orator sheweth that the said Ambrose Rookwood the younger haveing in his life time promised to give and did give unto your Orator all his Estate whatsoever and He dying intestate administration of all and singular his Goods and Chattles rights and Creditts was duely granted to your Orator in the prerogative Court of Canterbury As by Letters of Administration under the Seale of that Court dated the Thirtieth day of July One Thousand seaven hundred and Seaven ready to be produced to this honourable Court will plainely appeare. And your Orator sheweth unto your

Lordship that the said Thomas Rookwood and William Covill having not accounted with the said Ambrose Rookwood the younger in his life time nor your Orator since his Death for any part or share of the personall Estate of the said Ambrose Rookwood the Elder nor for the rents and profits of the said Mannor of Shriefs and Estate called Claverings and Barrowe into which the said Thomas Rookwood ent[e]red and received the rents and profits ever since the death of the said Ambrose Rookwood. and haveing not accounted for or paid your Orator his said Legacy of ffour Hundred pounds and the said William Covill being dead and in his life time transferred all his share and interest unto the said Thomas Rookwood or otherwise renounced the same. He your said Orator applyed him selfe unto the said Confederate Thomas Rookwood in a fair and friendly manner as well for his the said Thomas Rookwood for his coming to a faire and just account with your Orator in and about the Legacy given to him as aforesaid as also for your Orators Moyety or halfe or other part of the personall estate of the said Ambrose Rookwood the Elder and for the rents and proffits of the said Mannor of Shriefes and Estate called Barrowe ffarme as also for other the personall estate of the said Ambrose Rookwood the younger of considerable other value which He dyed possessed of interested in or intituled unto and which the said Thomas Rookwood respectively or some other person or persons' oyer with his Order disertion privity Knowledge consent approbation or procurement in trust for him or them or to his or their use thentofore had possessed himselfe off and converted to his own use or uses. And that the said Thomas Rookwood would pay satisfy unto your Orator what on the ffoot state or ballance of such account should appeare to be due unto him your said Orator together with interest for the same. But now soe it is May it please your Lordship that the said Thomas Rookwood designeing and intending to defraud and wrong your Orator of the Moneys due to him as aforesaid absolutely refused to come to any account with your Orator touching the same or to pay your Orator any part of the moneys thereon due or to give any account to your Orator of the personall estate of the said Ambrose Rookwood the Elder and Ambrose Rookwood the younger or of the rents and profitts of the said Mannor of Shriefes and Estate of Clavering and Barrowe ffarme, and some times pretends he is not in possession of the same or at least wise he took possession of the said Mannor of Shriefes but from the death of Ambrose Rookwood the younger tho[ough] he well knowes the contrary to be true and that he received the rents and profitts thereof from the death of the said Ambrose Rookwood the ffather. and att other times the said Thomas Rookwood pretends the said Ambrose Rookwood the younger made his Will and gave the premises to the said Defendant therefore he will not account for his Estate to your Orator Notwithstanding your Orator hath Letters of Administration granted to him thereof which are in force and unrevoked. and at other times the said Thomas Rookwood pretends he did in the lifetime of the said Ambrose Rookwood account with and pay to him his Moyety part or share of the personall Estate of the said Ambrose Rookwood the Elder and also for the rents and profits of the said Mannor of Shriefes and Claverings but refused to discover how or by what means or when where or in whose presence or in what manner such account payment or satisfaction was made. and the said Thomas Rookwood well knows he never came to any such account or made any such payment or satisfaction and hath been so sensible thereof he hath since the death of the said Ambrose Rookwood the younger paid your Orator ffour hundred pounds in part of the money due to your Orator out of his Estate and faithfully promised he would come to a fair and just account with your Orator for the residue and pay your Orator what should thereupon appeare due Notwithstanding the pretences aforesaid which He now setts upp to avoid comeing to such account. and the said Thomas Rookwood His Defend[an]t about five yeares since most wrongfully seized and possessed himselfe of one Sorell Mare with a Colt and Bay Mare, three holland shirts, one Silke Damask waistcoat, one shag pair of Brieches a Night Gown and cover and several other goods of value and a setting Dog all the proper goods of your Compl[ainan]t to the value of about one hundred pounds and never paid this Compl[ainan]t for any of them, or gave him any recompense for the same. All which actings and doings of the said Thomas Rookwood are contrary to Right Equity and [*illeg.*] and tend to your Orators apparent wrong and Injury. In tender Consideration whereof and for that your Orator is not releivable in the premisses at or by the rules of the Com[m]on Law thereat for that your Orators Witnesses who could and would prove the truth of all and singular the premises are sithes dead or in parts remote beyond the Seas unknowne unto your Orator. nor can your Orator make any discovery of the Estate of the said Ambrose Rookwood the Elder and Ambrose Rookwood the younger nor have an account of the rents or profits of the said Mannor of Shriefes and Claverings or have a discovery of other the premises aforesaid but by the Oathes of the said Thomas Rookewood in Equity before your Lordship nor else where compell the said Thomas Rookewood to come to a just and fair account with him touching the matters aforesaid and to pay him what shall thereupon appeare due To the one therefore that the said Thomas Rookwood may true perfect and direct answer make to and discover all and singular the premisses upon Oath as He knowes beleives or hath heard as to the place Quantity Quality manner and forme and all other the Circumstances thereof and that as Largely amply and particularly in every respect as if the same had been here again repeated and inserted in the prayer of this Bill. and that the said Thomas Rookwood may set forth and discover if the said Ambrose Rookwood the Elder did not make such Will as in herein below set forth and whether your Orator hath not Letters of Administrat[i]on granted to him of the Estate of the said Ambrose Rookwood that stand unrevoked. and that the said Thomas Rookwood may answer and sett forth a true particular and perfect account and Inventory all and every the personal Estate whereof or wherein his late ffather and Brother or any other person or persons and whom in Trust to them or either and which of them were at the time of their respective deaths any ways respectively possessed off Interested in or intituled unto and the true and full yearly or other value thereof respectively and wherein the same Consisted and what is become of the same and to whose hands Custody or possession the same was paid and delivered and how and to whom and when paid and distributed and may sett forth a true and exact account of the yearly rents and profitts of the said Mannor of Shriefes & C[l]averings and Barrowe ffarmes and what yearly rents in other profitt or advantage hath been made and by whom of the same since the death of the said Ambrose Rookwood the younger. And may sett forth whether he did at any time and when came to any account with him touching his said ffathers Estate or the rents and profitts of the said Mannor and ffarme and when where and in whose presence such account was made and if he did at any time and when where and in whose presence pay the said Ambrose Rookwood the younger any and what sume or sumes of Money for and in part of the moneys due upon such account or on the premisses aforesaid and that the said Thomas Rookwood may produce in this honourable Court his Receipts Discharges & Acquittances for such payment. And if he hath not since the death of the said Ambrose Rookwood the younger pay & your Orator the sume of ffour hundred pounds in part of his moneys due to your Orator out of his Estate as his Devisee and Administrator

as aforesaid. And that the said Thomas Rookwood this Def[endan]t may sett forth whether he did or not possess himself of two Mares and Colt and the Wearing Apparell of your Compl[ainan]t and other Goods as before set forth in this Bill. and what money \paid/ or other satisfact[i]on he hath made to your Compl[ainan]t for the same. And that the said Thomas Rookwood may come to a faire and just account with your Orator as well touching the said Legacy of ffour hundred pounds given to your Orator by his said ffather as aforesaid as also for a Moyety or half part of the Estate of the said Ambrose Rookwood the Elder and for all the Estate of the said Ambrose Rookwood the younger and for the rents and profitts of the said Mannor and ffarme from the death of the said Ambrose Rookwood the Elder and may pay for all the goods of the said Compl[ainan]t which the said Def[endan]t most wrongfully possessed himselfe of as aforesaid. And may be compelled to pay your Orator what shall appear due upon such accounts. And that your Orator may bee otherwise releived in all and singular the premises according to Equity and Conscience and the nature of this Case. May it please your Lordshipp [illeg.] & the premisses consider & to grant unto your Orators her Ma[jes]ties written writts of Subpena to be [illeg.] to Thomas Rookwood \& other [illeg.] Persons when discovered/ at a certaine day and under a certaine payne therein to be limited personally to be and appear before your Lordship is her Ma[jes]ties high and hon[oura]ble Court of Chancery then and there to answer all and singular the pr[emi]sses and further to stand to and abide such further Order and Direction therein as to your Lordship shall seem most agreeable to Equity and good Conscience. And your Orator shall ever pray &c:
Bawdes

19. [TNA C 6/469/70] *Thomas Rookwood's counter-appeal against Charles Rookwood, 14 May 1712*

The Plea of Thomas Rookwood Esq[ui]r[e] Def[endan]t to part And his Answer to the residue of the Bill of Complaint of Charles Rookwood Gent[leman] Compl[ainan]t

This Defendant by protestat[i]on not confessing or acknowledging all or any of the matters or things in the Compl[ainan]ts Bill of Complaint contained to be true in such manner and forme as the same are therein and thereby sett forth. As to so much of the said Bill as requires a discovery or account of the Moyety or halfe part of the Estate of Ambrose Rookwood (the Compl[ainan]ts and this Def[endan]ts late father dec[ease]d) or the Estate of Ambrose Rookwood (the Compl[ainan]ts and this Def[endan]ts late brother dec[ease]d) or any part or parts thereof respectively This Defend[an]t doth plead in barr And for plea saith That in regard the said Compl[ainan]t in and by the said Bill hath not derived or made out to himselfe any title of pr[e]tension to the said Moyety or any other part or share of or in his said ffathers reall or personall estate other than by from or under the said Ambrose Rookwood his brother. And for that the said Ambrose Rookwood (the Compl[ainan]ts and this Def[endan]ts late brother) in or about the ninth yeare of the reigne of his late Majesty King William the Third was at a sessions held at the Old Bayly in the said year for the County of Middle[se]x indicted for and convicted or attainted of High Treason for Conspiring the Assassination or death of his said late Majesty King Will[ia]m and dyed thereof convicted or attainted As by the record of his Convict[i]on or Attainder, relat[i]on being thereunto had, it doth and may more at Large appear. Therefore in case the said \Ambrose Rookwood the/ Compl[ainan]ts and this Def[endan]ts late brother was possessed of interested in or intituled unto any Reall or personall Estate whatsoever at the time of his said convict[i]on or Attainder (Which this Def[endan]t will not admitt) the same Reall and personall estate and every part thereof as this Def[endan]t is informed or advised did upon the said convict[i]on of the said Ambrose Rookwood the Compl[ainan]ts and this Def[endan]ts said brother become forfeited to the Crowne and consequently the Compl[ainan]t cannot have any lawfull title to the same or any part thereof. All which this Def[endan]t doth averr to be true and doth plead the same in Barr to so much of the said Bill as aforesaid And humbly prays the Judgement of this hon[oura]ble Court whether this Def[endan]t shall be compelled to make or give any further or other Answer unto the said Bill and the matters therein contained save as herein after is answered unto. And this Def[endan]t saving and reserving all and all manner of benefit and advantage of Exception to the incertaintyes and imperfections of the said Bill This Def[endan]t (not waving his said plea but relying thereon) doth for Answer say that He beleives it to be true That the said Ambrose Rookwood the Elder this Def[endan]ts late father dec[ease]d Did on or about the Eighteenth day of ffebruary which was in the year of our Lord One thousand six hundred and ninety two make his last Will and Testament and therein and thereby did give and bequeath unto his son Ambrose Rookwood all his Mannor of Shreiffes together with all the houses Lands and tenements scituate in Colne in the County of Essex in the occupant[i]on of the Widdow Wiltshire and Ham[m]ond with the Woods and Coppices thereunto belonging To hold to him and his heires for ever. And did also give and bequeath All his ffarme called Claverins in the parish of South Hawstead in the said County of Essex to his Exe[cuto]rs therein named to be sold by them and the money thereby arising to go and be for and towards the performance of his said Will. And this Def[endan]t further saith That the said Ambrose Rookwood the Elder did also by his said Will give severall Legacyes and particularly to the Compl[ainan]t did give and bequeath the sume of ffour hundred pounds to be paid within six months after his decease And did in and by his said last Will constitute and appoint this Def[endan]t and his said brother Ambrose Rookwood and Mr Will[ia]m Covell Ex[ecut]ors thereof. And this Def[endan]t further saith that he hath accounted with the Compl[ainan]t for all sume or sumes of money in any wise due to the said Compl[ainan]t by virtue of the said Will or otherwise to this Def[endan]ts knowledge or beleife and hath paid the same by the direct[i]ons of this hon[oura]ble Court to the said Compl[ainan]t or his order As by the Orders and Reports now remaining in this Hon[oura]ble Court to which for greater certainty this Def[endan]t ceaveth leave to referr himselfe and humbly submitts to the Judgement of this Court whether he shall be obliged to give any other Account thereof or further answer thereunto. And this Def[endan]t doth deny all and all manner of Combinat[i]on wherewith he is charged by the said Compl[ainan]ts said Bill of Complaint Without that that any matter or thing within the Compl[ainan]ts said bill of Complaint contained materiall or effec-tuall in the Law for this Def[endan]t to make answer unto and not herein answered or pleaded unto confessed or avoided traversed or denyed is true. All Which matters and things this Def[endan]t is ready and willing to averr maintaine and prove as this hon[oura]ble Court shall direct And humbly prays to be hence dismissed with his reasonable costs in this behalfe most wrongfully sustained

Hoc plitum & Responsio capt[atum] fuer[at] & p[rae]d[ict]us Thomas Rookwood Jurat[us] fuit ad veritat[em] eod[e]m apud Bury St Ed[mund]i in Com[itate] Suff[olciae] Decimo Quarto die Maii Anno r[eg]ni D[omi]n[a]e Ann[a]e R[egi]n[a]e

Magn[ae] Britann[iae] &c undecimo Annoq[ue] D[omi]ni 1712 cor[am] nobis[21]

John Wrighte
Bartho[lomew] Paman
B[enjamin] Muchall
Thomas Rookwood
Rich[ar]d Berney

20. [CUL Hengrave MS 1/4, fols 348–9] *Notes on Elizabeth Rookwood (from Thomas Gage, 'Some Account of the Manor and Parish of Hengrave in the County of Suffolk')*

Elizabeth Rookwood received all the advantages of the first Masters at Paris, whither her Father took her at six years of age – her Mother had died in Childbed of her – and her Father doatingly fond of this only child, spared no expence in her education – she returned from Paris at 16 excelling in the Graces – and possessing what was far more valuable strong principles, a superior Understanding, and a highly cultivated Mind,[22] Her Father on her return to England entered into a matrimonial Alliance for her, with a Catholic Baronet[23] of Fortune whose death prevented the Match from taking 'effect' – after this Event her father made difficulties for every proposal of marriage for his Daughter, and finding her society essential to his happiness, could not prevail upon himself to part with her, and at length denied every Suitor – Under these Circumstances, Elizabeth Rookwood attained her 30th year – At this Juncture, John Gage was an intimate Friend of Mr Rookwood's, and often on hunting parties at Coldham – his Merits and Accomplishments were not lost upon Elizabeth Rookwood – a Secret Marriage was effected between them, and it was not until Circumstances disclosed the event, that her Father was made acquainted with the Marriage.[24]

Thomas Rookwood remained long without being reconciled to his Daughter, and in his resentment is said to have married a young Wife in hopes of an Heir in which he was disappointed.

The couple went to live in a house at Fornham All Saints until 1726. This house was close to the gates of Fornham Park, a seat of the Duke of Norfolk, and was later turned into cottages in 'ornamental brick'. The Duke enjoyed pointing it out to John Gage the antiquary as the place where his great-grandfather, Sir Thomas Rookwood Gage, 5th Baronet was born.[25]

---

21 'This plea and answer had been taken [sic.] and the aforesaid Thomas Rookwood had been sworn [sic.] to the truth of the same at Bury St Edmunds in the county of Suffolk on the fourteenth day of May in the eleventh year of the reign of our Lady Anne, Queen of Great Britain etc. and in the year of our Lord 1712 before us:'

22 'The Information of the late Mrs Maxwell of Munches. She grew too masculine to be a Beauty and the Dowager Lady Gage had told the writer that she had the Air of an Empress but too much of the Hauteur to be agreeable' (Sir Thomas Gage's note).

23 'Mrs Maxwell's information' (Sir Thomas Gage's note).

24 'The Neighbourhood spoke of his Daughter being in the family way – and old Rookwood is said to have exclaimed "if Bess is with Child he could rely upon her honor that she was married" – his Daughter on her knees thanked him for doing Justice to her Character' (Sir Thomas Gage's note).

25 CUL Hengrave MS 1/4, fol. 349 (note in the hand of John Gage, dated 1843). The house still survives just north of the roundabout at the bottom of Shepherd's Hill.

21. [CUL Hengrave MS 76/1] *Catholic marriage certificate of John Gage and Elizabeth Rookwood, 7 January 1718*

Jan[uary] 7th 1717/8

This is to inform all whom it may concern, that Mr John Gage of Hengrave, and Mrs Elizabeth Rookwood of Coldham in Staningfield in the Countey of Suffolk were, this day, being the seventh of January an[no] 1717/8 married by me underwritten according to the rites of our Holy mother, the catholique church.

witness my hand   Hugh Owen

In presence of us,   Henrietta Gage
                        Nicholas Horsman

22. [CUL Hengrave MS 76/1] *Indenture settling Thomas Rookwood's estates on John and Elizabeth Gage, 12 April 1721 (summary by John Gage)*

12th April 1721 Ind[entu]re made between the s[ai]d Thomas Rookwood of the one part and John Gage therein described of Hengrave one of the sons of Sir William Gage Baronet and Elizabeth wife of the said John Gage therein described only dau[ghte]r of the s[ai]d Thomas Rookwood by Tamworth his late wife deceased of the other part, being a demise of the Manor of Mortimers for a term of years determinable on the death of the said Thomas Rookwood, and a settlement on the issue of the said John Gage and Elizabeth his wife of the £3000 provided for her portion.

23. [CUL Hengrave MS 76/1] *Summary of the marriage settlement of Thomas Rookwood and Dorothy Maria Hurst, 6 May 1721*

6th May 1721 Indenture made between Thomas Rookwood 1st part, John Poley Esq[ui]re 2d part, George Bate Gentleman & Francis Harvey clerk 3d part and Dorothy Maria Hurst spinster 4th part. Being the settlement in contemplation of the Marriage of the s[ai]d Thomas Rookwood with the said Dorothy Maria afterwards his wife. The family estates of the said Thomas Rookwood were limited, as to parts thereof To George Bate and Francis Harvey In trust by sale to raise £4000, of which £1000 to be paid in discharge of a Mortgage on the Essex estate & £3000 to John Gage Esq[ui]r[e] and Elizabeth his wife daughter of the said Thomas Rookwood for her portion, and subject to a further trust for sale with the consent of the s[ai]d Thomas Rookwood (and which was not executed) for raising a sum of £8000 for the s[ai]d Dorothy Maria in the event of her surviving. And as to the whole estate Upon trust for the benefit of the s[ai]d Thomas Rookwood and Dorothy Maria his intended wife and their issue male in strict settlement.

Plate I. The coat of arms of the Rookwood family, Argent six chess-rooks Sable, from *Vetustissima Prosapia Rookwodorum de Stanningefilde, in Comitatu Suffolciae* (1619). Reproduced by kind permission of the Syndics of Cambridge University Library

Plate II. Coldham Hall (built 1574–75), an early nineteenth-century watercolour after an earlier engraving (CUL Hengrave MS 1/4, between fols 362 and 363). Reproduced by kind permission of the Syndics of Cambridge University Library

Plate III. Portrait of Sir Robert Rookwood (IV), a copy of an original of 1660 by Joseph Richard Wright, painted by Herbert Luther Smith in 1841. The figure behind Sir Robert is a bronze figurine of the god Mars, suggesting martial prowess (in spite of the fact that he never fought in battle). Photographed by Mike Durrant and reproduced by kind permission of Moyse's Hall Museum, Bury St Edmunds

Thomas Rookwood Efq. *of Coldham, Suffolk.*
From an original picture at Coldham.

Plate IV. Thomas Rookwood (1658–1726), the long-exiled master of Coldham Hall. An 1818 watercolour by J. Linnell after an original painting at Coldham Hall (CUL Hengrave MS 1/4, between fols 349 and 350). Reproduced by kind permission of the Syndics of Cambridge University Library

Elizabeth wife of John Gage.
And only child of Thomas Rookwood Esq.ʳ

Plate V. Elizabeth Rookwood (1684–1759), only daughter and heiress of Thomas Rookwood. An 1818 watercolour by J. Linnell after an original 1748 painting by Heins at Coldham Hall (CUL Hengrave MS 1/4, between fols 351 and 352). Reproduced by kind permission of the Syndics of Cambridge University Library

Plate VI. Prayers for the Feast of St Thomas Becket from the Rookwood Book of Hours, CUL MS Add. 10079, fol. 23r, 1460's, once owned by Thomas Rookwood and possibly **RFP9** in this volume. Reproduced by kind permission of the Syndics of Cambridge University Library

24. [CUL Hengrave MS 76/1] *Will of Thomas Rookwood, 17 March 1725 (summary by John Gage)*

17th March 1725. The will of Thomas Rookwood of Coldham Hall Esq[ui]re whereby he charged all his personal estate (excepting his silver plate the use of which he gave his wife during her life) with his debts. He gave to each of his sisters Anne Rookwood and Margaret Rookwood for their lives an Annuity of fifty shillings. And after bequeathing certain pecuniary legacies to his servant therein mentioned and directing the usual dole given by him to be distributed at Christmas among the poor of Stanningfield. He gave the residue of his personal estate to his wife Dorothy Maria Rookwood for her [life] and in the event of her death without issue to his daughter Elizabeth Gage[;] and if she died in the life time of the testator or of his s[ai]d wife to his two Grandchildren Thomas and John Gage equally—And desiring to be decently interred in the Parish Church of Stanningfield among his ancestors he appointed his wife Dorothy Maria Rookwood sole executrix.

Proved in the Prerogative Court of Canterbury.[26]

25. [CUL Hengrave MS 76/1] *Indenture between John Gage and Sir Thomas Hanmer, 20 November 1726 (summary by John Gage)*

20th November 1726 Indenture made between John Gage therein described of Fornham St Martin in the County of Suffolk Esq[ui]re & Elizabeth his wife therein described as the only daughter & heir at law of Thomas Rookwood late of Coldham Hall in the parish of Stanningfield Esq[ui]re deceased of the one part and Sir Thomas Hanmer Bar[one]t of the other part, being a deed to lead the uses of certain fines levied by the said John Gage & Elizabeth his wife of the family Estates of the said Elizabeth Rookwood To ensure to uses in strict settlement for the benefit of the said John Gage & Elizabeth his wife & their issue. With power of revocation & new appointment to the said John Gage & Elizabeth his wife & the survivor of them.

26. [CUL Hengrave MS 76/1] *Summary of the will of Dorothy Maria Rookwood, 24 April 1727*

24. April 1727 Will of Dorothy Maria Rookwood of Coldham Hall widow whereby she charged her lands & tenements with Annuities of twenty pounds payable to each of her Aunts Jane Turner and Jane Throckmorton during their lives. And she directed her Executor among other legacies to pay ten pounds a piece to her uncle Francis Harvey & her Aunt Ann Harvey his wife for Mourning—she bequeathed her diamond ring, and diamond earrings, and a purple ring to her sister Elizabeth Hanford and gave a Mourning ring to Mr John Gage and Elizabeth his wife. And after giving legacies to her Aunt Elizabeth Bourke & Dr Pake and directing to be buried in the same Vault with her late husband Thomas Rookewood the testatrix appointed Edward Hanford of Woolashill in Worcestershire Esq[ui]re Ex[ecut]or of her will.

---

[26] Proved on 27 February 1728. The original will is PRO 11/614/103.

Proved in the Prerogative Court of Canterbury by the said Edward Hanford in the month of July 1727.

27. [CUL Hengrave MS 76/1] *Indentures of release, 29 and 30 August 1728 (summary by John Gage)*

Ind[entu]res of Lease & release dated 29th & 30th August 1728. The Ind[entu]re of release made between Elizabeth Gage widow & relict of John Gage Esq[ui]re dec[ease]d: of the 1st part, Thomas Gage Esq[ui]re & John Gage Gent[lema]n therein described as only children of the said Elizabeth Gage by the said John Gage dec[ease]d: of the 2d part, Sir Thomas Hanmer Bar[one]t & Sir Henry Bunbury Bar[one]t of the 3d part and Richard Whitborne Gent[lema]n of the 4th part, which Ind[entu]res are enrolled in Chancery. The family estates of the s[ai]d Elizabeth Rookwood were limited to use in strict settlement for benefit of the s[ai]d Elizabeth Rookwood and her sons the s[ai]d Thomas Gage & John Gage. And in the said Ind[entu]re of release is a condition that the said Thomas Gage and his sons when they should come into possession of the family estates by virtue of the limitations therein contained should respectively take upon himself the surname of Rookwood & use the arms of the Rookwood family.

28. [CUL Hengrave 76/2/29] *Notes on the Coldham estate in 1730*

An Account of All the Farmes belonging to the Estate of Eliz[abeth] Gage w[i]th the taxes & other incumbrances taken the the yeare of our Lorde – 1730 – when taxes wear att 2 sheelings in the pound & 4 for us

	£	s.	d.		£	s.	d.
John Murrills holds & farmes, that of Phillets, Paskes, & Highnotts, in all	152			the tax	23	16	10
Abraham Jourdans holds the Mannor farm of Preston, att	115			the tax	18	04	
the quit rents of the mannor are payd att Christmass & are	3	10		noe tax			
John Hayward holds Coldham; next Micklemass John Simson Junior	100			the tax	15	11	2
Window tax	1	10					
Robert Plumbs is att present but att the End of his Lease is to be att an Hundred a yeare as heretofore	90			the tax	15	1	11
Thomas Talbots holds the manor farm of Haningfield Hall att	70			the tax	10	9	

	£	s.	d.		£	s.	d.
The quit rents of the manor are yearly	17	1	10	the tax	1	2	6
Robert Londons is yearly	80			the tax	7	9	2
William Michall holds a farme near Lanham att	80			the tax	10		
William Venro holds a farm in Lawshall att	45			the tax	8		
John Nunns is yearly	32			the tax	5	2	2
Charls Brooks is yearly	25			the tax	4	1	7
Robert Bigsby is yearly	23			the tax	3	15	10
John Simson Senior is yearly he has itt in part of Weages	8			the tax	1	4	9
a tenement in Staningfeeld Lett to Francis Bullmor att	2						
Gorg Nunn holds a farm neare Mellon green in Whespted att he pays Lords rent 2 sheelings & 3 pence	15			the tax	1	16	2
in Essex Caniall Miller holds the Mannor the farm of Shrives & another Cald Wittles both att the yearly rent of	50			the tax	8	10	6
the quitt rents of the manor are yearly & is allowed 2 sheelings & 6 pence for gathering the quitt rents twoo years to come is payd	2	10					
John Sheely holds the mannor farm Cald Cleverings att out of w[hi]ch he pays a perpetuall anuity of 18 pounds to Lord Castlemaine, my Lorde paying the taxe of his sheare. He also pays Lords rent 3 sheelings & 2 pence	50			the tax	2	18	

The sume totall is [£]920 1[s] 10[d] Exclusive of the Woods

2 Acres is generally Cut Every yeare to allowe the tenants wheare there is a deficiancy of Cropings – 4 Acres more I Usialy Cut if I meet w[i]th a Chap th[a]t will give 5 pounds an Acre att II years grothe, other ways I Lett them stand

Theare is allso a Litill tenement in Staningfeeld w[hi]ch used to be Lett att 30 sheelings a yeare, w[hi]ch my Father Lett John Gough Live in gratis th[a]t he may Look after the woods & stope gaps

29. [Downside Abbey MS 70, fols 64–5] *Agreement between Francis Rookwood OSB and the South Province of the English Benedictine Congregation, 20 January 1737*

Of a Draught of Agreement stipulated Between Mr Francis Rookwood & this Province. Jan: 20. 1736/7.

Whereas Mr Francis Rookwood hath propos'd, & offer'd to place out the sum of one Hundred Pounds, in the Hands of Mr Gregory Greenwood, for the use & Benefit of this Province, on Condition, that the said Mr Gregory Greenwood, & his successors do Oblige themselves to the yearly Payment of Five Pounds on the 25th Day of December, unto the said Mr Francis Rookwood, during his Natural life. This is therefore to signify to all those, whom it may concern hereafter, that the said Mr Gregory Greenwood, with the advice, & Consent of Mr Maurus Rigmaiden, & Mr Richard Isherwood the two Definitors of the Province, hath accepted of the said Hundred Pounds, on the abovementioned Condition, obliging himself & his successors, to the due Payment of Five Pounds p[er] Annum, To the said Mr Francis Rookwood, on the day abovementioned. In Witness Whereof, He has hereunto set his Hand, & Seal, this 20th Day of January. 1736/7.

John Hardcastle.
Dom John Wythie. Depositarij Provinciae.
Dom Gregorius Greenwood Prov: Cant:

30. [from CUL Hengrave 77/1] *Authors listed in the Rookwood biobibliography, early eighteenth century*[27]

1.   William Allen, Cardinal (1532–94)
2.   John Aungell (d. 1566/8)
3.   Patrick Anderson SJ (1574/5–1624)
4.   Christopher Bagshaw (1552–*c.* 1625)
5.   David Augustine Baker OSB (1575–1641)
6.   William Rudesind Barlow OSB (1584–1686)
7.   Stephen Baron OFM (*fl.* 1508–13)
8.   Joshua Basset, convert (1641–1714)
9.   Richard Bradshaigh alias Barton SJ (1601/2–69)
10. Thomas Baylie, convert (*fl.* 1650s)
11. L. B. (author of *The Right Religion evinced*, 1652)

---

[27] The biobibliography consists of a list of books under each author's name with biographical information, although there is a great deal more detail on some authors than others. The entries, which are written on the blank pages of one of a pair of old music books, are roughly in alphabetical order; however, some names were clearly added later where there was a convenient space and the original order has been retained here. The latest date of death recorded is that of Lewis Sabran in 1732, suggesting an end point for the biobibliography during the lifetime of Elizabeth Rookwood (1684–1759). However, the compilation was probably made over a number of years and may have been begun by Thomas Rookwood (1658–1726). Spellings of authors' names have been changed to conform with those in the *ODNB*; dates of birth and death are taken from the same source. There are a few occasions where the same author is listed twice under a different alias, and I have removed these.

12. Ralph Baynes, Bishop of Coventry (d. 1559)
13. James Anderton alias John Brereley (1557–1613)
14. Laurence Anderton alias Scroop SJ (1575–1643)
15. B. C. (author of *Puritanisme the mother sin the daughter*, 1633)
16. Edmund Bonner, Bishop of London (d. 1569)
17. William Bishop, Bishop of Chalcedon (*c.* 1554–1624)
18. Richard Bristow (1538–81)
19. James Brooks, Bishop of Gloucester (1512–58)
20. Ralph Buckland, secular priest (1564–1611)
21. Thomas Buckland OSB (*fl.* 1630s)
22. Robert Buckland
23. George Bullock (1520/1–72)
24. Miles Pinkney alias Thomas Carr, secular priest (1599–1674)
25. Edmund Campion SJ (1540–81)
26. Roger Palmer, Earl of Castlemaine (1634–1705)
27. Anthony Champney, secular priest (1569–1644)
28. Robert Chambers (*fl.* 1600s)
29. Michael Walpole alias Christopherson (1570–1625)
30. John Christopherson, Bishop of Chichester (d. 1558)
31. Chandler, secular priest (*fl.* 1730s)
32. William Caxton (d. 1492)
33. Henry Cole (d. 1580)
34. Edward Coffin alias Hatton SJ (1570/1–1626)
35. John Colleton, secular priest (1548–1635)
36. Thomas Thorold alias Carwell (*c.* 1600–64)
37. Ramundus Cavan (*fl.* 1650s)
38. Alan Cape (d. 1580)
39. Richard Creagh, Archbishop of Armagh (d. 1585)
40. Hugh Serenus Cressy OSB (1605–74)
41. Joseph Creswell SJ (1556–1623)
42. Crosshon alias Shepherd (*fl.* 1710s)
43. W. C., secular priest (*fl.* 1670s)
44. C. W. (*fl.* 1620s)
45. Thomas Dorman (*c.* 1532–77)
46. Edward Dawson SJ (*c.* 1579–1622)
47. John Huddleston alias Shirley Dormer SJ (1636–1700)
48. Christopher Davenport OFM (d. 1680)
49. Charles Dodd alias Hugh Tootell, secular priest (1672–1743)
50. Edward Phillip (*fl.* 1600s)
51. Humphrey Ely, secular priest (*c.* 1539–1604)
52. George Etheredge (1519–*c.* 1588)
53. T. G. (*fl.* 1600s)
54. Arthur Laurence Faunt SJ (1533/4–91)
55. John Feckenham OSB, Abbot of Westminster (*c.* 1518–84)
56. John Fisher, Bishop of Rochester (1459/69–1535)
57. Henry Fitzsimon SJ (1566–1643)
58. Thomas Fitzherbert SJ (1552–1640)
59. Anthony Fitzherbert (*c.* 1470–1538)
60. Nicholas Harpsfield (1519–75)
61. John Harpsfield, secular priest (1516–78)

62. John Hay SJ (1566–1607)
63. Christopher Holywood alias Sacrobosco SJ (*c.* 1559–1626)
64. Richard Hopkins, translator (*c.* 1546–96)
65. Henry Holland
66. Richard Gibbons SJ (1547/53–1632)
67. Thomas Goldwell, Bishop of St. Asaph (d. 1585)
68. William Gonell (d. 1560)
69. Martin Green SJ (*fl.* 1650s)
70. Cuthbert Scott, Bishop of Chester (d. 1565)
71. John Story (1503/4–71)
72. Stephen Gardiner, Bishop of Winchester (1495/8–1555)
73. Thomas Tylden alias Godden (1622–88)
74. John Gother (d. 1704)
75. William Gifford, Archbishop of Rheims (1557/8–1629)
76. Richard Hall, Canon of Cambrai (*c.* 1537–1604)
77. Daniel Halseworth (d. 1595)
78. Thomas Heskyns OP (*fl.* 1560s)
79. John Heighem (*fl.* 1600s)
80. Thomas Harding (1516–72)
81. William Harris, secular priest (1546–1602)
82. Henry Hawkins SJ (1577–1646)
83. James Gordon Huntley (*fl.* 1610s)
84. Silvester Jenks alias Metcalfe, secular priest (1656–1714)
85. Rowland Jenkes (*fl.* 1570s)
86. George Keynes SJ (1628–58)
87. Vincent Canes OFM (1608–72)
88. Matthew Kellison, secular priest (1561–1642)
89. Edward Knott alias Matthew Wilson SJ (1581–1656)
90. Alban Langdale, Archdeacon of Chichester (*fl.* 1532–80)
91. John Lloyd, secular priest (*c.* 1630–79)
92. John Lewgar, convert (d. 1665)
93. Peter Manby, Dean of Derry (convert) (d. 1697)
94. Robert Manning, secular priest (1655–1731)
95. Sir Thomas More (1478–1535)
96. Walter Montagu, Abbot of St Martin (1604/5–77)
97. John Mush, secular priest (1552–1612)
98. Ann Owen, Protestant controversialist (*fl.* 1630s)
99. John Marshall (1534–97)
100. Sir Toby Matthew (1577–1655)
101. Thomas More SJ (*fl.* 1610s)
102. Henry More SJ (*c.* 1587–1661)
103. Gregory Martin, secular priest (*c.* 1542–82)
104. Thomas Martin (1520/1–92/3)
105. James Mumford SJ (*c.* 1606–66)
106. Joseph Mumford SJ (*fl.* 1680s)
107. Silvester Norris SJ (1572–1630)
108. Nicholas Morton, secular priest (1520/1–87)
109. Jerome Porter OSB (d. 1632)
110. Matthew Pattenson (*fl.* 1623)
111. Francis Porter OFM (*fl.* 1680s)

112.   Richard Pates, Bishop of Worcester (1503/4–65)
113.   John Bennett alias Price SJ (*c.* 1550–1625)
114.   Lewis Richcome (*fl.* 1610s)
115.   John Radford alias Tanfield SJ (*c.* 1562–1630)
116.   William Rowland, convert (d. 1659)
117.   Edmund Stratford, secular priest (*c.* 1586–1640)
118.   John Sergeant (1623–1707)
119.   Cuthbert Tunstal, Bishop of Durham (1474–1559)
120.   Thomas Thirlby, Bishop of Ely (*c.* 1500–70)
121.   Sir Henry Tichborne (1624–89)
122.   R. A. B. (translator of John Fisher's *Treatise of Prayer*, 1644)
123.   Richard Smith, Bishop of Chalcedon (1567–1655)
124.   William Peryn OP (d. 1558)
125.   Robert Poyntz (*c.* 1535–68)
126.   William Petre, 4th Baron Petre (1625/6–1684)
127.   Thomas Paynell OSA, translator (d. 1564)
128.   J. P. (author of *The Safeguarde from ship-wracke*, 1618)
129.   John Paunce (*fl.* 1605)
130.   Robert Persons SJ (1546–1610)
131.   John Pits, secular priest and convert (1560–1616)
132.   John Rastell SJ (1530–77)
133.   William Rastell, legal writer (1508–65)
134.   William Rainolds, secular priest and convert (*c.* 1544–94)
135.   Lewis Sabran SJ (1652–1732)
136.   Nicholas Sanders, secular priest (*c.* 1530–81)
137.   Richard Smyth, secular priest (1499/1500–63)
138.   Richard Stanihurst, translator (1547–1618)
139.   Thomas Stapleton, secular priest (1535–98)
140.   Richard Verstegan alias Rowlands (1548/50–1640)
141.   John Sanderson, secular priest (1540–1602)
142.   Robert Southwell SJ (1565–95)
143.   Robert Turner, secular priest (d. 1598)
144.   Peter Talbot, Archbishop of Dublin (1620–80)
145.   John Keynes alias Williams SJ (1624–97)
146.   John Williamson, secular priest (*fl.* 1640)
147.   J. W. P. (author of *The key of paradis*, 1631)
148.   J. W.[28]
149.   P. W., secular priest (*fl.* 1644)
150.   C. W. (author of *A summary of controversies*, 1623)
151.   Obadiah Walker, convert (1616–99)
152.   Richard Walpole SJ (1564–1607)
153.   John Warner SJ (1628–92)

---

[28] An annotation reads: 'there was a collection of St Lives written an[no] 1619 in the gatehouse prisoner for religion & and 1660 he wrot & finished May 15 the history of Nichodemus Gospel then in norwhich for religion[.] M/S in mr Rookwoods hands q[uar]to'. It is possible that the 'collection of St Lives' was *A Chayne of Twelve Links, to wit XII Catholick conditions* (1617), translated by 'I. W.' The book on the Gospel of Nicodemus was never published, it seems, and J. W.'s identity and connection with the Rookwoods is unclear. The 'mr Rookwood' mentioned was probably Thomas.

154.   Thomas Watson, Bishop of Lincoln (1513–84)
155.   John White, Bishop of Winchester (1509/10–60)
156.   Waller Whitford, sub-president of the Scots College, Paris (*fl.* 1657)
157.   Abraham Woodhead (1609–78)
158.   Edward Worsley SJ (1604/5–76)
159.   Phillip Woodward (*fl.* 1602)
160.   William Wright SJ (1563–1639)
161.   Thomas Worthington, secular priest (*c.* 1548–1626)

31. [CUL Hengrave 77/2, fols 8–25] *Inventory of the contents of Coldham Hall, 1737*

[fol. 8r] In the Brewhouse

	£	s.	d.
one Copper boiling a hogsh[ead] Cost 5:14:0 Irons & door 27sh	7	14	
one missing top & one other Large tubb holding a hogsh[ead] & 1/2 both of Deal Cost me 4:15:0 [*illeg.*] larder Bank 7:6:	4	2	6
A strainer 4:6: two jets 2:6. Copper Lead 5sh a larg tramel 3sh		11	
Tap husen 6d missen plate 6d		1	
One Larg tubb made of a stand hogset 6sh 2 other Larg tubs 6sh		12	
The powdering tubb with cover 30d 3 large keelers 5sh		7	6
three small Kellers 18d two more for dropings 4d 1 wossing keeler 5sh		6	10
An Ale stall under the missing tub i. sh.		1	
a Horse for linnine painted 30d		2	6
Sume	13	5	4
one Cooler bought of M[arshal]l 1738 8 shillings; & one tubb & Three Cheslers bought at Aunts 6 shillings a Coal Roo & Ruer for Copper 1 sh. vi[delicet] a fork for fire 2d An Iron hoop for to burn tobacco pipe 6		15	2
In the Cellar three half hogsh[ea]ts, beside that in the new house larder mentioned there, 19 shill. A stand hogs[hea]t 7sh. a quarter of a hogset 3sh a wine vessel with Iron hoops come with wine	2	2	
one Horn for Hogset, three Cock taps 5sh. 4 other taps 4d.		5	4
two Celler Locks 4 shill. two other Cock tappes 2 shill[29]		4	3
1739 Ap 4 I bought of prigg a ten Gallon vessel 28d			
Sume	2	13	4
Aug 3d another of the same bigness at the same price of ten Gallons		1	8
57 I bought of [*name left blank*] a new half Hogset 8sh			

---

[29]   Note in margin: 'see fol. 7. B.'

[fol. 8v] The Old Kitchen & passage thereto

	£	s.	d.
Two picture folding of our saviour & Lady on wood ore the door.		10	
A picture of Hesiod & frame 1s. a picture of virgil & frame ish		2	
A picture of the pope 3sh. family scutchions, & paper prints 5sh		8	
A lock & Barr for entry door 4sh A Ketch & hasps for [illeg.] 2sh		6	
A lock on the bottle Celler 4sh shelves rown the B[ottle] celler 5sh		9	
Bottles in the bottle Celler beside those in the new house 80qts 58 pints	7	7	6
The dressers in the Kitchen & Laders & shelves		12	
one large stone marble morter w[i]th black pestle 17sh another \30d/		19	6
with two hand Irons & fender 3sh. tongs & shovel 3sh. a tramell 18d		7	6
a Grid Iron smaller 1sh on pair of Iron shilliards 5sh. Larg bellows \5:6/		11	6
a dripping pan 28d a larg screene for rosting lined 9sh		11	4
A Lye trough 3:6 Leading thereof 15 shill. In all 18:6		18	6
three Iron Candlesticks 1sh. two druging boxes 10d a basting ladle 6d a Large frying pan 7:6 two other frying pans 8sh.		17	10
two Larg sauce pans Copper 7sh. 6d one smaller Copper sauce pan 2sh.		9	6
two Boilers one larg other small 19sh. a cullender 18d	1		6
a brass chafing dish, and another Larger, 9sh. three hues 3.6		12	6
A corner Cubbort Lock & Key 3sh. A warming pan 10sh		13	
one salt Box 1sh. a Tin sauce pan 6d a tin funnel 6s		2	
one larg Copper Jococale[30] pot 7:6 one larg Copper Coffy pote \3:6/		11	
one Copper Coffy pot smaler 3sh. 6d. a halve pint Copper pott 1sh		4	6
A trivet 8d Tinder box 8d 4 smoothing Irons 5 shil		4	6
4 pails 4sh. nutmeg greter, 3d one spit 1sh.		5	3
two Curtain Rods, & two Curtains 5sh three locks 3:6		8	6
one Tea Furnesh, Cost 45 one Copper tea Kettle 1tt	3	5	
one pewter bason 2sh. one brush for Bottles & hook for Corks 4d		2	4
Two tinn coffy potts 2sh. 6d. another Larger 3 shill.		5	6
Sume	23	6	7
one new Chopping block 10d		1	6
an[oth]er Chopping Knife bought of marshall feb 1736/37		1	3
another Chopping knife bought of Aunts 1 shill. hooks for trammels A 6d		1	6
4 small [illeg.] for birds 4d 2 Large ones for meat Iron all 5d			9
a flat fender ½ a trivet 6d, a brass handed Candlestick 12d			10
a lock Iron & 2 heaters 30d a round deal table [illeg.]		3	6
a new Coal great with Charles 14sh another for Irons 18d		15	6

---

[30] Chocolate.

	£	s.	d.
a 2d warming pann 3 shil a livery Cubbord 2:6 an oaken box with lock 1sh		16	6
3 smoothing Irons ish 1 brass candlestick small 1sh a brass Ladle 6d 1 [*illeg.*] & [*illeg.*] 3sh		5	6
a smooking chafindish brass 1sh a pestle & morter 30d mrs Harry			
another Lock Iron w[i]th 2 heaters of marden 30sh			

[fol. 9r] In The Cool Room, & Closet & stairs Case

	£	s.	d.
four & tweenty prints of the emperours & empresses w[i]th frams		12	
one Large print of the midnight entertainment & frame		2	
2 corner shelves 1sh three black Ch[a]irs 3sh.		4	
two whit curtains Rod & eyes		4	
one print of the south prospect of London 18d ketches for hats 6d		2	2
one Lock on door 3sh another on Closet 10d shetter & barr 2sh		4	10
In the Closet one pewter Case with dresser & 2 draws		9	
18 old pewter plats broad Rim'd with the Martin's arms at 8d ptt and one mustard plate of the same		16	2
twelve fine pewter with L[or]d monson's Corronet there on		15	
4 other old plates 4 pewter dishes marked G. W. J. one mark'd K. R. M. G. the 6th marked G. G. the 7th marked M. R. the 8th marked R. H. or[31]	1	3	
one New suppe dish Cost me 3sh.		3	
A pair of [*illeg.*]holes Iron beame; & Leaden weights 160tt		19	
A Tin toaster with 2 pair of feet 4s 6d two Lamps 3s 6d		8	6
A Tin quart measure 18d 38 pattapans 11sh 6d		13	
A fish Kettle strainer & Rover		4	
A vessel chain 6d one Cross Bow Inlead'd 15		15	6
a mustard Cherne 1sh six wedges & beetle 7sh or a [*illeg.*]		9	
sume	8	8	8
Eleven pattapans more & a picture of the french Court 5sh		5	
a four corner oaken table 1sh 6d		1	6
on the stair Case one picture of St Ignatius		10	6
two small Lanschips in Guilt frams 4sh		4	
on[e] picher of mrs Cary a nun[32] full length & frame		12	6
twenty prints of our savior's passion & frams		10	

---

[31] Note in margin: 'fol. 28'.
[32] Probably Anne Clementina Cary OSB (1615–71), the foundress of the English Benedictine convent in Paris (J. Gillow, *A Biographical Dictionary of the English Catholics* (London, 1885–1902), vol. 1, p. 417).

	£	s.	d.
22 prints of several subjects the same size		11	
one Clock with an Alarm made by blundell Cost 8tt	2	10	
one picture of our saviour on the crose Glass & frame		6	
4 more prints & frames 2sh <u>12</u> smaller picturs &c		6	
two Corner shelves 18d a painted bird cage pulley &c. 30d		4	
Two Blockd tin tea potts 5sh a brown stone one & 2 white tea pots 1sh		6	
three Indian Japannd sugar Capps now in use 3sh.		3	
	6	3	
a new Clock Case to the said Clock made by Corder black & 2 locks		8	

[fol. 9v] In the study

	£	s.	d.
one Large secretore w[i]th 10 Large drawers & 4 small ones and with 12 Locks 40sh	3		
A Lock to the door 3sh [*illeg.*] other Locks within 3sh.		6	6
one curtain Rodd & eyes 2sh & Curtain		2	
one pointed curtain for glass door 1sh shelves round & cubbords	1	1	
My Fathers picture[33] one closet door 1tt. one black Chire 1sh	1	1	
one Hand with Ink & sand 2sh psuter.		5	
The books in the s[ai]d study number 1755 w[hi]ch see below Catalogue page 28			
an oaken with Lock & Key 30d			

[fol. 10r] In the Chamber over the old Kitchen

	£	s.	d.
one new bedstead with falsen bottom	1	1	
A Curtain Rod for bed 4sh. 6d a set of Green valence, top &c.	2	12	
one feather bed Large & best no. VI weig[h]ing	6		
one bolster weighing [*left blank*] markd VI. one pillow		11	6
one flock bed 8sh. three blankets Bought of Oliver 20sh	1	8	
two Red & white good Carpets ag[ains]t the wall & other tepastry	1	10	
one curtain rod for the window & curtain & eyes 7sh. 2d		7	2
one Chest of drawers 25sh one black arm Chier 38d	1	7	6
one Chimney piece painted 10:6d tongs & shovel, 3shil.		13	6
a pair of bellows 4sh A portmantle trunk 7sh 6 brass ketches belong \18d/ &		12	6

---

[33] Probably the same picture that was lot 512 in the Hengrave sale of 1897 (*Catalogue*, p. 43) and hanging at Old Buckenham Hall in 1905 (Farrer (1908), p. 379). See Plate III.

	£	s.	d.
one oaken for linning 5sh. one brass lock Chamber door 5sh, one other 8s		11	
two Cross serves for windows \16s/ two shelters for windows 8sh.		9	4
2 hand serines 3d one brush for harsh 6d a small hanging shelve 6d		1	3
one wroght picture of our saviour & passion our Lady & st John o're Chimney	1		
one print of our saviour & st John Baptist saluting black frames & Glass		3	6
two prints of st mary magdeline smaller Glass & frames, & taking from the Cross		4	
three other small pictures & frams 6d one cloaths brush tortershel back 2s		2	6
one other hand brush for bed &c. 6d a Basket for dressing, & a Cover edged 10d		1	4
one Cushing 6d one lettle Leather trunk with lock 4sh.		4	6
shelves in closets 5sh.		5	
A new fashion stove green with brass with brass fender & poker	19	5	7
tis now in the best parlour & the firehearth is here & dogs	2		
a writing desk 30d a linen Hutch oak with Lock 5sh A trunk 2sh		9	6

[fol. 10v] In the dressing Room ore the old parlour

	£	s.	d.
Two pieces of Hangings on the two sides one representing venus and the other the Goddes Ceres	5	10	
one large Chimney piece painted 15sh. one large stove greet 28sh	2	3	
one brass fender 4sh. fireshovel & tongs 3d brass ketches 18d		8	6
fire purr or poker brass Knob[be]d 18 one fire Brush red painted 18		3	
two small Japan'd shelves 18d two Curtain Rods & eyes 4s. 4d		5	10
two brass serves for windows 3sh one carnet 3.6d		6	6
a brass lock into my Chamber 5:6d another Brass lock on the door 5.8		11	
one Oacken Burrow or Escr[i]ture w[i]th six locks & draws	2	5	
one Corner Cubbart Jappan[e]d in the entrance		10	
two [illeg.] cuts in Japan[e]d frams & glasses rack side the Chimney		8	
one pearl Cabinett with draws & three Locks & stand for the same	4		
two pair of damask painted Curtains and valance	1		
one pire Glass with black frame ore the tea table Cost	3	10	
one Tea Table right Indean the best	3		
six Tea Cupps redish flowerd finest old Cheney & seven sa[u]ccers	1	11	
Two black stands to the Glass one China sugarpott small & cover 1sh		9	
six low Backed Cane Chires bought at London at 5:6 each	1	6	
one Japan[e]d box 6sh one China large tea pot & plate 6		12	

	£	s.	d.
one lock on Closet door 20d silk hanging in the Closet & peggs 6sh		7	
one box done w[i]th Irons in the closet for writings w[i]th a very good Lock		5	
other Cheney in the passage 1 large fine dish flowerd 15 Inches wide		18	
a pair of cheney dishes flower[e]d different Colours old Cheney		14	
one Large blew & whit Bason ore corner Cubbart		5	
one blew & whit cupp ibid ish an Inkhorn & sand box Cheney 3sh		4	
A small oval table oak 4sh. one ebony & silver toaster 35sh	1	19	
what more China the account fol 22			
two Large silver Candlesticks weighing 33z 12oz: gr23. on the stand	10	1	1
two small tea Candlesticks on the 2 Japand shelves see acc[oun]ts of plate fol. 19.	1	14	2
sume	44	4	7
A tea kettle & lamp silver weighing 43 ounces 12 penney weight at 6d p[er] ounce	12	19	6
one four Legd black table on w[hi]ch the tea kettle stands		2	6
two damask Covers for the tea & Coffy tables		4	
sume	57	10	
one Red Cheney Tea pot with silver spout Late Lady Barnardiston's		10	6
a tea table for the Corner bought of Aunts 3 leged 5sh		5	
in the Closet one desk Lock & key with draws 5sh		5	
six Cushings 6sh a small stool 6			

[fol. 11r] In my Room & Closets

	£	s.	d.
one Bedstead & Cord 7.sh. one feather bed new token'd weighing 88tt at 10 p[er] tt 3:6:8 one Large Bol[s]ter, and three pillows 15. shill. blew Curtins valence tester, head &c. 3tt. one Counterpin dark velvet 1tt	8	8	8
three Blankets 12 shill. the old hangings ab[ou]t the room 1tt.	1	12	
two new peices of Hangings over part of the other & belonging to those in the dressing Room, one of Diana the other of Ariadne 4tt 10d	4	10	
a schutheon of my sisters[34] with Glass & Guilt fram & Card behind		6	
Two folding pich[ure]s part of an alter piece of the salutation & saviours [illeg.]	5		
two small picture[e]s of st Catharen & st Barbara under the Glass & frams		4	
one of Nuns work in Japan frame by bedside 6sh		6	

---

[34] One of Elizabeth Rookwood's seven sisters-in-law, the daughters of Sir William Gage, 2nd Baronet of Hengrave.

	£	s.	d.
one picture of our saviour carr[y]ing his cross Gilt frame & Glass	1	10	
a print of the saints of the dominicans &c and frame		2	
one print of a pope Gilt frame & Card behind		2	
one watch case 2 sh. 6d and old couch 18. one black corner shelve 1sh		5	
two Guns 42sh one close stool case 8.sh & pan 3sh. 6d			
a painted Chemney piece 7sh 6d tongs & shovel 3sh ketches brass 18d	2	13	6
a pair of bellows 3sh a broom for Hearth 6d		3	6
A Curtain Rod for bed 7sh 2 Curtain rods for windows & eyes 4/		11	
two painted window curtains 13sh. one Bell 3shil.		10	
one Large Looking Glass In Guilt frame ore the table	4		
one tinder box pitter fashion 5sh an Angling Rod can ways 5sh		10	
one table 4 legs under the Glass with draw 8sh; \[illeg.]/ an old table 5sh 6d \Bought [illeg.]/		13	
one large Cabinet & chest of drawers wallnut tree	3		
one wallnut tree Eleutrer or Cabinet with drawers	1	2	
six skye Colour[e]d, patten Cushings on couch 18. Shill. & one pillow of the same 5sh.			
one pillow of the same 5sh.	1	3	
three door Locks & two Cubbart Locks 11sh.		11	
one arm Chire cover'd with bren Cheney 7sh on other of the same 3		10	
one Japan Indian Tea bord 12sh one small picture of Christ & virgin 8d		12	8
one brass stand or buger for wax Candle 18d one Cane with silver handle 8sh 6d another Cane only a silver piece at handle 2sh. 6d		11	
one Tea chest with 3 Canisters tin for tea & sugar		14	
Two silver flat Candlesticks w[i]th my father & mothers arms on 5.6d	2	15	2
2 Larg Glasses holding each ab[ou]t a gallon, & six open mouths bottles for tea		4	
A pewter pint measure an half pint a 1/3 & 2 1/2 5sh no. V.		5	
One Cocoa Cup made out of the shell trim[me]d with silver & silver [illeg.]	1	6	
One small cupp ditto the inside silver cased 7:6d 4 knives & forks silver Handles 9s		16	6
One black rownd 4 legg[e]d table In corner 30d	10	02	6
One Larg down Cushing for the great Chire covered with the same blew Cheney		5	6
	42	4	8

	£	s.	d.
Pair of Dogs with brass Nobbs bought of porlet 3 shillings & a quilt for my bed for Common use bought at melford fair for ten shillings		18	
A [*illeg.*] Cubbard 10sh. 6	43	12	

[fol. 11v] In dark Closet

	£	s.	d.
one Trunk Leather with Lock & Key no draw		11	
In the said trunk Linnen used in the oratory w[hi]ch see below p. 18		14	6
shelves p[er] totum & hanging Impliments for vestments with hooks		6	
The vestments & their appurtenances see below page 18	40	19	6
The plate see below page 19th	110		
	162	11	2

[fol. 12r] In the Red Closet

	£	s.	d.
one Black Arm Chair 3sh a green & whit Cover w[hi]ch hangs down 18d		4	6
one picture of Christ Crucified & frame 30d a Guilt Crucifix 18d		4	
one print of the visitation & frame 18 one tall Candle stick w[i]th socketts		2	6
three red velvet Cushings 5sh one large Red Cushion 5sh		10	
one large Green velvet Cushion 7sh 6d one large Cushion yellow on one side 5s		12	6
my newest port mantle Trunk Cost 13 shilings		6	
one old trunk 1 sh. one pewter Bason 3sh with drawers		4	
one large Trunk without draw Lock & Key 13sh		13	
one other Trunk with out drawers 3sh one Ladder 6d		3	6
a lock on the Inner Closet door 3s one bedstead behind the door 5sh		7	6
one set of Laths for bed beside w[hi]ch belongs to the other bedstead 1sh		1	
a deal box with wax flowers to be made up for alter &c.		10	6
Shelves 1sh. The linni[n]g in the Best trunk see below p. 21	43		
Red hangings ish. one Black G[r]ound 7sh. 6d.		8	6
one print of St mary magdeline & fraim 6d			6
sume	46	8	6
In the Inward Closet a deal box with lock w[i]th odd fringes, old point & other piec[e]s &c		5	8
one side table with draw ish one Large work[e]d Cushin Long 2sh three black & white 20d.		6	6
2 livery Cubbords 3sh. 6 one stool 2d		3	8

[fol. 12v] In the Hall Room

	£	s.	d.
one Large High table & a Large Guilt frame before it		12	
one other table by the window of deal 2sh.		2	
two steps Guilt framed 4sh Three Cards Guilt frames 5sh		5	
one little tabonacle &c 5sh two sconces french mettle Guilt 6sh		11	
two pieces in Guilt frames nuns work 10sh 2 black Candlesticks 30d		12	6
4 marble Images 3sh. two Carpets 6sh. one stool 3d		9	8
three Large Cushions & 7 small ones 30sh all Cover[e]d	1	10	
two pictures with out frames on bord 18d one scuthion & frame 6d		2	
one poor's box & lock 3sh. one arm black Chire 30d.		4	6
on Ivory Crucifix & Cross Inlead tortor shell with foot	2		
one crocifix brass Guilt & black cross	1	2	
one antient folding piece the middle part of the 3 Kings		7	
one wall [*illeg.*] frame or Couch for the larg Cushions		15	
painted hangings round the Room 35 yards	1	15	
some pictures on that staircase ish six locks 6sh.		7	
In the Closet behind one bedstead		6	
one Greet Irons for still & Iron bead made for the elembeck		7	6
one Large curtain Rodd		2	6
one picture on wood of our Lady our Saviour standing in her lapp w[i]th frame		10	
one tapastry Cushion in the arm Chire 1sh. one brass crucifix & cross ore [*illeg.*]		3	
sume	2	8	8
three pictors in Guilt frames of our Saviour's nativity, ecce homo, a madonna	5		
two small Chirs or stools 1sh. & white ribbed bazon		1	

[fol. 13r] In the first Garratt and shopp

	£	s.	d
one bedstead 2sh 6d. one large bolster 8sh. 2 Blankets 30d		13	6
one large trunk with 3 locks 10sh. one green curtain round the bed ish		11	
one small tin tunnel 2d. 16 Canisters 5sh.		5	2
In the [*illeg.*] trunk one large Red silk quilt for bed 2tt one fender ditt.	3		
one white stiched petticote w[i]th pocket. [*illeg.*] the same & an old shift[35]		10	

---

[35] Note in margin: 'Now in my Chamber'.

	£	s.	d.
one Lock on the Closet or shop door 1sh		1	
one large deal box in the Closet, & five small ones		4	
one box with brass weichts averdepois & Troy & two pair of ballance		14	
six Large syrapp patts with Covers entitled		6	
17 Large Glasses entitled from 2 quart to 4 quarts	1		
20 smaller 6sh. 3 power vials belley'd 9d.		6	9
vialls more of different sizes 30. 3sh		3	
a marble slab almost 2 foot 6sh a plaster knife 6d		6	6
a Curtain Rod Eyes & Curtain 2sh. open mouth Glasses		6	
shelves & table or counter 3sh all the druggs about 30sh	1	13	
two sives for shape 18d. one Casting net in the box 3sh		4	6
two pair of Gold weiths & Choles with cases 7sh.		7	
one feather bed	10	11	5

[fol. 13v] In the farthest Garratt

	£	s.	d.
one bedstead with Green & whit Curtains 9sh Bed rods new 6sh		15	
one bolster 7sh. 1 Blanket w[i]th one Green rug ish.		12	
two leather Trunks with lock & keys 6sh		6	
one window rod & curtain 3sh a lock on the door 18d		4	
a Cellar for bottles or strong waters with lock & key 6sh w[i]th Bd		6	
a large old trunk with Iron Ribles 1sh. one small hanging shelve 6d		1	6
	2	5	
one Feather bed	2		

[fol. 15r][36] In the Green house stables & over them

	£	s.	d.
In Green house one table with draw oak & 4 brass nobs for hats		3	10
one lock on door next the yard 22d a lock on the passage door 3sh		4	10
one breeding Cage bough[t] of uncle 7sh 6, one other for 4 birds 4sh		11	6
2 curtain rods & eyes 4sh In the green house & 2 painted curtains & valence 4sh		8	
ore the stairs one breeding cage large fixed		17	
one other cage longish halve dark jsh		1	
	2	6	2
one large Hutch with Lock & key			
one pallet bedstead			

---

36 There is no folio numbered 14.

	£	s.	d.
over the stable is one Copper pott belonging to the Elimbeck[37] and on the stair case there is the head of pewter	1	15	
one large painted new Ladder 15sh. & one short one 18d		16	6
one Rack & manger 6sh. a Corn brass [*illeg.*] sive is		7	
7 hammers, plains, saws, & other tools		10	6
A Garden Saw 3sh. 6d		3	6
In the stable one spade 18d. two other Ladders 3sh. 6d		3	6
one corn Hutch 18. 3 pit[c]h forks 18d a bushel 2sh.		5	
five halters 1sh. a good sadle 14sh an old sadle 2 shil. Three bridles 3sh.		17	

[fol. 15v] At Kilbers house[38]

	£	s.	d.
one press bought of mrs Osborn it stands over the shop		6	
one Bedstead & one bord or shelve in the beforehand appartment		3	6
several Lumes bought of mr Basset's sail ibid			

[fol. 16] Account of Ch[apel] stuff vestments & Linning

	£	s.	d.
one Large Holland surplus[39] Laced	1	1	
one Callico surplus 6sh		6	
4 Holland Albs,[40] two of w[hi]ch are Laced	3	10	
one Large Alter cloath for any by Alter Laced to the ground round 4sh. 5 holland Alter Cloaths, one of w[hi]ch is laced, 15ll. 3 damask alter Cloath, 18sh. two diaper, 6sh. one Callico alter Cloath another of scotch Cloath and another of Lawn, Large 8sh 6d. In all 13	2	11	6
five comm[o]n Cloaths 2 holland & 3 damask		7	6
Eleven Amicts[41]	16	6	
three broad Lace Corporals[42] 10sh three edged, 6sh. ten large & nine smaller, & one all Lace 20sh. in all 26	16 1		
Eight purificatories[43] 2sh. 8d.		2	8
three large towels & nine others In all twelve		12	
two Covers wrought with black for stools		2	
a Chryth[enin]g Handcerchife[44]		2	

---

[37] Alembic.
[38] Probably a house on the estate occupied by a servant.
[39] Surplice.
[40] Alb: a long white robe worn underneath vestments.
[41] Amice: a white cloth worn around the neck and shoulders underneath vestments.
[42] The corporal is a square linen cloth on which the chalice and paten rest during the mass.
[43] Purificators: the cloths used to wipe the sacred vessels.
[44] Perhaps a christening robe.

	£	s.	d.

[fol. 17] one black velvet vestment Burs[45] & antipendium[46] the same — 6

one of Crimson velvet wrot with Gold antipendium & cushions &c — 8

three white vi[delicet] one [*illeg.*]ably antipendium & Cushion[47]: — 6
one set with needle work & one embroider[e]d with antipend[ium] fixed

one Red silk with Lace with flower w[i]th ordinary antipendium — 2

one Green w[i]th w[hi]t[e] Lace & antipend[ium] & cusshion 30sh. — 1 10

one purple damask dyed from yallow antipend[ium] & cushion — 5

one Blew wrote with Gold, wanting a new ground — 5

one ordinary black with whit Lace almost new & antipend[ium] — 1 1
cushion

one white of flower[e]d silk with silver Lace antipend[ium] & — 6
Cushion, and lined with Red silk 6ll with Burse proper

one antependium w[hi]ch suits none of white satten w[i]th wrott sprigs, green & Red 6sh. 6d.

Small cushion Green fellows none 2sh. — 8 6

as to the Burses here unto belonging one generally serves two — 40 19 6
vi[delicet] The Black velvet & whit Tabby 2. purple damask &
ordinary black. 3. Red gold wrot & red silk. 5sh of gree[n] silk & — 11 52
white. 5sh to the crimson velvet, & flower[e]d white imbroder[e]d.
6sh is proper to the last above mentioned.

sume — 52 4 8

[fol. 18] Things for the Chap[e]l bought of Mrs Marg[are]tt Martin executive of my Aunt who [*illeg.*]

	£	s.	d.

a vestment stole maniple[48] burse vail[49] corpsieulum [corporal?] of a — 12
whit mock damask

an Alb of scots Cloath 3 shil 4 Alter Cloaths 5sh 3 Amicts 18 2 — 19 4
Communion Cloaths 5sh 3 Corporals 5sh 3 other towels 1sh two
purificatories 4d a Crusifix brass 3 Cards for A[l]ter two Girdles a box — 5
for bread & pin Cushen 3sh. a red & w[hi]t[e] Calico antipendum and
alter ston[e][50] 18d a red silk Cushen & Green stand for booke one darke
Burse 3 other Cooper cushins one red one white & one w[hi]t[e] w[i]th

---

45 Burse: a stiff card envelope covered in cloth (often decorated), used to hold the corporal before and after Mass.

46 Antependium: an altar frontal.

47 Probably the cushion on which the missal lay open on the altar, in the same liturgical colour as the chasuble and altar frontal.

48 Maniple: a small vestment worn over the priest's right arm.

49 Veil: the humeral veil, a cloth in the liturgical colour of the season, which covers the chalice and paten before and after Mass.

50 According to canon law, Mass could only be celebrated on a consecrated stone altar. Because this was not possible in England, consecrated portable altar stones were often placed on an ordinary table so that Mass could be said over them.

	£	s.	d.

red Crosse 2sh a small [*illeg.*] Colour[e]d Curtain 4 black & w[hi]t[e] Cushing one wrot silk and 5 others

	£	s.	d.
sume	1	16	4

Another Black velvet vestment with Bugels silver laced,[51] stole manuple Burs vail Antipendium, paten of the same — 4 10

Another silk damask ground whit Brocaded red and Gold w[i]th gold lace, vaile, burs stole & manuple all new with a red Cushin no Antipendium, never had tho I believe there is one. — 4 10

[fol. 19] Account of plate I have this Aug[us]t 1737

	oz.	pw.	gr.
Two flat Candle sticks with father and mothers arms on th[e]m weigh.	10		22
one sucking spout 1oz. 10p[enny]w[eight] 6 gr[ains]. two exit[n]guis[h]ers 2:01:0	3	11	
one cup w[i]th patten Guilt with in	8	4	12
another Cupp with patten also guilt with in old Aunts	9		
another w[hi]ch was Lady monson's with patten Guilt with in now at B[eyto]n	13	3	
3 small boxes for oils[52] 2:12:0 one pixis[53] 19p[enny]w[eight]	3	11	
a prefum box one the topp of Cane 1:05:05 & inside of cup 9p[enny]w[eight] 17g	1	14	22
a chain, small cross, watch case, & other small things	10	18	
sume of ounces	60	3	8
Two Large Candesticks Lady monson's	33	12	23
one stand Candlestick	9	12	9
one Tea pott bought an[no] 1710	11	3	12
one Counter box, with 35 Counters with Reresbies & the Tamworth arms & sixty three old shillings &c. weighing	17	17	12
one large Coffy pott with arms	23	9	
one milk pot with arms	6	3	
seven new fashion Large spoons six wherof with arms	14	9	12
eight tea spoons Guilt 2:5:6. six other tea spoons tongs & poker newly bought 2:3:22 a new fashion tea tongs 17p[enny]w[eight]	5	6	4
one snuff box Guilt with in 2:01:0. a patch box 1:5.2	3	6	2

---

51 Elizabeth, sister of Ambrose Rookwood (I), married Christopher Forster of Copdock, whose arms were argent three bugle horns stringed sable (Gage (1835), p. 143). Black vestments were worn for requiem Masses.

52 These boxes would have contained the three kinds of consecrated oil kept in all Catholic churches: the oil of catechumens (for anointing at baptism), oil of chrism (for anointing at ordination) and oil of the sick (for anointing in the last rites).

53 Pyx: a box used for the reservation of the consecrated sacrament.

	oz.	pw.	gr.
of plate to the ebony Toster	4	11	12
sume of ounces	129	12	14
six new fashion glasses for salvers	35	5	1
Three Casters for sugar pepper & mustard	24	8	1
four salts 6:19:8 4 salt spoons g.p[enny]w[eight] 22. supe Ladle 8:5:12	15	14	18
one pair of snuffers & stand	7	14	12
four other new Candlesticks these bought together	36	12	
sume of ounces	119	14	8
Two silver Canns 13:06:12 A punch Ladle 3:08:0	16	14	12
one pair of spurs	4	18	
one scollasted plate or Bason with arms	9	18	
one Clapp for Bell & 2 hafts for knives 2:16 Clasp for Gowns 6 p[enny]w[eight]	3	2	
Two Tea Candlesticks 6:14:0 A small Canaster Guilt 3:1:8	9	15	8
one sugar Capp with Cover	05	10	
sume of ounces	49	17	20
4 sumes above	359	6	2

[fol. 20] Plate not before mentioned in my possession

	oz.	pw.	gr.
Of mr Angiers a silver two eared Cup with the Daniels armes[54]	7	19	
two silver spoons marked G. A. A.	2	18	
a snuff box with stone a mour[n]ing ring & an old watch upon all w[hi]ch I lent him 5 Gunies december the 2d 1748	5	5	
And march the 18 1748/9 he left with me three silver spoones more upon w[hi]ch I Lent him twenty shillings marked as the above 2. The 3 last weighs 4oz:14 p[enny]w[eight]:0	1		
Of mr J[oh]n Taybers eight floer spoons six flat marked two new fashion a pair of buckets ½ silver a gold lace, 2 Gold mourning rings with stones & a silver Ring with red stones upon w[hi]ch I lent him four Gunies may 21. 1745 for a month all return[e]d	4	2	
A pair of spurrs he sent march 16 1748/9 & desired six shillings for a week w[hi]ch I Lent him & a pair of Bucles the same time these last are return'd	8	3	
Elizabeth Strutt left with me two silver spoons one marked R. F. G. S. the other M. B. G. S. they weighed 11:11 p[enny]w[eight]:10 gr[ains]. I let her share have twelve shillings. she since owes more ab[ou]t 2tt.	1	1	
I have still one spoon knobed of peggys \abs Bell/ she having borrowed the Childs spoon & two others & the Corall of me since the[y] all weight oz.15p[enny]w[eight] tis letter[e]d at topp J. C.			

---

54 The Catholic Daniell family of Acton, near Sudbury.

mrs Harrisson has her sister betty's silver Cup & her silver spoons marked M. S. G. S. flat Handled

found of mrs Harrissons six silver spoons three with Knobbs, 3 flatt

[fol. 21] An Account of the Linning

Damask Table Cloaths Large 12: smaller 4

Damask napkings 46

Diaper Table Cloaths Large 9. smaller 2

Diaper napkings 41

Holland sheets six pair

Hempen sheets seven pair & an odd one

Blew striped Napkings 24

Towels five & tweenty

pillobers 22. bolster casses six

Large Baggs seven

Corse towels for servants 2

This parcel of Linning may be cominted to be worth at second hand at the Lowest, most of the Damask & holland being very fine, at 43tt B. Book p. 159.

[fol. 22r] An Account of the China ware I have this Aug[us]t 1737

	£	s.	d.
Two pair of very fine Colour[e]d old basons	1	10	
one pair of blew & white Basons		5	
one large Blew & white Bason		4	
one other Blew Bason the Bottom somew[ha]t defective		3	
one other white, with a green & red ringm broken at top		1	
one pair more of blew & white bazons the same as above		5	
one dozen of blew & white China plates	1	4	
two white plates with Blew edgings deep for fruit		5	
one smaller blew & white plate		1	6
four Blew & white China supe plates		14	
four white chocolate old China Cups w[i]th 3 saucers the same	1		
six more Colour[e]d chocolate Cups w[i]th two saucers of the same old		12	
one square old colour[e]d chocolate cup small solo		3	
one large Green Cup		2	6
two Greenish cups edged blew within		2	6
two Blew & white cups		2	
one small white cup		1	
three large blew & white Cups for sauce		3	

	£	s.	d.
six very fine red edged with Gold China tea Cups with seven saucers to them in dressing room	1	10	
six blew & w[hi]t[e] tea cups with six saucers to them China		6	
A smaller Blew & white with five saucers		6	
two odd saucers flower[e]d red bought 1732		2	
one large tea pot China blew & white		4	6
one small blew & white tea pot		3	
one stand for tea pot china & one boat for spoons		2	6
two China sconces in old parlour		5	
two China Inkhorns one round the other square & one sand box		3	
one large dish china fine 15 Inches wide flower[e]d		16	
two china dishes diffiren[t] colours fine fellows		12	
one large china dish now some w[ha]t broken		4	
sume total	11	13	6
one small sugar pot & Cover ish. one Red Chiny tea pot val[ue]d at 10:6 w[i]th silver spout in the dressing room		11	6
total summe	12	5	
[fol. 22v] January 1742/3 six tea Cupps blew & sausers & two basons bought		16	

[fol. 23] An Account of w[ha]t Glasses I have this Aug[us]t 1737

	£	s.	d.
small drinking wine Glasses in the 2 boofets 2 doz[en] & 4: at 3d		7	
4 ditto Larg stone Glasses either for wine or beer at 5d		1	8
2 quart decanters 7sh. 2 pint decanters 4 shil.		11	
one pint flowered decanter with [illeg.]		1	10
4 large cut flowered German water Glasses 5sh 4 smaller ditto 4sh		9	
8 Hatt bottom cutt bier Glasses		3	4
one large flower water Glass with handle 7d one dram glass 2d			9
20 sweet glasses of different sizes		5	
	1	19	7
3 glasses for mustard, sugar, pepper with covers & silent waiter		6	6
sume	2	6	1

[fol. 24] An Account of my pewter w[hi]ch see p. 9th

Twelve fine pewter plates with a Corronet on th[e]m

Eighten broad ringed with arms of our family, & a mustard plate w[hi]ch I bought of Sarah Carley & had been my Aunts at 8d p[er] tt

four other platts bought of Nichonson an[no] 1714

Two more new plates marked on the Back R. M.

four Large dishes marked G. w. J.

one large dish marked K. R. m. G.

one dish mark[e]d G. G.

one dish marked M. R.

one dish marked H. H.

one supe dish not marked, but w[i]t[h] the stamps, new

[fol. 25] Goods bought at Aunts 9br [September] 25 1741 not otherways mention[e]d

	£	s.	d.
a large oval table w[i]t[h] draw oak		7	
another oval table Less also oak 5sh		5	
eight Rush bottom[e]d Chiers 8sh two Leather Chiers 30d two other Rush bottom[e]d 2sh one oak two arm Chier 3sh. three other Rush Chiers 30d ditto 3 more white ones 2sh	1		
a Larg screen of paper two Coolours 6sh. 13 small prints 30d.		8	6
one Larg one of the Court of france 2sh. Cobb Irons, fender and 2 brasses for tongs & shovel 3sh tea table 2sh 6d		7	6
a pair of bellows & purr 3sh. A tinned blower for stove ish.		4	
4 window Curtains in her parlour & valence 3sh four more in her parlour Chamber 5 shillings five Curtain Rods 4sh		12	
A Iron Crest fixt in parlour Chamber 10sh & sixpence. a small one in Aunts Chamber of small barrs 18d. A firepan & tongs 2sh. an Iron grate for heaters & hooks 2sh		16	
Coal great in Kitchen five barrs, two Cheeks 12sh. a Long fender ish. a. purr 6d a trivet ish. a long fender ish. an other fire pan & tongs 18d. Chopping Knif[e] ish. an Iron scure 6d		17	
a press with 3 Loks 4 shill. a looking Glass oval 2sh		6	
a trammel ish. A Chicken Coop 18d		2	6
a pestle & morter bell mettle 4sh 6d		4	6
for a Copper weighing 5tt at ish p[er] pound sold by me to \mr George Kedington/	2	11	
for the Copper Irons & Copper Leads		14	
for the Green bed Courtains & valence upper & Lower head & tester trimed with red 8sh Curtain rod new fashion 6sh bed stead Cold straw bed & bolster 3sh and cors Cloath over tester		17	
sume	9	12	
a swinging Iron in Kitchin for tramel &c 3sh a wheelbarrow & pitchfork 2sh. a bell & pullies 2sh. a pair of old Cob Irons 6d		6	6
14 pictures in parlour Chamber with fram[e]s some Glassed 2sh		2	

32. [CUL Hengrave MS 77/2, fols 28v–55v] *English Catholic books and manuscripts in the library at Coldham Hall, 1737*[55]

[fol. 28r] A Catalogue of my Library an[no] 1737
In folio

				£	s.	d.
RFP1	60	**[fol. 28v]** Harpsfildij Historia Ecclesiastic[a] Anglicana et Campiani de divorsio[56]	1622		1	

[fol. 30r] In quarto

				£	s.	d.
RFP2	4	Verstegan Theatrum Crudelitatis Haereticorum antiq[uorum][57]	1592		6	6
RFP3	12	Campiani Rationes 10, et withakerij responsio &c.[58]	1617		2	6
RFP4	71	**[fol. 30v]** Joannes pitseus de Rebus Anglicis[59] Pariis	1619		10	6
RFP5	74	P[atris] Henrici Fitz Simon Britannomachia ministroru[m][60] \duaci/	1614		3	

[fol. 31r] Libri Latini in 8° et 12°

RFP6	81	**[fol. 31v]** Joan[nes] Roffensis de veritate Corporis et Sanguinus &c[61]	1527		1	6
RFP7	82	eiusdem psalmi seu precationes et Th[omae] mori[62] Impl. Lugd[uni]	1598			6
RFP8	223	**[fol. 33r]** Stonihursti dei patientis Historia editio 3a[63]	1670		2	

55 Books included here fall into the following categories: books included in the standard lists of English Catholic books (Allison and Rogers (1956), Clancy (1974), and Blom et al. (1996)); books published before 1559 that were significant to the Catholic community; Latin works by English Catholic authors; manuscripts, and books of Jacobite interest. I have excluded Catholic books whose subject matter pertains principally to Ireland, but not Irish authors who were read by English Catholics. The numbering of books in the original MS is not always consistent and I have made no attempt to correct this in transcription. I have listed as separate entries books bound together and listed in the MS as one entry, distinguishing them by letters after the numbers. Dates of publication were not always accurately recorded and I have not corrected these, although I supply them in square brackets where they are lacking. This list is designed to be read in conjunction with Allison and Rogers, Clancy and Blom et al. and details of books can be checked against these standard lists.

56 Nicholas Harpsfield, *Historia Anglicana Ecclesiastica* (Douai, 1622).

57 Richard Verstegan, *Theatrum Crudelitatis Haereticorum Antiquorum* (Antwerp, 1592). This was a companion volume to Verstegan's account of martyrdoms in England, *Theatrum Crudelitatis Haereticorum Nostri Temporis* (Antwerp, 1592).

58 William Whittaker, *Ad Rationes Decem Edmundi Campiani ... responsio Guilielmi Whitakeri, theologiae* (London, 1581). There is no 1617 edition of this work in the British Library Catalogue.

59 John Pits, *Relationum Historicarum de Rebus Anglicis* (Paris, 1619), 2 vols.

60 Henry Fitzsimon, *Britannomachia* (Douai, 1614).

61 John Fisher, *De Veritate Corporis et Sanguinis in Eucharistia* (Cologne, 1527). See here Plate 6.

62 John Fisher, *Psalmi seu Precationes* (Lyons, 1598).

63 William Stanihurst, *Dei Immortalis in Corpore Mortali Patientis Historia* (Antwerp, 1670).

ꝗDE VERI-
TATE CORPORIS
ET SANGVINIS CHRISTI IN EVCHA
riſtia, per reuerendum in Chriſto patrem, ac dominum
D. Iohãnem Roffenſem Epiſcopum, aduer-
ſus Iohannem Oecolampadium.

ARMA ∗ REGIS ∗ ANGLIE ∗ ET ∗ F

Coloniæ, Anno domini, M. D. XXVII.
AEDITIO PRIMA.

Plate 6. **RFP6**. Frontispiece of John Fisher, *De veritate corporis et sanguinis Christi in Eucharistia* (Cologne, 1527), one of the oldest printed books in the former library at Coldham Hall. This copy in Cambridge University Library reproduced by kind permission of the Syndics of Cambridge University Library

			£	s.	d.
RFP9	263	Liber precum manuscript[64]		2	
RFP10	268	Manuscriptio S. J. variarum Rerum &c Motus Reg[ulae] S. Ignatij		8	
RFP11	270	privilegia et facultates Soc[ietatis] Jesu manuscript		6	

[fol. 34r] Folios in English, French &c

				£	s.	d.
RFP12	16	Causins Holy Court english[e]d by T. H.[65] Lond[ini]	1634		7	6
RFP13	17	And ditto the 4th part or Tome by the same[66]	1638		2	6
RFP14	67	**[fol. 34v]** Cresses's Church History of England[67]	1668		12	6
RFP15	82	Sanders Acc[oun]t of the English sc[h]isms translated manuscript		1		
RFP16	83	B[isho]p Fisher's life by his Co[n]tempory In manuscript		1		
RFP17	94	**[fol. 35r]** Heskings parliament of the sacrament[68] o[riginal] p[rinting] antw[erp]	1566		3	6
RFP18	95	T. C.'s Dr Lauds Labyrinth vi[delicet] Carwell[69] parisiis	1658		2	6
RFP19	96	S[i]r Thomas Mor's 2 tomes of his works[70]	1557		2	6
RFP20	101	of transubstantiation between harlow and Goodman manu[script]			8	
RFP21	123	Mr Dods Church History vol[ume] ist[71] \Brussels/ only three published	1737	1	4	6

---

64 This may be the Rookwood Book of Hours, purchased by Cambridge University Library at Sotheby's Sale of Medieval and Renaissance Manuscripts as Lot 51 on 2 December 2014 and now CUL Add. MS 10079. This contains the inscription 'Thomas Rookwood his Book / June 1726' on fol. 136v. Thomas's signature appears also on fol. 1v although 'Thomas' has been erased with ink. The MS was illuminated in the southern Netherlands, probably at Bruges, c. 1460–70, for the English market. Unusually for an English book of hours, however, the prayers for the feast of St Thomas Becket beginning on fol. 23r (see here Plate VI) have not been defaced (following royal instructions in 1537), leading the expert at Sotheby's, Mara Hofmann, to conclude that the book was preserved by an English recusant family. This is confirmed by additional quires inserted in the MS (fols 2r–5v, 81r, 132r–138r) in which the name of Queen Mary has been erased and replaced in one instance by that of Elizabeth. The name 'Martyn' appears in a fifteenth-century hand in the centre of fol. 1v and 'Roogers' on fol. 138r, making it possible that the prayers were composed in Mary's reign by the long-lived recusant Roger Martyn (c. 1527–1615) of Long Melford, an ancestor of Thomas Rookwood's wife Tamworth.

65 Allison and Rogers 219.

66 Allison and Rogers 220.

67 Clancy 258.

68 Allison and Rogers 393.

69 Clancy 173.

70 Thomas More, *The VVorkes of Sir Thomas More Knyght, sometyme Lorde Chauncellour of England, wrytten by him in the Englysh tonge* (London, 1557).

71 BBKS 2769.

				£	s.	d.
RFP22	132	Mr Dods 2d vol[ume] of Church History[72] Brussels	1739	1	4	6
RFP23	142	**[fol. 35v]** Mr Dods 3d volum[e] of Church History[73]	1742	1	4	6
RFP24	152	The lives of S[ain]ts with other feasts of the year&c.written in Spanish by Peter Ribadeneyra Translated by william petre.[74] Edit[ion] 1669 cum figures	[1669]	2		

[fol. 36r] Quarto's in English French

				£	s.	d.
RFP25	3	The new & Old Scriptures by the Coledge of Rhems[75]	1609	1	1	
RFP26	4	Woodwards Historical narration of the life & death of J[esus] Ch[rist][76]	1685		6	
RFP27	5	Ejusdem Exhortations on the Council of Trent Being &c.[77]	1687		5	
RFP28	6	Ejusdem of the succession of the Clergy being the 2d Edit[ion][78]	1688		1	
RFP29	7	Ejusdem the 3d tract on the succession ag[ains]t some late Authors[79]	1688		1	6
RFP30	8	Ejusdem A Relation of the English Reformation & its Lawfulness[80]	1687		3	6
RFP31	9	Ejusdem 2 discourses of the Adoration of our saviour in the Sacram[ent][81]	1687		1	6
RFP32	10	Ejusdem 2 discourses of the sp[iri]t of Martin Luther; & Celab[ac]y of the Clergy[82]	1687		2	
RFP33	11	Ejusdem Compendius discourse of the Eucharist & 2 appendices[83]	1689		3	
RFP34	12	Ejusdem concerning Images & Idolatry potius walkers[84]	1689		1	

---

72 BBKS 2769.
73 BBKS 2769.
74 Clancy 832.
75 Allison and Rogers 107.
76 Clancy 1118.
77 Clancy 1112.
78 Probably Clancy 1127.
79 Probably Clancy 1128.
80 Clancy 1107.
81 Clancy 1129.
82 Clancy 1131.
83 Clancy 1108
84 Clancy 1109.

				£	s.	d.
RFP35	14	F[ather] Talon's Holy History translated by marq[uess] of winch[este]r[85]	1653	4		
RFP36	16	Fr parsons discussion of Barlows Answer[86]	1612		3	6
RFP37	17	Ejusdem Answer to S[i]r Edw[ar]d Cooke 5th part of Rep[ort][87]	1606		8	
RFP38	18	Ejusdem A quiet & sober Reckoning ag[ains]t Morton[88]	1609		3	6
RFP39	19	Ejusdem of mitigation ag[ains]t morton & others[89]	1607		3	6
RFP40	20	Ejusdem a warn word to S[i]r Francis Hastings wastword[90]	1602		2	
RFP41	21	Ejusdem a temporal ward word to the watch word of S[i]r Fra[ncis][91]	1599		1	
RFP42	22	J. B.'s Reply to a notorious libel ag[ains]t sec[ular] pri[es]ts[92]	1603		1	
RFP43	23	Wards History of England's Reformation[93]	1710		5	
RFP44	24	T. Bailys end of Controversy Between the R &c.[94] Doway	1654		5	
RFP45	25	Bonner's profitable & necessary doctrine[95]	1555		2	
RFP46	26	Sander's Supper of our Lord[96] Lovain	1566		2	
RFP47	27	Hardings Answer to Jewel's Reply[97]	1568		2	
RFP48	28	Q[ueen] Marys prisoner with a treatise of Mass & Sacram[ent][98]	1553		1	6
RFP49	29	Stapleton Staphilus of Scripture & disagree[ment] am[on]gst prot[estants][99]	1565		1	6
RFP50	30	Fitz Simon's Justification of the Mass, & Rules &c[100]	1611		1	6

---

[85] Nicholas Talon, *The Holy History* (London, 1653); not listed in Clancy.
[86] Allison and Rogers 628.
[87] Allison and Rogers 611.
[88] Allison and Rogers 635.
[89] Allison and Rogers 641.
[90] Allison and Rogers 642.
[91] Allison and Rogers 639.
[92] Allison and Rogers 236.
[93] BBKS 2917.
[94] Clancy 83.
[95] Edmund Bonner, *A profitable and necessarye doctrine with certayne homelies adioyned thervnto* (London, 1555).
[96] Allison and Rogers 752.
[97] Allison and Rogers 377 or 378.
[98] I find no reference to this book in any catalogue.
[99] Allison and Rogers 794.
[100] Allison and Rogers 320.

				£	s.	d.
RFP51	31	Kellison's Survey of the New Religion, detecting &c[101]	1605		2	6
RFP52	32	Eiusd[em] Reply to sutclifs Answer to the Servey[102]	1608		1	
RFP53	33	Breleyly's protestant Apologie for R[oman] Cath[olics][103]	1608		5	
RFP54	34	Knots Breleyly abreviated or prot[est]ancy Condemn'd[104]	1654		2	6
RFP55	35	Ejus[dem] Charity maintaynd by Catholicks ag[ains]t potter[105]	1634		1	
RFP56	36	Walsingams search into Religion dedicated to K[ing][106]	1609		4	
RFP57	37	Bishops reformation of a Cathol[ic]k deform[e]d or Reprooff of Dr Abbots defence of the Catholick deform[e]d. And likeways the 2d p[ar]t of the Reformation of a Cath[olic]k Deformed[107]	1608		2	6
RFP58	38	ejusdem the former part of a reformation of a Cath[olic]k deform[e]d[108]	1607		1	6
RFP59	39	grounds of the old & new Religion 2 parts w[i]th appendix[109]	1608		1	6
RFP60	40	Anderson's Ground of the Catholick & Roman Religion[110]	1623		1	6
RFP61	41	N. N's Triple Corde proving Religion by script[ure] &c[111]	1634		2	6
RFP62	42	Worthingtons Anker of Christian doctrine[112]	1618		1	6
RFP63	43	Fisher ag[ains]t white into the 9 points of Controversy[113]	1626		2	6
RFP64	44	of R[ome]'s overthrow of the protestant pulpet Bable[114]	1612		1	6

---

[101] Allison and Rogers 429.
[102] Allison and Rogers 426.
[103] Allison and Rogers 132.
[104] Clancy 1102.
[105] Allison and Rogers 897.
[106] Allison and Rogers 875.
[107] Allison and Rogers 116.
[108] Allison and Rogers 117.
[109] Allison and Rogers 493.
[110] Allison and Rogers 20.
[111] Allison and Rogers 25.
[112] Allison and Rogers 910.
[113] Allison and Rogers 605.
[114] Allison and Rogers 326.

				£	s.	d.
RFP65	44a	And an oration of Cardinal peron Translated[115]	1616			
RFP66	45	**[fol. 36v]** Ed[ward] Worsleys Truth will out ag[ains]t Jeremy Tayler[116]	1665		1	6
RFP67	46	S. N's Guid of Faith or Antidote ag[ains]t &c 3d part[117]	1621		1	6
RFP68	47	Eiusdem appendix to the Antidote[118]	1621		1	
RFP69	48	Thomas Martin ag[ains]t priests marriage ag[ains]t poynet[119]	1544		1	6
RFP70	50	K[ing] Hen[ry] 8th seven sacraments ag[ains]t Martin Luther[120]	1687		5	
RFP71	51	Gother's papist represented & misrepresent[ed] 1st p[ar]t[121]	1685		1	6
RFP72	52	Ejusdem the third part[122]	1687		1	6
RFP73	53	Ejusdem papists protesting ag[ains]t protestant popery[123]	1686		2	
RFP74	53a	Ejusdem An amicable accommodation of the difference[124]	1686			
RFP75	53b	Ejusdem A Reply to the Answer of the Amicab[le] accommod[ation][125]	1686			
RFP76	54	Ejusdem Advice to the pulpets deliverd in Cautions[126]	1687		1	
RFP77	55	Hudleston's short & plain way to the Faith & Church[127]	1688		1	
RFP78	56	Sargaints Antimortonus or Apologie in defence of the f[aith][128]	1640		2	6
RFP79	57	Eiusdem 5 Catholik letters of w[hi]ch 2 are sargaints[129]	1687		1	

---

[115] Allison and Rogers 287.
[116] Clancy 1136.
[117] Allison and Rogers 574.
[118] Allison and Rogers 575.
[119] Thomas Martin, *A Traictise Declaryng and plainly provyng, that the pretended marriage of Priests and professed persones is no marriage* (London, 1554).
[120] Clancy 496.
[121] Clancy 455–9.
[122] Clancy 462.
[123] Clancy 463.
[124] Clancy 433.
[125] Clancy 472.
[126] Clancy 438–9.
[127] Clancy 520–3.
[128] Allison and Rogers 679.
[129] Clancy 883.

				£	s.	d.
RFP80	58	The schism of the English Church demonstrated[130]	1688		1	6
RFP81	58a	Also The English donatizin[g] Church: In point of schisme[131]	168–			
RFP82	59	A. pulton's Remarks on B[isho]p Teneson's narrative&c[132]	1687		1	
RFP83	60	Meredith Some further Remarks \and Reflections/ on Dr Fenelon's acc[oun]t \And total defeat/[133]	1688		2	
RFP84	62	Richom's pilgrime of Loretto[134] paris	1629		1	6
RFP85	63	Ejusdem Holy pictures of the Sacrame[n]t[135]	1619		1	6
RFP86	76	Dods Certamen utriusq[ue] ecclesiae, or a lists of all the emine[nt writers][136]	1720			6
RFP87	77	Cressey's two questions[137]	1686		1	
RFP88	78	The use & moment of the notes of the Church[138]	1687		1	6
RFP89	78a	vindication of St Gregory's dialogues[139]	1660			
RFP90	78b	& manuscrip[t] of the invocation of saints				
RFP91	82	[fol. 37r] Roman Catholick sermons before the King &c vol 2[140]	[1741]		2	6
RFP92	83	Idem one preach'd by N. Hall before her majesty[141]	1686			6
RFP93	84	B[isho]p of Condom's pastoral letter to the new Catholicks[142]	1686		1	6
RFP94	85	ejusdem exposition of Christian doctrine &c	1687		2	6
RFP95	86	ejusdem of Communion under both kinds &c	1687		2	6
RFP96	87	Smith's prudential balance second part[143] doway	1631		3	6
RFP97	88	Barkley's discourse of the sacrament. & a rational disc[ourse] [illeg.][144]	1688		1	6

---

130 Clancy 920.
131 Clancy 1276Z.
132 Andrew Pulton, *Remarks Upon Dr. Tho. Tenison's Late Narrative* (London, 1687), omitted by Clancy.
133 Clancy 662.
134 Allison and Rogers 715.
135 Allison and Rogers 714.
136 BBKS 2768.
137 Probably Clancy 267.
138 Clancy 990.
139 Clancy 704.
140 BBKS 2522.
141 Clancy 481.
142 Clancy 124.
143 Allison and Rogers 777.
144 Clancy 77.

				£	s.	d.
RFP98	93	Flowers of the lives of the most Renownd Saints English[ed][145]	1632		7	6
RFP99	94	Fitzerbe[r]ts policy & Religion first part[146]	1606		4	
RFP100	96	venerable Bede's Ecclesiastical History Stapl[eton][147]	1565		5	
RFP101	98	[Dryden] The Hind & panther & remarks on't[148]	1687		4	6
RFP102	120	Exposition of the 7th psalm	1525		1	6
RFP103	123	Alph[onso] Rodrigues three vols of Christ[ian] perfect[ion][149]	1699	1	1	
RFP104	127	[fol. 37v] Fr michael's Admirable History o. p. of a possessed[150]	1618		2	
RFP105	128	Acts of the General Assemble of the french Clergie[151]	1685		1	6
RFP106	131	F. Canne treatise ag[ains]t the o[a]th of alleigiance	1674		1	6
RFP107	133	The Jesuit's Loyalty vi[delicet] 3 treatises ag[ains]t the oath w[i]th preface[152]	1677		2	6
RFP108	133c	the Jesuits Reasons unreasonable[153]	1662			
RFP109	135	Roquet's brief History of the life & death of k[ing] James 2d[154]	1713		1	6
RFP110	136	Five pamphlets vi[delicet] a new test of the Church of Eng[lan]ds Loyalty[155]	1687			2
RFP111	136a	A vindication of the Rom[an] Catholick[s] in England[156]	1660			
RFP112	136d	5 a Clear vindecation of Rom[an] Catholiks[157]	1659			
RFP113	136e	Rom[an] Catholick principles to God & to the King[158]	1680			

---

[145] Allison and Rogers 658.

[146] Allison and Rogers 311.

[147] Allison and Rogers 82.

[148] Clancy 327–31.

[149] Clancy 837.

[150] S. Michaelis (trans. 'W. B.'), *The Admirable History of the Possession and Conversion of a Penitent Woman* (London, 1613). This book does not appear in Allison and Rogers, but I have argued elsewhere that the translator was probably a Catholic (Young (2013a), p. 150).

[151] Clancy 12.

[152] *The Jesuits Loyalty, manifested in Three several Treatises lately written by them against the Oath of Allegeance* (London, 1677). This was an anti-Catholic republication of Catholic pamphlets with a critical preface.

[153] Clancy 551.

[154] A later edition of BBKS 2479 or 2480.

[155] Clancy 717–18.

[156] Clancy 172.

[157] Clancy 302.

[158] Clancy 248–9.

				£	s.	d.
RFP114	138	Six pamphlets ag[ains]t persecution & penal laws	1687		2	
RFP115	139	Leyseisters Common wealth supposed to be F[ather] parson[s][159]	1641		4	
RFP116	145	Wal[t]er Hiltons Ladder of perfection[160]	1533		1	6
RFP117	151	Causin's Holy Court the first part[161]	1626		2	6
RFP118	167	R[ichar]d Verstegan's Restitution of decayd Intelligence[162]	1634		3	6
RFP119	230	[fol. 38v] Some Queries to the protestants Concerning the English reformation by T. W.[163] Gent.	1687		2	
RFP120	234	3 Cases ab[ou]t the Talbot family & the Jesuits B[isho]p Chalender supposed[164]	1744	3		
RFP121	235	Gathers papist represented & misrepresented & Stillingfleet expos[ed][165]	1687		1	
RFP122	236	A Supplement to the reply in vindication the kindred of the late mr Talbot[166]	1741		4	
RFP123	237	Britannia Sancta or the lives of the most celebrated British English Scottish & Irish Saints &c In two parts[167]	1745		2	
RFP124	238	The seeker's Request to Cathol[ic]k priests & protestant ministers[168]	1687		1	
RFP125	239	T. J. Adjo[inde]r to the suppliment of Fr parsons discourse[169]	[1613]		1	
RFP126	240	Fr Alphonsus villegas St Lives 2 vols by Heigham[170]	1630		1	

[fol. 39r] In 8° et 12°

				£	s.	d.
RFP127	3	R[ichar]d withams annotations on the new testament tow volums[171]	1730		8	

---

159 Clancy 1353W.
160 Walter Hilton, *Scala Perfectionis* (London, 1533). This was the second edition from the press of Wynkyn de Worde.
161 Allison and Rogers 217.
162 Allison and Rogers 846.
163 Clancy 1043–4.
164 BBKS 61, 62, 63.
165 Clancy 455–9.
166 BBKS 2616
167 BBKS 506.
168 Clancy 878.
169 Allison and Rogers 309.
170 Allison and Rogers 857.
171 BBKS 2951.

			£	s.	d.
RFP128 6	The Council of trents Cathecisme in English[172]	1687		3	6
RFP129 11	Bed's ecclesiastical of the English nation by Stevens[173]	1723		4	
RFP130 12	Burgis's Annals of the Church 3 first ages[174]	1712		3	
RFP131 13	du pin's Church History volum 3 & 4th from the begining &c[175]	1712		3	
RFP132 15	Thom[as] Ward's History of Reformation In four Canto's[176]	1715		5	
RFP133 16	du pin's evangelical History or life of Jesus &c[177]	1694		2	6
RFP134 23	Jo[h]n Christoferson B[isho]p of Chisester ag[ains]t Rebellion Dedicat[ed] to Q[ueen] Mary[178]	1554		2	
RFP135 24	Dr Bristow motives of faith to move one to beleve the Cath[olike faith][179]	1599		1	
RFP136 25	Ejusdem his demand to be propounded to Hereticks[180]	1623			6
RFP137 26	Smith's defence of the Blessed Sacrament of the Alter[181]	1546		1	6
RFP138 27	Ejusdem his defence of the mass[182]	1546		1	
RFP139 28	Ejusdem Treatise of traditions or Brief treatise &[c]	1547		1	
RFP140 29	B[isho]p Gardner of the blessed sacrament[183]	1546		1	
RFP141 30	Ejusdem his Answer to Cranmer Sacrament[184]	15[51]			6
RFP142 31	Cardinal Allen's defence of purgatory[185]	1564		1	
RFP143 32	Ejusdem his defence of Lawfull power of priesthood[186]	1667		2	
RFP144 33	Ejusdem his Apologie for the two English Colledges[187]	1581		1	6

---

[172] Clancy 184.
[173] BBKS 219.
[174] BBKS 377.
[175] BBKS 955.
[176] A non-Catholic edition of BBKS 2917.
[177] Not recorded in Clancy.
[178] John Christopherson, *An Exhortation to all Men to take heed agaynst Rebellion* (London, 1554).
[179] Allison and Rogers 147.
[180] Allison and Rogers 148.
[181] Richard Smith, *The Assertion and Defence of the Sacrament of the Altar* (London, 1546).
[182] Richard Smith, *The Defence of the Mass* (London, 1547)
[183] Stephen Gardiner, *An Explicatio[n] and Assertion of the True Catholique Fayth, Touchyng the Moost Blessed Sacrament of the Aulter* (London, 1546).
[184] Published as part of the second edition of *An Explicatio[n] and Assertion* (London, 1551).
[185] Allison and Rogers 10.
[186] Allison and Rogers 11.
[187] Allison and Rogers 6.

			£	s.	d.
RFP145 34	Rastal his beware of Jewel[188]	1565		1	6
RFP146 35	Gregory Martin's corrections of protestant scripture[189]	1582		3	
RFP147 36	Ejusdem his treatise of schisme[190]	1578		3	
RFP148 37	Ejusdem his treatise of Christian peregrination[191]	1583		1	
RFP149 38	Ejusdem his treatise of the love of the soul &c[192] Roan	1578			6
RFP150 39	John Angell's Agrement of the holy fathers & doctors[193]	1554		10	
RFP151 40	An Apology ag[ains]t the defence of schisme[194]	ab[ou]t 1590		1	6
RFP152 41	A Treatise of Christian Renuntiation &c w[i]t[h] declaration of [the fathers of the Councell of Trent][195]	1580		3	
RFP153 44	william perin o. p.'s spirituall exercisses[196] Caen	1598		2	6
RFP154 45	B[isho]p watson's two notable sermons of the reall presence[197]	1554		1	6
RFP155 46	Thom[as] paynyll's 16 sermons in Q[ueen] marys days[198]	1555		1	
RFP156 47	Reynalds ag[ains]t whitaker of Reims anotations[199]	1583		1	6
RFP157 48	Ejusdem concerning the Catholick faith in the holy sacrafice &c[200]	1593		1	6
RFP158 50	**[fol. 39v]** Fr person's Reasons why Catholicks refuse to go to Ch[urch][201]	1580		2	
RFP159 50a	& a Brief Censure in defence of Campion answer[202]	1581			

---

[188] Allison and Rogers 709.

[189] Allison and Rogers 525.

[190] Allison and Rogers 535.

[191] Allison and Rogers 534.

[192] Allison and Rogers 526.

[193] John Aungell, *The Agrement of the Holye Fathers, and Doctors of the Churche, upon the cheifest articles of Christian religion* (London, 1555).

[194] Allison and Rogers 353.

[195] Allison and Rogers 357.

[196] Allison and Rogers 643.

[197] Thomas Watson, *Twoo Notable Sermons made the thirde and fifte Fridays in Lent last past, before the Quenes highnes, concerninge the reall presence of Christes body and bloude in the blessed sacrament* (London, 1554).

[198] Thomas Paynell, *Certaine Sermons of Sainte Augustines translated out of latyn, into Englisshe, by Thomas Paynyll* (London, 1557).

[199] Allison and Rogers 702.

[200] Allison and Rogers 703.

[201] Allison and Rogers 616.

[202] Allison and Rogers 615.

				£	s.	d.
RFP160	51	Ejusdem his defence of the said Censure[203]	1582		1	6
RFP161	52	Ejusdem his conference ab[ou]t the next succession to the Crown[204]	1594		3	
RFP162	53	Ejusdem's Apologie for ecclesiastical subordination[205]	1601		1	
RFP163	54	Ejusdem An Apologetical epistle to the Queens privy Council[206]	1601		1	
RFP164	57	Ejusdem's three Conversions of England three volums[207]	1603		15	
RFP165	58	Ejusdem A Review of 10 publick disputation[208]	1604		3	
RFP166	58a	& a Relation of a tryal before the K[ing] of france& a defence others of[209]	1604			
RFP167	59	Ejusdem Christian directory Bunney's edition[210]	1584		1	
RFP168	60	Ejusdem Christian directory sine titulo[211] ab[ou]t	1687		3	6
RFP169	61	Ejusdem Leycesters Com[mon]wealth & Leycester's Goals[212]	1612		1	6
RFP170	62	B[isho]p Smith his prudential ballance first part[213]	1609		2	6
RFP171	63	Dr Harding's Answer to Juelles Challenge[214]	1565		1	
RFP172	64	A Treatise of the possibility & conveniency of the Real pr[esence][215]	1596			6
RFP173	65	S[i]r Thom[as] Mors Comfort ag[ains]t Tribulation[216]	1554		1	
RFP174	66	Nicholas Sanders's Rock of the Church, & primacy[217]	1567		1	
RFP175	68	L[or]d Chancell[or] Heath speech ag[ains]t Elizabeth supremacy &c[218]	1559			6

---

[203] Allison and Rogers 626.
[204] Allison and Rogers 271.
[205] Allison and Rogers 613.
[206] Not listed in Allison and Rogers.
[207] Allison and Rogers 640.
[208] Allison and Rogers 638.
[209] Allison and Rogers 637.
[210] Allison and Rogers 621.
[211] Clancy 769.
[212] Allison and Rogers 261. No edition of 1612 is listed in Allison and Rogers.
[213] Allison and Rogers 777.
[214] Allison and Rogers 372.
[215] Allison and Rogers 925.
[216] Thomas More, *A Dialog of Comfort against Tribulacion, made by Syr Thomas More Knyght* (London, 1553).
[217] Allison and Rogers 750.
[218] Nicholas Heath, *A Speech made in the Upper House of Parliament against the Supremacy to be in her Majesty By N H Lord Chancellor of England* (London, 1558).

			£	s.	d.
RFP176 69	The mirrour of the new Reformation in her own words[219]	1634		7	
RFP177 70	B. C.'s puritanisme the mother sin the daughter[220]	1633		1	
RFP178 71	Woodward's detection of divers notable untruths[221]	1602		1	
RFP179 72	Fraser his learn'd epistle[222]	1605			6
RFP180 73	Tutchit his Historical Collections of the Change of Rel[igion][223]	1674		4	
RFP181 74	N. N. his treatise of Faith & Haeresie[224] Rouen	1657		3	6
RFP182 75	N. N. his polititians Catechisme[225] Antwerp	1658		3	
RFP183 76	R. Walpole's brief confutation of sutclife[226]	1603		2	
RFP184 77	Turbavill's manual of controversyes[227] Doway	1654		2	6
RFP185 78	C. W.s Summary of Controversies[228] St Omers	1623		1	
RFP186 79	Gorden Huntley's summary of controversies[229]	1618		1	
RFP187 80	L[or]d Castlemains apology for Catholick & Reply 3d ed[ition][230]	1674		4	
RFP188 83	Dr Godin's Catholick's no Idolaters[231]	1672		1	6
RFP189 84	Ejusdem his Just discharge to Stillingfleet[232]	1677		1	6
RFP190 85	J. Williams his Stillingfleet ag[ains]t Stillingfleet[233]	1671		1	6
RFP191 86	Ejusdem his second Stillingfleet \still/ ag[ains]t Stillingfleet[234]	1675		1	
RFP192 87	Antony Champny's pilkintons parallela disp[aralleled] with whithalls discourses[235]	1620		2	
RFP193 88	Erastus senior scholastically demons[trating] ag[ains]t ordination of the protestant Bishops[236]	1662		3	6

---

[219] Allison and Rogers 135.
[220] Allison and Rogers 185.
[221] Allison and Rogers 906.
[222] Allison and Rogers 346.
[223] Clancy 970.
[224] Clancy 939.
[225] Clancy 396.
[226] Allison and Rogers 874.
[227] Clancy 984–6.
[228] Allison and Rogers 867.
[229] Allison and Rogers 365.
[230] Clancy 176.
[231] Clancy 420.
[232] Clancy 421.
[233] Not listed in Clancy.
[234] Clancy 1056.
[235] Allison and Rogers 232.
[236] Clancy 590.

				£	s.	d.
RFP194	89	[fol. 40r] Knots Charity mistaken or Catholicks unjustly charg'd[237]	1630		2	
RFP195	90	Godden his Catholicks no Idolaters[238]	1686			6
RFP196	91	protestant plea the second part[239]	1625		2	6
RFP197	92	Spenser's Scripture mistaken[240]	1655		2	
RFP198	93	James Mumford's Question of Questions 2d edit[ion][241]	1687		2	6
RFP199	100	W. Johnson his Novelty Represt or[242]	1662		2	
RFP200	101	J[oh]n Sergeant his Schisme disarmed ag[ains]t Hammond[243]	1655		1	6
RFP201	102	Ejusdem schisme dispatched[244]	1657		2	6
RFP202	103	Ejusdem's sure footing 2d edition[245]	1665		2	6
RFP203	104	Ejusdem his letter of thanks to J. T.[246] paris	1666		1	6
RFP204	105	Ejusdem his Faith vindicated Lovain[247]	1667		1	
RFP205	106	Ejusdem error nonplus Lond[on][248]	1673		1	6
RFP206	107	Ejusdem's method to arrive at satisfaction in Relig[ion][249]	1673			8
RFP207	108	Ejusdem Reason against Raillery[250]	1672		2	
RFP208	109	Ejusdem of divotion[251]	1678		1	
RFP209	110	Ejusdem Raillery defeated by Calm reason[252]	1699		1	
RFP210	111	Kellingson Jurisdiction of prelat & prince[253]	1621		2	
RFP211	112	Ejusdem of the Heirarchy of the Church[254]	1629		2	
RFP212	113	The unerring & venerable Church or exp. J. S.[255]	1675		1	6
RFP213	114	Richlieues points of faith defended ag[ains]t 4 minist[ers][256]	1635		2	

---

[237] Allison and Rogers 892.
[238] A later edition of Clancy 420; not listed in Clancy.
[239] Allison and Rogers 169.
[240] Clancy 922.
[241] Clancy 700.
[242] Clancy 556.
[243] Clancy 896.
[244] Clancy 897.
[245] Clancy 903.
[246] Clancy 887.
[247] Clancy 881.
[248] Clancy 880.
[249] Clancy 890.
[250] Clancy 895.
[251] Clancy 893.
[252] Clancy 894.
[253] Allison and Rogers 427.
[254] Clancy 431.
[255] Clancy 147.
[256] Allison and Rogers 289.

				£	s.	d.
RFP214	115	Ejusdem's Christian doctrine translated by Carr[257]	1662		1	
RFP215	116	G. P.'s safe gard from Shipwrack[258] doway	1618		1	6
RFP216	117	T. H.'s first motive to suspect the protestant Rel[igion][259]	1609		1	6
RFP217	118	H. Leech his Triumph of Truth[260]	1609		1	
RFP218	120	S. Cressy's Answer to piercys court sermon[261]	1663		2	6
RFP219	121	Ejusdem his Apologeticall epistle of Still[ingfleet][262]	1674		1	
RFP220	122	Ejusdem's Question why are you a Catholick[263]	1672			6
RFP221	123	An answer to a question where upon depends &c[264]	1628			6
RFP222	123a	also questions proposed for Resolution of &c[265]	1657			
RFP223	124	F. S.'s disputation wherein the Old Religion &c[266]	1632		1	6
RFP224	125	Ejusdem Relection of Certain Authors[267]	1635		1	
RFP225	126	W. W.'s of Transubstantiation answer to Cosen[268]	1657		1	
RFP226	127	A Consultation about Religion[269]	1693		1	6
RFP227	128	**[fol. 40v]** A Secure and prudent Choice of beliefs[270]	1639			6
RFP228	128a	an answer to one question on w[hi]c[h] all depends[271]	1628			
RFP229	129	L[or]d Castlemains Reply to the Answered first edit[ion] [272]	1668		1	6
RFP230	130	J. Caumont his firm foundation of Catholick Faith[273]	1665			6

---

257 Clancy 834.
258 Allison and Rogers 647.
259 Allison and Rogers 397.
260 Allison and Rogers 450.
261 Clancy 273.
262 Clancy 260.
263 Clancy 270.
264 Allison and Rogers 31.
265 Clancy 919.
266 Allison and Rogers 443.
267 Allison and Rogers 446.
268 Clancy 1098.
269 Edmund Lechmere, *A Consultation about Religion, or, What religion is best to be chosen* (London, 1693). Not listed in Clancy.
270 Allison and Rogers 330.
271 Allison and Rogers 31.
272 Clancy 180.
273 Allison and Rogers 213.

				£	s.	d.
RFP231	132	Covent's Enchiridion of Faith[274]	1655		1	
RFP232	134	ph[illip] scot his schisme of England[275] amsterd[am]	1650			
RFP233	136	R. F.s missale Romanum vindicatum ag[ains]t[276]	1674		1	
RFP234	137	J. L s only way to Rest of the soul in Religion[277]	1657		1	
RFP235	138	Kaine's compendious way to convince[278]	1674			6
RFP236	140	Dr Carrier's missive to King James the first edit[ion][279]	1687			10
RFP237	141	mount syon shewing the Church[280]	1658			6
RFP238	142	A discourse of Infalibility in Religion[281]	1652		1	
RFP239	143	whit's Rushworth's dialogues edition[282]	1654		1	6
RFP240	144	white his apology for the said dialogues[283]	1654		1	
RFP241	145	Ejusdem his Christian doctrine 2d edit[ion][284] paris	1659		1	
RFP242	146	R everard his epistle to the nonconformists[285]	1664		1	
RFP243	147	J. B.'s tradidi vobis or traditionary[286]	1662		1	
RFP244	148	H. T.'s Reason for Religion[287]	1673			
RFP245	149	Turbavill's Catachisme 3d edition[288] doway	1650		1	
RFP246	150	A. R. B.'s treatise of Indulgences[289] St Omer	1623		1	
RFP247	151	L. J.'s Relection of a Conference of the Real pres[ence][290]	1665		1	
RFP248	152	F[ather] veron his Rule of Faith[291] paris	1660		1	
RFP249	153	w. Birchley Christian moderator[292]	1652		1	
RFP250	155	Warner's Antihamaman ag[ains]t B[isho]p Burnett[293]	1679		1	6

---

[274] Clancy 304.
[275] Clancy 871.
[276] Clancy 400.
[277] Clancy 591.
[278] Clancy 573.
[279] Clancy 169.
[280] Clancy 694.
[281] Clancy 318–19.
[282] Clancy 845.
[283] Clancy 1064.
[284] Clancy 1066.
[285] Clancy 366–7.
[286] Clancy 91.
[287] Clancy 962.
[288] A later edition of Clancy 974.
[289] Allison and Rogers 711.
[290] Allison and Rogers 447.
[291] Clancy 1001.
[292] Clancy 52.
[293] Clancy 1050.

			£	s.	d.
RFP251 156	a net for fishers the old edition 2d edit[ion] Nath[aniel] Thompson[294]	1686		1	
RFP252 157	C. T.'s Layman his Ritual in two parts & of the Ceremonies[295]	1698		2	
RFP253 158	Hudleston's short & plain way & acc[oun]t of K[ing] Charles[296]	1688		1	
RFP254 159	A missive of consolation to the Catholicks[297]	1647		1	
RFP255 160	A defence of the Catholicks persecuted[298] doway	1630		1	
RFP256 161	An epistle of Comfort to the persecuted for Relig[ion] in Queen Elizabeth her days[299]			1	
RFP257 162	The great sacrafice of the new law expounded[300]	1685		2	
RFP258 163	B[isho]p of Condom's explication of the Catholick F[aith][301]	1686		1	
RFP259 164	H. W.'s meditations on the marks of the Church[302]	1655		1	
RFP260 166	J. M.'s Rememberance to pray for the dead 2 vols[303]	1660		2	
RFP261 167	Maria Triumphans or vindication of B. V. M.[304]	1635	1	6	
RFP262 171	[fol. 41r] Vaux's Christian doctrine[305]	1620			6
RFP263 172	Bellarmine ample Declaration of the Cathol[ick] doctrine[306]	1620			6
RFP264 173	Catachisme of the Christian doctrine[307] paris	1637			6
RFP265 174	Turbavill's abridgment of Christ[ian] doctrine[308]	1708			6
RFP266 175	A short & easy Introduction to the true faith of Christ	1692	1		8
RFP267 175a	Item an easy Guid to the true faith of Christ Church[309]	1692			

---

[294] Clancy 540 (second edition only).
[295] Clancy 969.
[296] Clancy 520–3.
[297] Clancy 655.
[298] Allison and Rogers 154.
[299] Allison and Rogers 781–3.
[300] Clancy 336–8.
[301] Clancy 120–2.
[302] Clancy 1099.
[303] Clancy 702.
[304] Allison and Rogers 562.
[305] Allison and Rogers 842.
[306] Allison and Rogers 92.
[307] Allison and Rogers 888.
[308] BBKS 2801.
[309] Neither 175 nor 175a appears in Clancy or in the British Library catalogue but it is likely that they were Catholic catechetical works in pamphlet form.

			£	s.	d.
RFP268 175b	Item an Abstract of doway Catachisme[310]	1688			
RFP269 176	Fleury's Historical Catachisme[311]	1704			4
RFP270 180	K[ing] Henry's primer Reprinted[312]	1545		1	6
RFP271 181a	Savonorola's verity of the Christian faith o. p.[313]	1651		2	
RFP272 181b	St Augustin's profit of believing[314]	1651			
RFP273 181c	& his care for the dead translated[315]	1651			
RFP274 182	The non entity of protestancy or discourse[316]	1633		1	
RFP275 183	of the sacrafice of the mass a manuscript				
RFP276 184	A Relation of a Conference before K[ing] James 2d printed 1722[317]	1686		1	6
RFP277 186	Edw[ard] Tesk's Armour of patience[318]	1558			6
RFP278 187	Lanspergius's epistle of J[esus] C[hrist] to the faithfull[319]	1595		1	
RFP279 188	J. Heigham's exposition of the Holy mass[320]	1614			8
RFP280 190	V. B.'s Catachisme of penance[321]	1685			6
RFP281 191	La selle his way to hear Mass[322]	1644		1	
RFP282 195	a primer of divout prayers[323]	1604		1	6
RFP283 196	A manual of prayers & litanies[324]	1614		1	
RFP284 197	Molina's spiritual Guid & dayly Common[325]	1688		1	6
RFP285 199	J. S.'s Invitation to a seeker[326]	1670		1	
RFP286 200	N. Smith alias Knot modest & brief discussion[327]	1630		3	
RFP287 201	Ejusdem's defence of the same discussion[328]	1631		1	
RFP288 324	[fol. 41v] St Gregory his dialogues translated[329]	1608		2	

---

[310] Clancy 9.
[311] BBKS 1052.
[312] *The Primer, set forth by the King's Majesty and his clergy* (London, 1545).
[313] Clancy 863.
[314] Clancy 45.
[315] Clancy 46.
[316] Allison and Rogers 22.
[317] BBKS 2451.
[318] I find no record of this book in the British Library catalogue.
[319] Allison and Rogers 438.
[320] Allison and Rogers 390.
[321] Clancy 185.
[322] An earlier edition of Clancy 581.
[323] Allison and Rogers 681.
[324] Allison and Rogers 509.
[325] Not listed in Clancy.
[326] Clancy 847.
[327] Allison and Rogers 898.
[328] Allison and Rogers 894.
[329] Allison and Rogers 367.

				£	s.	d.
RFP289 333	The roman martyrologe[330] st omer's	1667	2			
RFP290 334	The English martyrologe[331]	1640	2			
RFP291 335	Miracles wrought at our Lady of Montague[332]	1606	1			
RFP292 338	M. G.'s Acc[oun]t of the Jesuits life & doctrine[333]	1661	1			
RFP293 346	Martin Green's Answer to the provincial letters[334]	1679	3			
RFP294 348	A Case of Conscience signed by fourty of paris[335]	1703	1			
RFP295 384	[fol. 42r] Rules of the english sodality of the Conception[336]	1618		4		
RFP296 385	an abridgement of the said Rules[337] st omer	1672		2		
RFP297 386	The society of the Rosary, the pop's epistle &c[338]	1605		1	6	
RFP298 387	The Garden of the confraternaty of mount Carmel[339]	1652		6		
RFP299 388	The confraternaty of the Cord of St Francis[340]	16[54]		2		
RFP300 389	A. F.'s manual of the \3d/ order of St Francis[341]	1649	1			
RFP301 393	The Infallibility of the C[atholic]k ab[ou]t Rom[a]n Church proved out of the word[342]	1631		6		
RFP302 395	The prayers of St Brigit in honour of the sacred wounds[343]	1686		3		
RFP303 396	The manner of performing the novena &c to St F[rancis] Xaverius[344]	1700		4		
RFP304 397	Bona Mors or Art of dying happily in the congregation[345]	1714		8		
RFP305 398	An Account of the Conference in Nicholas Lane Feb[ruary] 13[346]	1735		6		
RFP306 399	divout Invocations of the most Holy name of Jesus[347]	1605		1		

---

330 Clancy 474.
331 Allison and Rogers 890.
332 Allison and Rogers 578.
333 Clancy 474.
334 Clancy 1299Y.
335 BBKS 465.
336 Allison and Rogers 744.
337 Possibly an earlier edition of BBKS 6.
338 Allison and Rogers 355.
339 Not listed in Clancy or the British Library catalogue.
340 Clancy 651.
341 Clancy 652.
342 Probably Clancy 1133.
343 Clancy 140.
344 Clancy 629.
345 BBKS 300.
346 *An Account of the Conference held in Nicholas-Lane, February 13th. 1734–5. Between Two Romish Priests, and some Protestant Divines* (London, 1735); not listed in BBKS.
347 Not recorded in Clancy or in the British Library catalogue.

				£	s.	d.
RFP307	402	Rules & Instructions for the sodality of the Im[maculate] concep[tion] w[i]th Appendix[348]	1703		1	
RFP308	405	The perfect Christian living & dying in contemplatio[n][349]	1700			3
RFP309	406	a short Catechism or abridgm[en]t of Ch[ristian] doctrine from french[350]	1687			2
RFP310	409	a short Christian doctrin of Bellarmine[351]	1674			4
RFP311	410	An Abstract of Douay Catachisme[352]	1725			2
RFP312	411	a short abridgm[en]t of Christian doctrine edit[ion] 7.[353]	1726		2	
RFP313	415	**[fol. 42v]** R Chandlers Catholick Christian Instructed in the sacraments[354]	1737		2	
RFP314	418	A manuscript of Controversie with an acc[oun]t of the Jesuits' order			1	
RFP315	421	A Caution ag[ains]t prejudice perticularly in matters of divotion[355]	1740			6
RFP316	423	D[r] Christ[opher] potter's want of Charitie Justly Charged &c[356]	1634			10
RFP317	424	A net for fishers of men[357] printed anno	1686		1	
RFP318	425	The Right Religion Evinced by L. B.[358] paris	1652		1	
RFP319	440	The Catholicks mirrour or Looking Glasse for protestants[359]	1662			10
RFP320	441	J. R. West Radfordus directory or discourse ag[ains]t the Heresies of the times[360]	1599		10	
RFP321	443a	Chalenders answer[361] [to C. Midleton's *Letter from Rome* (1729)]	1741			6
RFP322	443b	& Typper's answer anno[362]	1741			

---

[348] *Rules and instructions for the Sodality of the Immaculate Conception, of the most glorious and ever Virgin Mary, mother of God* (Dublin, 1703); not listed in BBKS.

[349] Christopher Tootell, *The Perfect Christian Living and Dying in Contemplation of Christ's Doctrine and Example* (London, 1700). Not listed in Clancy.

[350] Probably Clancy 980.

[351] Clancy 88.

[352] BBKS 10 (or similar).

[353] Probably BBKS 2536.

[354] BBKS 508.

[355] BBKS 275.

[356] Allison and Rogers 897.

[357] Clancy 540.

[358] Clancy 754.

[359] Clancy 187.

[360] Allison and Rogers 701.

[361] This was printed as an appendix to BBKS 508.

[362] Robert Pinkard, alias John Typper, was a Catholic translator; not listed in BBKS.

			£	s.	d.
RFP323 445	B[isho]p Chalender's martyrs 2 vol[umes] or memoirs of missionary pr[ie]sts[363]	1742		11	6
RFP324 448	Dod's reply to Constable in defence of his Church History intitled an Apology[364]	1742		3	6
RFP325 449	mr Cartiel's ord[inis] S[ocietatis] J[esu] entitled a short explanation of Indulgences[365]	1742		1	8
RFP326 450	B[isho]p Stoner's exercise of devotion for Sunday& holiday mornings &c[366]	1742		1	6
RFP327 451	The old religion by mr Chalender alias B[isho]p Fisher at augusta[367]	1742		2	6
RFP328 453	A selection of Catholick sermons 2 vols[368]	1741		11	
RFP329 454	The Spiritual Combat Englished by J. T.[369]	1742		2	6
RFP330 455	Mr Challender's letter to a frind concerning the Infallibility of the Church[370]	1743			4
RFP331 457	B[isho]p Bossuet's His History of the variations &c translated by mr musson S. J. 2 vol[umes][371]	1743		11	
RFP332 458	popish pagan refiction of a protestant heathen by Fr[ancis] Loraine ord[inis] St Francis[372]	1743		4	
RFP333 465	Mr Clarkson's letter ab[ou]t worship & invocation of Angles &c[373]	1742		1	

[fol. 44r] English 8° et 12° History Controversy &c

			£	s.	d.
RFP334 35	King James the second his life[374]	1705		3	6
RFP335 169	**[fol. 45r]** Memoirs of the Chevalier de St George[375]	1712		1	6
RFP336 169a	Item Jus sacrum or a discourse wherein &c[376]	1712			

---

[363] BBKS 607.
[364] Not listed in BBKS.
[365] Not listed in BBKS.
[366] BBKS 2606.
[367] BBKS 588–9.
[368] BBKS 2522.
[369] BBKS 2495.
[370] BBKS 693 (or similar).
[371] BBKS 333.
[372] Phillip Loraine, *A Popish Pagan the Fiction of a Protestant Heathen* (London, 1743); not listed in BBKS.
[373] Not listed in BBKS.
[374] Probably BBKS 2479 or 2480.
[375] *Memoirs of the Chevalier de St George with some private passages of the life of the late King James II. never before publish'd* (London, 1712); not listed in BBKS.
[376] *Jus Sacrum: or, A discourse wherein it is fully prov'd and demonstrated, that no Prince ought to be depriv'd of his natural right on account of Religion* (London, 1712); not listed in BBKS.

				£	s.	d.
RFP337	169b	Item a memorial of the Cheval[ie]r De St George[377]	1720			
RFP338	342	**[fol. 47r]** Cornucopia or Collection of Remarkable manuscript				6
RFP339	343	Choice Collections till an[no] Mundi 2526 manuscript				6
RFP340	344	a writting book with various Coppys	16			6
RFP341	351	St Francis Sales Intertainments[378]	1632		1	
RFP342	352	Ejusdem of the love of God by Carr[379]	1630		2	
RFP343	353	Ejusdem his spiritual director[380]	1703		1	
RFP344	354	Ejusdem his Introduction to a divout life[381]	1686		1	6
RFP345	356	St Bonaventure's Guid of divine love[382]	1642		1	6
RFP346	357	Fr Causin's Christian diary[383]	1648			6
RFP347	358	mr Austins devotions by way of Antient Office[s] [384] 12° Ant[werp]	1672			
RFP348	362	F. p.'s Christian sodality 1st p[ar]t in 3 volums[385]	1652		3	6
RFP349	364	de Avila his spiritual epistles[386]	1631		2	
RFP350	368	Whole Duty of a Christian as to faith & piety[387] Antwerp	1684		1	
RFP351	369	Southwell his works title page wanting[388]	16		1	6
RFP352	370	Ejusdem peters complaint & magdalins tears[389]	1620			6
RFP353	372	V. C.'s Christian Rules[390]	1659		1	
RFP354	373	Hilton his Ladder of perfection in 12°[391]	1659		2	
RFP355	374	B[isho]p Fisher his treatise of prayer[392]	1640		1	
RFP356	375	The poor man his mite concerning the Rosary[393]	1625			6

---

[377] *The Memorial of the Chevalier de St George, on occasion of the Princess Sobieski's retiring into a nunnery; and two original Letters, written by the Chevalier to the said Princess, to dissaude her from that design* (London, 1726); not listed in BBKS.
[378] Allison and Rogers 337.
[379] Allison and Rogers 343.
[380] BBKS 1113.
[381] Clancy 391.
[382] Clancy 113.
[383] Clancy 189.
[384] Clancy 57.
[385] Clancy 413.
[386] Allison and Rogers 54.
[387] Clancy 1097.
[388] Allison and Rogers 788–91.
[389] Allison and Rogers 786.
[390] Clancy 228.
[391] Clancy 498.
[392] Allison and Rogers 305.
[393] Allison and Rogers 74.

				£	s.	d.
RFP357 377	Fr Parsons his directory[394]		1650		3	6
RFP358 378	[fol. 47v] Fr Lud[ovici] Granatensis o.p. memorial of C[hristian] life vol 1[395]		1698		7	
RFP359 379	Ejusdem the second volum[e][396]		1699			
RFP360 381	Gobinet's Instruction of youth two volum[es][397]		1687		8	
RFP361 383	A spiritual retreat for one day in the month[398]		1704		2	
RFP362 385	Albertus magnus o.p. of adhering to God & Confer[ence with a lady][399]		165[4]		1	
RFP363 386	A. C. & T. V.'s dayly exercise of a divout Christ[ian][400]		1669		4	6
RFP364 387	Ejusdem Christian pilgrimage in his conflict[401]		1652		3	6
RFP365 388	The Key of paradise[402]		1631		1	6
RFP366 391	W. C. his little manual of the poor man's divotio[n][403]		1671		1	6
RFP367 392	The spiritual director for th[e]m that have none[404]		1703		1	6
RFP368 393	pious exercisses or divotion to the passion[405]		1687			6
RFP369 394	Vincent Bruno's meditation 4th part[406]		[1599]			6
RFP370 395	Granad's Rule o.p. or spiritual doctrine[407] Lovan		1599		1	6
RFP371 396	pensez bien or think well ont[408]		1673		1	
RFP372 397	The dayly exercise of a Christian life[409] paris		1684		1	6
RFP373 398	Burenzo his practice of meditation[410] mech[elin]		1613		1	
RFP374 399	Blosius his 7 exercises or meditations[411]		1686			6
RFP375 400	Bona Mors or art of dying happyly[412]		1709		1	
RFP376 401	Mr Gothers Instruction on the epistles[413]		1698		2	

---

[394] Clancy 766.
[395] Clancy 607.
[396] Clancy 608.
[397] Clancy 419.
[398] *A Spiritual Retreat for one day in every month* (London, 1703); not listed in BBKS.
[399] Clancy 19.
[400] Clancy 280.
[401] Clancy 872.
[402] Allison and Rogers 432.
[403] Clancy 231.
[404] BBKS 2781.
[405] Clancy 783.
[406] Allison and Rogers 175.
[407] Allison and Rogers 479.
[408] Clancy 77.
[409] Clancy 713.
[410] Allison and Rogers 106.
[411] Clancy 105.
[412] BBKS 298.
[413] Probably Clancy 449A.

				£	s.	d.
RFP377	402	Ejusdem Instructions for perticular estates[414]	1699		2	
RFP378	404	Ejusdem his afternoon Instructions two volum[e]s[415]	1699		4	
RFP379	406	Ejusdem Instructions for feasts two volum[e]s[416]	1699		4	
RFP380	407	Ejusdem his practical Catechisme[417]	1701		2	
RFP381	408	Ejusdem his Instruction for mass & Confession[418]	1705		2	
RFP382	409	Ejusdem his Rules for the Gosple[419]	1700		2	
RFP383	410	Ejusdem his instruction for the afflicted & sick[420]	1702		2	6
RFP384	411	Ejusdem his prayers for Lent[421]	1702		2	6
RFP385	413	Ejusdem prayers for sundays & holydays two volum[e]s[422]	1704		4	6
RFP386	414	Ejusdem Instructions for sundays on Gosples[423]	1698		2	
RFP387	415	Ejusdem his Instructions for Lent[424]	1704		4	
RFP388	416	Ejusdem his sinners Complaint[425]	1704		2	
RFP389	417	F. p's Christian solality 3 p[ar]ts in one volum[e][426]	1652		6	
RFP390	418	divotions to St Joseph[427]	1700		1	
RFP391	419	Thom[as] A Kempis of the Imitation of Christ[428]	1624		1	
RFP392	420	J W P's Key of paradise guilt[429]	1675		2	6
RFP393	421	[fol. 48r] Fotrias's little manuall of penance[430]	1621		1	6
RFP394	423	Causin's Christian diurnal Englished by J. H.[431]	1632		1	
RFP395	424	Kempis his Judg translated by G. M.[432]	1621		1	
RFP396	425	portha's spiritual Conflict[433]	1613			8

---

[414] Clancy 443.
[415] Clancy 431.
[416] Clancy 449.
[417] BBKS 1302.
[418] BBKS 1256.
[419] Clancy 469.
[420] BBKS 1237.
[421] BBKS 1306.
[422] BBKS 1309.
[423] Clancy 449A.
[424] BBKS 1272.
[425] BBKS 1322.
[426] Clancy 413.
[427] Clancy 76.
[428] Allison and Rogers 819 or 820.
[429] Clancy 571.
[430] Not listed in Allison and Rogers or the British Library catalogue.
[431] Allison and Rogers 215.
[432] Allison and Rogers 37.
[433] Allison and Rogers 761.

				£	s.	d.
RFP397	427	Card[ina]l Bona his Guid[e] to heaven In English[434]	1672		1	
RFP398	428	Thom[as] A Kempis his soliloquies translated by Carre[435]	1653		1	6
RFP399	429	St Augustin's Confessions translated by Wale[436]	1650		1	6
RFP400	430	de la serres sweet thoughts of death[437]	1632		1	
RFP401	431	A Kempis of the Immitation of J[esus] C[hrist] old edition[438]	1585			6
RFP402	433	2 books entitled manuscripts blank paper			5	
RFP403	434	sermons & prayers a manuscript			1	
RFP404	438	Austin his divotions in the Ancient way of offices paris[439]	1668		2	6
RFP405	439	A Christian directory &c divided into 3 book[s] F[ather] parsons Louv[ain][440]	1598		1	6
RFP406	442	F[ather] Causin his entertainments for Lent translated by a protestant[441]			1	
RFP407	443	Villa Castin his manual of divout meditations & exercises[442]	1618		1	
RFP408	454	A true Relation of the death of 2 Catholicks who suffered 1628[443]	1737		1	
RFP409	456	Clarkson's book of the Rosery or Introduction to the Celebrated dev[o]tion[444]	1737		1	
RFP410	457	Contemplations on the life & glory of holy mary mother of Jesus by J. C. DD.[445]	1685			4
RFP411	464	F Burgis his Annals of the Church five volum[e]s London[446]	1738	1	5	
RFP412	467	John Heigham's live of St Catharine of siena in 4 parts translated from Dr Catherinus Serensis by John Fene priest[447]	1609		1	8

---

[434] Clancy 110.
[435] Clancy 959.
[436] Clancy 1156W.
[437] Allison and Rogers 441.
[438] Allison and Rogers 814.
[439] Clancy 56.
[440] Probably Allison and Rogers 621.
[441] Clancy 195–201.
[442] Allison and Rogers 848.
[443] *A True and Exact Relation of the Death of Two Catholicks* (London, 1737); not listed in BBKS.
[444] BBKS 717.
[445] Clancy 679.
[446] BBKS 379.
[447] Raymond of Capua, *The Life of the Blessed virgin, Sainct Catharine of Siena Drawne out of all them that had written it from the beginning. And written in Italian by the reuerend Father, Doctor Caterinus*

			£	s.	d.
RFP413 469	[fol. 48v] A devout paraphrase on the 7 penitential psalms[448]	1741	1		
RFP414 470	The life of Christ & doctrine of our saviour J[esus] C[hrist] w[i]th short reflections for mental prayer in two parts[449] Gant	1656	1		
RFP415 471	Thom[ae] mori vita est exitus or the history of S[i]r Thom[as More][450]	1652	1	6	
RFP416 472	The Christian pilgrim in his Conflict & Conquest by A. C. et G. V. dub[lin][451]	1642	2	6	
RFP417 473	Mr Buckland's plain way to heauen (on the Gosples)[452]	1634	1	6	
RFP418 474	The primer an old edition of Roan[453] anno	1632		6	
RFP419 481	mr Rob[er]t mannings three volum[e]s of moral e[n]tertainments on the most [important practical truths of the Christian religion][454]	1742	10	6	
RFP420 492	The decalogue explained in 32 discourses &c by J. H.–C. And Hornyold[455]	1744	5		
RFP421 519	A Important enquiry of the nature of the Church reformation fully Cons[idere]d[456]	1751	2	1	
RFP422 520	William Wright's Consultation what Religion &c. translation from Lessius[457]	1621	1		

[fol. 49r] English 8° et 12° physick &c

			£	s.	d.
RFP423 83	[fol. 49v] Hunters manuscript			6	
RFP424 473	[fol. 50v] Instructions & Regulations 1754 by B[isho]p Chandler	[1754]		4	
RFP425 475	C[hall]anders Grounds of the old religion 2d edit[ion] 1742 Augusta	[1742]	2	6	
RFP426 478	The miraculous powers of the Church of Christ by walton[458]	[1756]		4	

Senensis. And now translated into Englishe out of the same Doctor, by Iohn Fen priest & confessar to the Englishe nunnes at Louaine (Douai, 1609). Not listed in Allison and Rogers.
[448] BBKS 276.
[449] Not recorded in Clancy or the British Library catalogue.
[450] Clancy 502.
[451] Clancy 872.
[452] Allison and Rogers 398.
[453] Allison and Rogers 694.
[454] BBKS 1746.
[455] BBKS 1461.
[456] BBKS 2423.
[457] Allison and Rogers 457.
[458] BBKS 2910.

				£	s.	d.
RFP427	489	A caveat ag[ains]t the Methodists by B[isho]p Challoner 1760	[1760]			8
RFP428	491	Granatensis sinner Guid[459] edition 1761 4sh 6d	[1761]		4	6

[fol. 51r] Books as duplicat[e]s & not mention[e]d in the Catalogue before & pamphlets

In folio

				£	s.	d.
RFP429	1	Heskings parliament of Christ ag[ains]t Juell[460] Antwerp	1566		3	6

In quarto

				£	s.	d.
RFP430	1	Fisher agaynst white the nine points of Controv[ersy][461]	1626		2	6
RFP431	2	worthington's Anker of Christian doctrine[462]	1618		1	6
RFP432	3	Kellingson again[s]t sutcliff[463]	1608		1	
RFP433	4	Richom's pilgrime of Loretto[464]	1629		1	6
RFP434	5	Gothers good advice to the pulpets[465]	1687		1	
RFP435	7	Fr parson's discussion[466]	1612		1	6
RFP436	8	Cressey his two Questions[467]	1686		1	
RFP437	9	Gother's protesting ag[ains]t protestant popery[468]	1686		1	6
RFP438	10	Rational discov[e]ry Concerning transubstantiation[469]	1676			6
RFP439	11	B[isho]p Meaux his pastoral Letter to the new Cath[olics][470]	1686		1	6
RFP440	12	A vindication of the Rom[a]n Catholicks of the Eng[lish] Nation[471]	1660			6

---

[459] BBKS 1689.
[460] Allison and Rogers 393.
[461] Allison and Rogers 605.
[462] Allison and Rogers 910.
[463] Allison and Rogers 426.
[464] Allison and Rogers 715.
[465] Clancy 438–9.
[466] Allison and Rogers 628.
[467] Probably Clancy 267.
[468] Clancy 463.
[469] Clancy 530.
[470] Clancy 124.
[471] Clancy 172.

				£	s.	d.
RFP441	19	Six more of Ward's History of Reform[ation] In canto's[472]	1710	1	10	
RFP442	30	[fol. 51v] Dryden's Hind & Panther[473]	1687		1	6
RFP443	35	Introductio ad philosophiam manuscript	1684		1	6
RFP444	36	Logica Aristotelis &c manuscrip[t]	1684			

In octavo

				£	s.	d.
RFP445	2	Manning his Case stated answer to Lesley two volum[e]s[474]	1721		10	
RFP446	9	The Roman martiologey[475] dupl[icate]	1667		1	6
RFP447	10	L[or]d Castlemains Apologie 3d edition	1674		4	
RFP448	11	N. N.'s polititians Catachisme[476]	1658		3	
RFP449	12	The Colledge of Turney's Catechisme[477]	1647		1	
RFP450	16	J. Sim[pson] Catholicks not Idolaters[478]	1688			4
RFP451	17	Kains's Catholicon first part[479]	1672			6
RFP452	18	A Consultation ab[ou]t Religion[480]	1693		1	
RFP453	19	Cressy's R[oman] Catholick doctrine no novelties	1663		1	6
RFP454	24	Sargent Reason ag[ains]t Raillery[481]	1672		1	
RFP455	25	ejusdem his letter of Thanks[482]	1666		1	
RFP456	26	Cain's fiat Lux[483]	1662		1	
RFP457	27	Rushworth's dialogues[484]	1640		1	6
RFP458	28	scots treatise of scisme[485]	1650		1	
RFP459	29	Veron his Rule of faith[486]	1668		1	
RFP460	41	[fol. 52r] Catachisme of the Councel of trent english[487]	1687		2	

---

[472] BBKS 2917.
[473] Clancy 327–31.
[474] BBKS 1737.
[475] Clancy 474.
[476] Clancy 396.
[477] Clancy 312.
[478] A later edition of Clancy 420; not listed in Clancy.
[479] Clancy 167.
[480] Edmund Lechmere, *A Consultation about Religion, or, What religion is best to be chosen* (London, 1693). Not listed in Clancy.
[481] Clancy 895.
[482] Clancy 887.
[483] Clancy 162.
[484] Allison and Rogers 745.
[485] Clancy 871.
[486] Clancy 1001.
[487] Clancy 184.

				£	s.	d.
RFP461 46	Rules of the sodality of Immaculate Concep[tion][488]	1659				2
RFP462 47	Bona Mors, or Art of dying Happily[489]	1710				9
RFP463 48	Rules of the sodality of Im[maculate] Concept[ion] edition[490]	1623				1
RFP464 49	Bona his Guid to Heaven In English[491]	1672			1	
RFP465 50	Francis sales spiritual directer[492]	1704				1
RFP466 51	Bossuet's exposition of the doctrine of the Cath[olic] Church[493]	1786			1	
RFP467 54	The society of the Rosary reprinted[494]	1687			1	
RFP468 59	Candler's profession of faith extracted &c three[495]	1732			1	6
RFP469 64	The society of the Rosarie[496] st omer's	1624				6
RFP470 65	A primmer sine titulo[497]	1600			1	
RFP471 66	A manual of prayers [*illeg.*][498] \Given to m. nice/	1671			1	
RFP472 67	mr mannings England's conversion & reformation Compared[499] \given to nice/	1725			4	
RFP473 69	Gothers Instructions for Sundays Gosple & epistles two vol[umes][500]	1698			1	6
RFP474 70	puente's first part of meditations on the mysteries of faith[501]	1610			1	
RFP475 71	Chandler's specimen of the spirit of the dissenting teachers[502]	1736			2	
RFP476 72	ditto	1736			2	
RFP477 73	ditto	1736			2	
RFP478 80	[fol. 52v] abstract of doway Catachism for Children[503]	1725				2

---

[488] A later edition of Allison and Rogers 744, not recorded in Clancy.
[489] BBKS 299.
[490] A later edition of Allison and Rogers 744, not recorded in Allison and Rogers.
[491] Clancy 110.
[492] BBKS 1113.
[493] BBKS 328.
[494] A later printing of Allison and Rogers 355, not recorded in Clancy.
[495] BBKS 624.
[496] A later printing of Allison and Rogers 355, not recorded in Allison and Rogers.
[497] Probably Allison and Rogers 680.
[498] Probably Clancy 640A.
[499] BBKS 1739.
[500] Clancy 447.
[501] Allison and Rogers 696.
[502] BBKS 662.
[503] Not listed in BBKS; possibly an earlier edition of BBKS 13.

				£	s.	d.
RFP479	81	Bellermin's short Catachism Revised[504]	1688			2
RFP480	93	Ten more books of the Rosary by Clarkson[505]	1737		10	
RFP481	95	first volum[e] of mr Burgis's Annal of the Church edit[ion] dup[licate][506]	1737		2	6
RFP482	96	A short & easy Method of Catechising lesser children &c manuscrip[t]			2	
RFP483	101	F[ather] parsons Christian directory[507] (Lent to marshall) 12°	1622		1	6
RFP484	104	Lud[ovicus] Granada of prayer & meditation[508] Imperfect Rouen	1584			6
RFP485	112	Chambers translation of the miracles of numan dup[licate][509]	1606		1	
RFP486	114	The only way to Rest of the soule in Religion &c missing title page[510]	1657			2
RFP487	114	Godden's just discharges ag[ains]t stillifleet dup[licate][511]	1677		1	6
RFP488	115	[fol. 53r] Gother's Instructions for Lent on the epistles dup[licate][512]	1695			6
RFP489	116	J.'s Invitation to a Seeker dup[licate][513]	1670			6
RFP490	117	N. N.'s Method to arrive at satisfaction in Religion dup[licate][514]	1677			4
RFP491	124	The following of Christ, st Barnards epistle, Mirandula rules[515]	1615		1	
RFP492	125	Jasper Loarte exercise of a Christian life[516] supra 486	1579			6
RFP493	125	first volum[e] of missionary priests by Chanlender[517]	1741		5	6
RFP494	126	Rushworth's Dialogues paris edition by white[518]	1654			6

---

504 Clancy 90.
505 BBKS 716 or 717.
506 BBKS 378.
507 Allison and Rogers 624.
508 Allison and Rogers 477.
509 Allison and Rogers 578.
510 Clancy 591.
511 Clancy 421
512 Clancy 445 or 446.
513 Clancy 847.
514 Clancy 890.
515 Allison and Rogers 816.
516 Allison and Rogers 462.
517 BBKS 607.
518 Clancy 845.

				£	s.	d.
RFP495	128	Instructions for the whole year by Gother part 2 et 4th 2 vol[umes][519]	1698		1	6
RFP496	129	Gother's Instructions for Confession & Communion dup[licate][520]	1692			6
RFP497	130	Turbovill's abridgment of Christian doctrine with proofs &c[521]	1661			10
RFP498	131	Sales's Introduction to a divout life fine title page				6
RFP499	133	Roman martyologie[522]	1627			6
RFP500	135	The office of the Blessed virgin mary 12vo[523]	1633			2
RFP501	136	ditto without title page	[1633]			2
RFP502	138	A Catalogue of divers visible professors of the Catholick faith &c[524]	1614			2
RFP503	139	pia desideria by Hermanno Hugo ant[werp][525]	1645			6
RFP504	144	Luke pinellis meditations on the B[lessed] sacram[en]t by J. W.[526]	1622			4
RFP505	146	devout treateses by John Heigham[527]	1624			6
RFP506	148	Cressy's questions why are you a Catholick, why a protest[ant] 2d edit[ion][528]	1673			6
RFP507	154	two of mrs Gother's sincere Christian's Guid[e] edit[ion][529]	1744		3	
RFP508	155	A friend of mr Chandler's Grounds of the Old Religion[530]	1741		1	6
RFP509	169	[fol. 53v] Instructions for the time of the Jubely 1751 with meditations &c by B[isho]p Chandler[531]	[1751]			6
RFP510	172	Mr Chandler's profession of Catholick 2d[532]	1732			6
RFP511	176	Ordo Baptizandi aliaq[ue] sacramenta administrandi et officia quaedam ecclesiastica &c.[533]	1686		1	

---

[519] Clancy 447 and 449A.
[520] An earlier edition of BBKS 1256; not recorded in Clancy.
[521] Clancy 975.
[522] Allison and Rogers 536.
[523] Allison and Rogers 684 or 687.
[524] Possibly Allison and Rogers 916.
[525] An earlier edition of Clancy 526; not recorded in Clancy.
[526] Allison and Rogers 649.
[527] Probably Allison and Rogers 391.
[528] Clancy 266.
[529] BBKS 1320.
[530] BBKS 588.
[531] BBKS 602.
[532] BBKS 624.
[533] Clancy 746.

			£	s.	d.
RFP512 177	Ordo missae aliorum sacramentorum pro Anglia by Benedi[ct XIV][534]			1	6
RFP513 181	Instructions & advice to Catholicks on the occasion of the late dreadfull earth quakes by mr Chandler vi[delicet] another edit[ion] of the Instr[uction] for the Jubely as above no 169[535]	[1750]		1	6

[fol. 55r] quartos

			£	s.	d.
RFP514 4	Roman Catholick principles in Reference to God& the King[536] an[no]	1688		2	
RFP515 5	A letter to both houses concerning proceedings ag[ains]t R[oman] Catholicks[537]	1679		2	
RFP516 16	Fell's s[ain]ts lives 4 volum[e]s twoo tomes[538]	1729	10		
RFP517 19	Fitzherbets suppliment to parsons discussion 1613 q[uar]to[539]	[1613]		3	6
RFP518 20	Fitz Herbets adjoynder to the supplement 1613 supra 240. p. 38. and no. 16 pag[e] 36 parsons discussion edit[ion] 1612[540]	[1613]		2	6
RFP519 20a	Talen's Holy History by wincester quarto 1653[541] well Bound	[1653]		5	

[fol. 55v] In octavos & 12°s

			£	s.	d.
RFP520 20	Meigham's Catalogue 1749 1d[542]	[1749]			1

---

[534] BBKS 2104–8.
[535] BBKS 596.
[536] Clancy 251.
[537] Clancy 750.
[538] BBKS 1035.
[539] Allison and Rogers 318.
[540] Allison and Rogers 309.
[541] Nicholas Talon, *The Holy History* (London, 1653); not listed in Clancy.
[542] Thomas Meighan (d. 1753) was one of the principal Catholic publishers in mid-eighteenth-century England (BBKS, p. xi).

33. [CUL Hengrave MS 76/1] *Marriage settlement of Thomas Rookwood Gage and Lucy Knight, 28 February 1746 (summary by John Gage)*

28th February 1746. Indenture of appointment between Lucy Knight the elder of Kingerby in the County of Lincoln widow of William Knight of Kingerby Esq[ui]re deceased 1st part, Lucy Knight Spinster daughter of the said Lucy Knight 2d part, Elizabeth Gage widow and Thomas Rookwood otherwise Gage eldest son and heir apparent of the said Elizabeth Gage 3d part, George Markham Esq[ui]re, John Southcote Esq[ui]re and James Ward Gentleman 4th part, Sir Robert Throckmorton Bar[one]t and James Boulton Doctor of Physic 5th part, the Hon[oura]ble Marmaduke Langdale 6th part and Sir Cordel Firebrace Bar[one]t 7th part. Being a settlement in contemplation of the marriage of the said Thomas Rookwood Gage with the said Lucy Knight the younger of her Estate consisting of the fourth part of the Manor of Imingham and the fourth part of the Rectory and Advowson of Imingham & certain farms in Imingham & other Parishes in Lincolnshire, which heredit[ament]s had been conveyed to or in trust for the said Lucy Knight the younger under Ind[entu]res dated 26 & 27 July 1744 by her only surviving brother Richard Knight (on his entering the Society of Jesus) & which heredit[ament]s descended to him by virtue of certain Ind[entu]res therein recited, particularly, Ind[entu]res of Lease & Release dated 24 and 25 March 1724, the Release made between Edward Greathead D[octo]r in Physic and Henry Boulton Gentleman 1st part, the s[ai]d William Knight and Lucy his wife & William Knight the younger since dec[ease]d son of the said William Knight & Lucy his wife & the said Richard Knight and Lucy Knight the younger 2d part & William Claux of Caversfield in the County of Buckingham Gent[leman] 3d part.

34. [CUL Hengrave MS 76/1] *Will of Elizabeth Rookwood, 16 November 1758 (summary by John Gage)*

16 Nov[embe]r 1658 [sic] Will of Elizabeth Gage late of Coldham Hall widow whereby she ordered her body to be buried in the same tomb with her late husband John Gage in the Church of Stanningfield in the most private manner, with six of the poor men of the parish to carry her to her grave, to each of whom she desired that 5 shillings might be given. among other legacies she bequeathed to her son John Gage £100, besides certain annuities which she had settled upon him. she bequeathed to her son Thomas Rookwood otherwise Gage all her silver plate (excepting such articles as are therein specified which she gave to her son John Gage) and the plate, furniture & household linen which the testatrix left at Coldham in the year 1749: and after directing a legacy of fifty pounds to be paid to her little God-daughter Elizabeth Gage, when she attained 21 years of age, the testatrix gave the residue of her personal estate to her eldest son Thomas Gage, appointing him and her son John Gage Ex[ecut]ors.

16 Nov[embe]r 1658 [sic.] Codicil to the Will whereby she made a further provision for her son John Gage and gave him & her son Thomas Rookwood Gage certain specific legacies therein mentioned. The Will & Codicil were proved by the said Thomas Rookwood otherwise Gage in the Prerogative Court of Canterbury 3rd Sept[ember] 1762.

35. [CUL Hengrave MS 76/2/31] *Will of John Martin of Long Melford, 24 June 1757*

In the Name of God Amen I John Martin of Long Melford in the County of Suffolk Gentleman Do make this my last Will and Testament in the manner following, that is to say, In the first Place I bequeath and recommend my Soul to God the Almighty my Maker and my Redeemer by whose Merits I hope for Pardon and Life Eternal and my Body I leave to the Earth to be privately yet decently interred at the Will of my Executors hereafter named or to be named. And as to such Estate with which it has pleased God to bless me I thus dispose of it / that is to say / In the first Place it is my express Will and Desire that all my just Debts due at the Time of my death should be discharged and justly paid. Item to the Servant living with me at the time of my death I give a Years Wages over and above what then shall otherways be due. Item I give and bequeath to Thomas Gage Rookwood of Coldham Hall Suffolk Esq[ui]r[e] and to Mr Antony Hatton now or late of Tong in Yorkshire Gentleman my funeral Charges being first duly paid all the Residue and Remainder of my Estate be it personal Copyhold or real or of whatsoever Nature they shall be with all my Monies Houses Goods Bonds Debts Mortgages Credits or other Estate whatsoever I shall at the Time of my death be possessed of with all Interest every Right and Title whether in Possession reversion or Remainder thereunto belonging for and to the sole Use and Behoof of them the said Thomas Gage Rookwood Esq[ui]r[e] and Antony Hatton their Heirs and Assignees for ever not expressly otherways mentioned and disposed of in this my last Will and Testament. Lastly I do hereby make Constitute and appoint nominate and ordain Thomas Gage Rookwood Esq[ui]r[e] and Antony Hatton Gentleman both above mentioned and Mrs Elizabeth Pittman Widow of Salisbury to be the three Executors of this my last Will and Testament which I do hereby declare and publish as such revoking likewise hereby all other Wills Testaments and Executors by me before this time willed or bequeathed all which I do now annul and make void hereby ratifying and confirming this to be my last Will and Testament bearing Date this twenty fourth of June One thousand seven hundred and fifty seven. In Witness whereof I the said John Martin have to this my last Will and Testament set my Hand and Seal John Martin

Signed sealed published delivered and declared by the said John Martin for and as his last Will and Testament in our Presence and imediately afterwards in the Presence of the said John Martin this last Will was attested and subscribed by us Benj[amin] Carter Hard. S. Richardson. Dansie Carter.[543]

---

[543] Proved on 9 April 1761. The original will is PRO 11/864/261.

36. [CUL Hengrave MS 76/2/32] *Indenture for the sale of lands inherited from John Martin, 29 March 1761*

Articles of Agreement indented made concluded and agreed upon this Twenty Ninth day of March One thousand Seven hundred and Sixty one Between Thomas Rookwood Gage of Coldham Hall in the County of Suffolk Esquire one of the two Devisees of the Real Estate of John Martin late of Long Melford in the same County Esquire deceased of the one part and Rogers Jortin of the Exchequer Office Lincolns Inn in the County of Middlesex Gentleman of the other part as follow (vi[delice]t)

First the said Thomas Rookwood Gage in consideration of the Sum of Two hundred and twenty three pounds to be paid to him by the said Rogers Jortin pursuant to the Covenant and agreement herein after in that behalf contained for the Purchase of the \Moiety of the/ Freehold and Copyhold Lands and Hereditaments in the County of Suffolk hereinafter mentioned and of the Sum of Twenty Seven Pounds to be in like manner paid to him for the purchase of the Freehold Messuage or Tenement and premisses in the County of Essex herein after also mentioned for himself his Heirs Executors and Administrators Doth Covenant promise and agree to and with the said Rogers Jortin his Heirs and Assigns by these presents That he the said Thomas Rookwood Gage or his Heirs Shall and will at his and their own Expence on or before the Twenty Ninth day of September now next ensuring by good and effectual Conveyances Surrenders and Assurances in the Law well and effectually Convey Surrender and assure or Promise to be well and effectually Conveyed Surrendered and assured unto and to the use of the said Rogers Jortin his heirs and Assigns for ever \or to such other person or persons as he or they shall direct and appoint/ free from Incumbrances The Moiety or one full undivided half part the same into two equal parts to be divided of the ffreehold \and/ Customary \or/ Copyhold Lands and Hereditaments herein after mentioned and devised bv the Will of the said John Martin (vi[delice]t) of a ffreehold Messuage or Tenement and Garden and of about Three acres of Land with the Appurtenances late in the Possession of the said John Martin and estimated to be worth to be let about the yearly Rent of ffifteen pounds and of a ffreehold Messuage or Tenement with the Appurtenances now divided into four Tenements \such tenements/ now or late Separately rented by Henry Norman at Two Pounds ten Shillings a year Thomas North at Two pounds ffifteen Shillings a year Thomas Airy at one pound & eighteen Shillings a year & William King at Three pounds & twelve Shillings a year and of a Customary or Copyhold Messuage or Tenement with the Appurtenances now divided into two Tenements such Tenements now or late Separately by John Blyth at Two pounds & ffifteen Shillings a year and John Metcalfe at Two pounds a year and of a Customary or Copyhold Messuage with the Appurtenances now divided into Three Tenements such Tenements now or late Separately rented by Ambrose Martin at Two pounds & ten Shillings a year Edmund Totman at one pounds & Seventeen Shillings a year and Isaac Lewis at two Pounds a year and of a Customary \or/ Copyhold Messuage or Tenement with the Appurtenances now divided into two Tenements such Tenements now or late Separately rented by Mrs Dow Widow at Two pounds \&/ four Shillings a year and Zephaniah Langley at Two pounds & four Shillings a year and of a Customary or Copyhold Messuage or Tenement with the Appurtenances now divided into two Tenements such Tenements now or late Separately rented by Peter Lee at Two pounds and ten Shillings a year and James Salter at Two pounds a year All which said Several Messuages or Tenements Lands and Hereditaments are Situate and being in Melford and County of Suffolk \aforesaid/ and also of a piece of Ground Situate in Glemsford in the \said/ County of

Suffolk on which latly stood a Copyhold or Customary Messuage or Tenement with a Croft and Pightle of Land and Pasture called Pondwick Pightle estimated half an Acre with the Appurtenances Situate in ffoxhearth in the County of Essex now rented by Elizabeth Macro at Two Pounds five Shillings and three pence a year.

And the Said Rogers Jortin for and in Consideration of the said Conveyances and Surrenders so to be respectively made as aforesaid for himself his Heirs Executors and Administrators Doth Covenant Promise and Agree to and with the said Thomas Rookwood Gage his Executors Administrators and Assigns by these presents That he the said Rogers Jortin his Heirs Executors Administrators or Assigns shall and will immediately at and upon the making and executing such Conveyances and Surrenders respectively as aforesaid of the said Moiety of the said Premisses in the said County of Suffolk well and truly pay or cause to be paid unto the said Thomas Rookwood Gage his Executors Administrators or Assigns the said Sum of Two hundred and twenty three \pounds/ for the purchase of the same Moiety and immediately at and upon making and executing such Conveyance as aforesaid of the said Moiety of the said Premisses in the said County of Essex well and truly pay or cause to be paid to the said Thomas Rookwood Gage his Executors Administrators or Assigns the said Sum of Twenty Seven pounds for the purchase of the same Moiety.

And it is hereby agreed That the said Rogers Jortin his Heirs Executors Administrators or Assigns shall have and be intitled to the Rents Issues and profits of the said Moiety of the said premisses in Suffolk and Essex so Contracted to be Sold to him as aforesaid to arrive and become due at Michaelmas next old or New Stile as the same shall happen to become due and payable. In Witness whereof the parties to these presents have hereunto Set their hands and Seals the day and year first above written.

Tho[ma]s Rookwood Gage
Rogers Jortin

Sealed and Delivered by the above named Thomas Rookwood Gage and Rogers Jortin being first duly Stamped with a ffive Shillings Stamp in the presence of us \ [*illeg.*] the name – Rogers Jortin – being first wrote on a raisure throughout And the words – 'Or to such other person or persons as he or they shall direct and appoint – and also several other Words being first interlined/

Hen[ry] Hutton
James Hutton

37. [Birmingham Archdiocesan Archives C2240] *'Memoirs of the Family of Rookwood of Stanningfield in Suffolk' (extracts) by John Gage, 2 March 1818*

[fol. 1r] Sir Alan de Rokewode in the 30th year of King Edward I[544] was seized of lands in Acton, Suffolk, in right of his wife Elizabeth daughter & coheir of Walter son of Henry de Clerbecke of Acton, which Elizabeth surv[iv]ing Alan de Rokewode married Walter de Hadbovil. Rokewode bore for arms six Chef Rooks Sable. Clerbecke, ermine three bars gules, upon each, three crosses patés or. Sir Alan de Rokewode by Eliz[abe]th left issue Robert de Rokewode, who married Marg[are]t daughter of Sir Michael de Bures K[nigh]t whose coat was ermine on a chief indented sable, two Lions Rampant or. Margaret de Bures was the widow of John de Scotland of Stoke Nayland and her son William de Scotland in the 9th y[ear] of King Edward III released to his mother and her husband Robert de Rokewode [fol. 1v] The manor of Scotland Hall which remains in possession of the representative of the Rookwood family. There was issue of Robert de Rokewode by Marg[are]t, several children of whom Sir Robert de Rokewode the eldest in the 21. Edward III represented together with Sir Robert de Howel the Shire of Suffolk. By Mariatta d[aughte]r of Sir — Waylande K[nigh]t whose shield displayed on a crosse gules, five escallops or, he had issue Richard the son of Edmund de Ilighe K[nigh]t in the 32. Edw[ard] III granted the Manor of Stanningfield with the app[ur]t[enances] in the towns of Stanningfield, Brockley, Little Whelnetham, Great Whelnetham, Ilighe Combust, and Bury St Edmunds in Suffolk. Which Manor continues Vested in the representative of the family. In the 34th Edw[ard] III Sir John de Rokewode & Richard de Martlesham were Knights of the Shire of Suffolk. And in the 42 y[ea]r of the same reign he and Sir Richard [fol. 2r] de Hamenhale represented the County. Cavendish Lord Chief Justice of England who was murdered at Bury St Edmunds app[oin]t[e]d Sir Robert Swynborne & Sir John de Rokewode w[itnesse]s of his will dated in 1381. By Joan d[aughte]r of Sir Rob[er]t Swynborne whose arms were Or a chevron sable three bears heads couped or Sir John de Rokewode had issue Thomas who died without issue and Sir John de Rokewode the y[ounge]r who married Eleanora d[aughte]r & coheir of Sir William de Burgate K[nigh]t by Eleanora d[aughte]r of Sir Thomas Visdelou K[nigh]t which Sir William de Burgate was son & coheir of Peter Burgate whose father Baldwin de Burgate married the Heiress of Robert de Swynford. The shield of Sir William de Burgate was quarterly 1st and 4th paly of six argent and sable for Burgate. 2nd and 3d a chevron between three bears heads gules for Swynford.

[fol. 2v contains a family tree of the medieval Rookwoods]

[fol. 3r] Ambrose Rookwood the 6th son born the 20th September 1664 had the Command of a Brigade in King James II Guards & followed that Monarch to St Germains[.] This officer was implicated in what is called the Barclay Conspiracy. On the 21. April 8th y[ea]r of King William III he was Indicted together with Major Lowick and Charles Cranburn for high treason in conspiring the death of his Majesty[.] The overt acts were consulting and agreeing how to kill the King and finding arms and horses for the purpose. Rookwood pleaded not guilty & requested that his brother might come to him in prison & that he might be allowed the use of pen Ink & paper which were granted. After an adjournment of the Court Rookwood was brought to the bar Sir B Shower & Mr. Phipps were his Counsell & the witnesses for the prosecution

---

[544] John Gage's note: 'From a MS Intituled "Vestustissima Prosapia Rokewodorum de Stanningfeld in Comitate Suffolciae" in the possession of Robert Gage Rookwood Esq. of Coldham Hall Suffolk'.

were Capt[ai]n Harris & Capt[ai]n Porter both of Rookwoods Brigade. It appeared in evidence that at a meeting at the Kings Head tavern Capt[ai]n Porter putting the question to Ambrose Rookwood if they were to be the murderers of the Prince **[fol. 3v]** of Orange Rookwood said "I am afraid we are drawn into some such business but if I had known it before I had come over I should have begged her Kings \pardon/ at St Germains & not have come over hither." That at a meeting in Red Lion fields on the remonstrance of Harris, that it was a barbarous act, Major Lowick Answered, they were to obey orders. And Rookwood on their appealing to him, exclaimed "It was a barbarous thing but he was sent over to obey Sir John Barclays orders which he was resolved to do. And that at a meeting at the Globe Tavern Rookwood remonstrated with Sir George Barclay who turning to him said he must obey his orders for he held a commission for the purpose to which Rookewood replied in French "There's is an end of it," a chief point in evidence against Rookewood was his delivering some written orders from Sir John Barclay cont[ainin]g a list of the names of those persons who were to be under the immediate command of Rokewood. The Jury retired for a quarter of an hour and found Rokewood guilty & the next day he, Cranburne, and Lowick, were sentanced to be hung drawn & quartered which sentance was executed on the 29th of the same month of April at Tyburne. Rookwood at the place of execution delivered an address which after his death was printed in the following form.

[fol. 4r is a transcription of Ambrose Rookwood's final speech, reproduced in this volume as document 9]

[fol. 4v] The seventh son of Ambrose Rookwood and Elizabeth Caldwell before ment[ione]d was John born 13th February 1665 and living in 1730. he was a Religious of the order of St Francis.

Charles Rookwood the 8th son was born april 21. 1671.

[fol. 5r] Ambrose Rookwood the 7th in lineal descent from Sir John de Rokewode & Eleanor Burgate was implicated in the Gunpowder plot and suffered death 31. Jan[uary] 1605. Dod says "The Indictment against Ambrose Rookwood was being acquainted with the treason, taking the Sacrament And an oath of secrecy. he owned thus far that he was privy to the transaction being drawn in by Mr Catesby but it did not appear that he had any knowledge of the design ag[ains]t the Parliament house." The State trials give the following report of the speech made by Ambrose Rookwood at his trial. "he first excused his denial of the Indictment for that he had rather lose his life than give it. thus did he acknowledge his offence to be so heinous that he justly deserved the indignation of the King and of the Lords And the hatred of the whole Commonwealth yet could he not dispair of mercy at the hands of a Prince so abounding in grace and mercy And the rather because his offence though it was incapable of any excuse yet not altogether **[fol. 5v]** incapable of some continuation in that he had been neither Author nor Actor but only persuaded & drawn in by Catesby whom he loved above any Worldly Man And that he had concealed it not for any malice to the person of the King or to the state or for any Ambitious Respect of his own but only drawn from the tender respect and the faithful and dear affection he bore Mr Catesby his friend whom he loved more than any thing in this world. And this mercy he desired not for fear of the image of death but for grief that so shameful a death should leave a perpetual blemish and blot unto all ages upon his name and blood" &cc.

at the place of execution he delivered a speech much to the same effect, which is reported in a scarce tract Intituled "The Arraignement and execution of the late traytors With a relation of the other traytors which were executed at Worcester the 27 of January last past, London Imprinted for Jeffrey Chorlton And are to be sold at his shop at the Great North doore of Powles 1606."

Ambrose Rookwood married Elizabeth **[fol. 6r]** daughter of Robert Tyrwhitt of Kettleby in the County of Lincoln <Esq> whose ancient coat of arms in gules three cranes or. probably this Robert Tyrwhitt is the personage of whose sufferings for the Catholic Religion Dod speaks \in his/ 1st Vol[ume] p. <56>. <and> \or/ perhaps it was the marriage of Ambrose Rookwood and Elizabeth Tyrwhitt that gave rise to the following occurrence

"William Tyrwhite[545] son of Sir Robert Tyrwhite accused for having heard mass at his sisters Wedding was carried prisoner to the Tower notwithstanding he was actually sick with a high fever And the Physicians declared he was a dead man if they removed him <from> \to/ prison in that condition. his friends offered any bail for his appearance as soon as he should recover but all in Vain he was hurried away sick as he was and died within two days. his Robert Tyrwhite was also for the same cause cast into prison and there died".

[fol. 6v] may not the mind of Ambrose Rookwood have been inflamed by the Severity with which the penal laws had been exercised against his Wife's relations? if thei had no operation, the reader shall draw what Conclusion he pleases from the following facts connected with the history of the Rookwoods.

[fols 6v–8r contain a digression on the Rookwoods of Euston]

[fol. 8r] To return to the family of Rookwood of Stanningfield. Ambrose by Elizabeth Tyrwhit had issue Sir Robert Rookwood <Knighted by King Charles> and Henry.

Sir Robert Rookwood of Stanningfield knighted by King Charles Ist married Mary da[ughter] of Sir Robert Townsend Kt whose arms were azure a chevron ermine between three escallops arg[en]t by her he had a numerous issue Robert the second son born Nov[embe]r 12th **[fol. 8v]** 1624 was a capt[ain] in the army and fell at Oxford in the Royal Cause. of the daughters Mary the eldest born 17 Nov[ember] 1723 and Frances born 8th Feb[ruar]y 1725 were nuns & both became Superiors of the English poor Clares at Dunkirk. See Dods Church History.

Ambrose Rookwood of Stanningfield the eldest son of Sir Robert Rookwood who died in the year 1679, married Eliz[abe]th the d[aughte]r and coheir of Caldwell whose arms were or a cross formé sable. he had issue eight sons and five daughters.

Robert the eldest died without issu. Ambrose the second son died an infant. Thomas the 3d And eldest surviving son became heir to his father. Henry the fourth son born 8th Nov[embe]r 1659 was a priest of the Society of Jesus and dying in <the year> 1730 was buried at Stanningfield April 21 in the same year. Francis Rookwood the 5th son <living in 1730> was a religious.

[fol. 9r] of the daughter of Ambrose Rookwood & Elizabeth Caldwell. Mary the eldest born 10th Nov[ember] 1654. Anne the third daughter born 28th January 1661 and Margaret the 4th daughter born April 7th 1663 were nuns at Dunkirk among the Eight Poor Clares. Eliz[abe]th second daughter and Catharine the youngest died unmarried.

Thomas Rookwood of Coldham Hall, Stanningfield the eldest surviving son and heir of Ambrose Rookwood & Eliz[abe]th Caldwell married Tamworth d[aughte]r of Sir Roger Martin of Long Melford in Suffolk Baronet, by Tamworth d[aughte]r of

---

[545] John Gage's note: 'Extracted from Memoirs of Missionary priests 1 Vol. p. 36'.

Edward Horner Esq of Mills in the Co. of Somerset by Elizabeth his wife daughter of Sir George Reresby of Thriburg in the Co. of York Kt which Elizabeth before her marriage with Edward Horner was the wife of Sir Francis Foljambe of Aldwark, Bart. and surv[iv]ing her second husband married successively Sir William **[fol. 9v]** Monson Viscount Castlemain and Sir Adam of Felton of Playford in the Co. of Suffolk Bart.

Eliz[abe]th Reresby's brother was the loyal Governor of Hull and she herself gave a singular proof od her attachment to the Royal Cause. <It happened that> her 3d husband Sir W[illia]m Monson had been created <by King Charles> Visc[oun]t Castlemain, \by King Charles/ receiving other marks of favor from that Monarch, and he afterwards was base enough to sit in the lower house and to sign the warrant for the death of the King. <Lady Monson in her indignation> On his return home from signing the warrant it is related that his wife in her indignation tied him to a bed post and in the presence of her household stripped & Whipped him with Rods. Hudibras has this ludicrously noticed this extraordinary action.

Did not a certain Lady whip
of late her husbands own Lordship
and tho' a grandee of the house
clawed him with fundamental blows.
[fol. 10r] tied him stark naked to a bed post
and firked his hide as if she'd rid post.
And after in the Sessions Court
wher whippings praised had honour for't.

at Coldham Hall is a portrait by Sir Peter Lely of Lady Monson.[546] The sides of the picture frame represent bed posts entwined with cords & rods, and beneath the painting are the lines quoted from Hudibras.

Thomas Rookwood had issue by Tamworth Martin an only child Elizabeth the wife of John Gage, younger son of Sir William Gage 2d Bart of Hengrave Suffolk. Tho[ma]s Rookwood subsequently married Dorothy Maria Handford wife of Compton Handford Esq of Woolushill in the Co. of Worcester. by her he had no issue and dying 31st Aug[us]t 1726 left his daughter <u>Elizabeth Gage</u> the heir **[fol. 10v]** General of the house of Rookwood. her eldest son Sir Thomas Rookwood Gage 5th Bart whose second son Robert Gage Rookwood \of Coldham Hall/ In pursue of the Will of Eliz[abe]th Gage and of subsequent settlements has by Virtue of his Majesty's licence assumed the name & bears the arms of Rookwood.

John Gage
Lin[coln's] Inn
Mar[ch] 2d 1818.

---

[546] John Gage's note: 'Lord Castlemain was degraded from his honors & with Sir Henry Mildmay & Mr Wallop was drawn on a sledge with a Rope about his neck from the Tower to Tyburn & back'.

BIBLIOGRAPHY

MANUSCRIPT SOURCES

Birmingham Archdiocesan Archives
C2240: 'Memoirs of the Family of Rookwood of Stanningfield in Suffolk' by John Gage, 2 March 1818

Cambridge University Library
Add. MS 4403/27: Unknown correspondent to Edmund Bohun, 30 November 1688
Add. MS 10079: Rookwood Book of Hours
Hengrave MSS 21: Papers of John Gage the antiquary
Hengrave MSS 69: Diary of Dom Alexius Jones, 1732–43
Hengrave MSS 76: Rookwood family papers
Hengrave MSS 77: Rookwood family papers
Hengrave MSS 88: Gage family correspondence

Downside Abbey, Abbot's Archives
Benedictine mission register for Hengrave and Bury St Edmunds, 1734–51 (Hengrave Register) with the North Province Cash Book 1806–9
South Province Book R, 1717–1826 (books of accounts)
Downside Abbey MS 70: South Province Contract Book

The National Archives, Kew
C 6/470/4: Thomas Rookwood's reply to Charles Rookwood's complaint against him in the Court of Chancery, 13 March 1709
C 6/469/70: Charles Rookwood's appeal to the Lord Keeper of the Great Seal against Thomas Rookwood, 16 July 1711; Thomas Rookwood's counter-appeal against Charles Rookwood, 14 May 1712
C 11/34/25: Thomas Rookwood's reply in Chancery against the plea of Mary Beach-croft, 1720
E 134/1Geo1/Hil 7: Richard Babbage's plea in Chancery against Thomas Rookwood, 1715
E 178/4006: Act of Attainder against Ambrose Rookwood, 8 May 1606
PRO 11/614/103: Will of Thomas Rookwood, 17 March 1725
PRO 11/864/261: Will of John Martin, 24 June 1757

Private Collection, Bury St Edmunds
Jesuit mission register for Bury St Edmunds 1756–89 (Bury Register)

Suffolk Record Office, Bury St Edmunds branch
326: Documents relating to the Coldham Hall estate
449/4/19: Settlements on John and Elizabeth Gage, 1726
558/1: Recusants presented at the Bury St Edmunds quarter sessions, 1674
D8/1/3 bundle 2: Constables lists of popish non-jurors in Bury St Edmunds, 1745
E2/41/5: Correspondence of Henry Jermyn, Lord Dover with John Stafford
HD526: Papers of Edmund Farrer of Hinderclay
J552/8: Stanningfield parish registers (microfilm)

Archives of the Archbishops of Westminster
A 40/97: Alban Butler to Bishop John Hornyold, 23 December 1753

PRINTED SOURCES

Allanson, A. (ed. A. Cranmer and S. Goodwill), *Biography of the English Benedictines* (Ampleforth, 1999)
Allison, A. F. and Rogers, D. M. (eds), *Catalogue of Catholic Books in English Printed Abroad or Secretly in England 1558–1640* (Bognor Regis, 1956), 2 vols
Anon., *A Catalogue of the Whole of the Very Interesting and Historical Contents of Hengrave Hall, Bury St Edmunds* (London, 1897)
Anon., 'The Coldham Hall Estate', *The Bury and Norwich Post*, 27 March 1918
Anon., *A Complete Collection of State-Trials and Proceedings upon High Treason* (London, 1730)
Anon., 'The Condition of the Archdeaconries of Suffolk and Sudbury in the Year 1603', *PSIA* 11 (1903), pp. 2–46
Anon., 'Hengrave Hall manuscripts saved', *Cambridge University Library Readers' Newsletter* 34 (October 2006)
Anon., *Historical Manuscripts Commission, 5th Report* (London, 1876)
Anon., *The London Gazette*, 23858 (17 May 1872)
Anon., *Miscellanea V* (London, 1908), CRS 5
Anon., *Miscellanea VI: Bedingfield Papers, &c* (London, 1909), CRS 7
Anon., *Miscellanea VIII* (London, 1913), CRS 13
Anon., 'Obituary: John Gage Rokewode, Esq.', *Gentleman's Magazine* (December 1842), pp. 659–61
Anon., 'Popish Recusants in Suffolk', *EANQ* 1 (1885–86), p. 345
Anon., *A Stanningfield Century 1837–1939: A Portrait of a Suffolk Village* (Bury St Edmunds, 1997)
Anstruther, G., *The Seminary Priests: A Dictionary of the Secular Clergy of England and Wales, 1558–1850* (Ware, 1969–77), 3 vols
Ashbee, A., 'Jenkins, John' in *New Grove*, vol. 12, pp. 946–8
Ashton, J., 'Jesuit Fathers to leave Bury', *The Bury and Norwich Post*, 23 September 1927, p. 10
Asquith, C., *Shadowplay: The Hidden Beliefs and Coded Politics of William Shakespeare* (New York, 2005)
Bellenger, D. A., *English and Welsh Priests 1558–1800* (Bath, 1984)
Bernardi, J., *A Short History of the Life of Major John Bernardi* (London, 1729)
Birt, H. N., *Obit Book of the English Benedictines, 1600–1912* (Edinburgh, 1913)
Blackwood, G., *Tudor and Stuart Suffolk* (Lancaster, 2001)
Blom, F., Blom, J., Korsten, F. and Scott, G. (eds), *English Catholic Books 1701–1800:*

A Bibliography (Aldershot, 1996)

Blomefield, F., *An Essay towards a Topographical History of the County of Norfolk* (London, 1805–10), 11 vols

Boaden, J. (ed.), *Memoirs of Mrs Inchbald* (London, 1833), 2 vols

Boothman, L. and Hyde Parker, R. (eds), *Savage Fortune: An Aristocratic Family in the Early Seventeenth Century* (Woodbridge, 2006), SRS 49

Brooke, C., *A History of Gonville and Caius College* (Woodbridge, 1985)

Callow, J., *King in Exile* (Stroud, 2004)

Clancy, T. H., *English Catholic Books 1641–1700: A Bibliography* (Chicago, Illinois, 1974)

Coleman, S., 'Three Seventeenth-Century Rectors of Euston and a Verse in the Parish Register', *PSIA(H)* 37 (1992), pp. 134–43

Collinson, P., 'Barrow, Henry (c. 1550–1593)', in *ODNB* vol. 4, pp. 95–6

Collinson, P., *From Cranmer to Sancroft* (London, 2006)

Copinger, W. A., *The Manors of Suffolk* (Manchester, 1910), 7 vols

Courthope, W., *Synopsis of the Extinct Baronetage of England* (London, 1835)

Dijkgraaf, H., *The Library of a Jesuit Community at Holbeck, Nottinghamshire (1679)* (Tempe, Arizona, 2003)

Dilworth, M., 'Forbes, John (1570/71–1606)' in *ODNB*, vol. 20, pp. 294–5

Dodd, C. [Hugh Tootell], *The Church History of England* (Brussels, 1742), 4 vols

Dovey, Z., *An Elizabethan Progress: The Queen's Journey into East Anglia, 1578* (Stroud, 1996)

Durrant, C. S., *A Link between Flemish Mystics and English Martyrs* (London, 1925)

Edwards, F., *The Enigma of Gunpowder Plot, 1605: The Third Solution* (Dublin, 2008)

Errand, J., *Secret Passages and Hiding-Places* (Newton Abbot, 1974)

Estcourt, E. E. and Payne, J. O., *The English Catholic Nonjurors of 1715* (London, 1885)

Evans, N. (ed.), *The Wills of the Archdeaconry of Sudbury 1630–1635* (Woodbridge, 1987), SRS 29

Farrer, E., *Portraits in Suffolk Houses (West)* (London, 1908)

Fea, A., *Secret Chambers and Hiding-Places* (London, 1908)

Fea, A., *Rooms of Mystery and Romance* (London, 1931)

Field, C. D. S., 'Simpson, Christopher' in *New Grove*, vol. 23, pp. 408–11

Foley, H., *Records of the English Province of the Society of Jesus* (London, 1877–83), 8 vols

Fraser, A., *The Gunpowder Plot* (London, 1997)

Gage, J., *The History and Antiquities of Hengrave in Suffolk* (Bury St Edmunds, 1822)

Gage, J. (ed.), 'Pedigree and Charters of the Family of Rookwood' in *Collectanea Topographica et Genealogica*, (London, 1835), vol. 2, pp. 120–47

Gage, J., *The History and Antiquities of Suffolk: Thingoe Hundred* (London, 1838)

Gerard, J. (ed. J. Morris), *The Condition of Catholics under James I: Father Gerard's Narrative of the Gunpowder Plot* (London, 1871)

Gerard, J., *The Autobiography of an Elizabethan* (London, 1951)

Gillow, J., *A Biographical Dictionary of the English Catholics* (London, 1885–1902), 2 vols

Glickman, G., *The English Catholic Community 1688–1745: Politics, Culture and Ideology* (Woodbridge, 2009)

Green, M. A. (ed.), *Calendar of Proceedings of the Committee of Compounding,*

1643– 1660 (London, 1889–92), 5 vols

Guilday, P., *The English Catholic Refugees on the Continent 1558–1795* (London, 1914)

Gumbley, W., *Obituary Notices of the English Dominicans from 1555 to 1952* (London, 1955)

Hervey, S. H. A., *Horringer Parish Registers: Baptisms, Marriages and Burials, with Appendixes and Biographical Notes 1558 to 1850* (Woodbridge, 1900)

Hervey, S. H. A. (ed.), *Suffolk in 1674, being the Hearth Tax Returns* (Woodbridge, 1905)

Hervey, S. H. A. (ed.), *Biographical List of Boys Educated at King Edward VI Free Grammar School, Bury St Edmunds from 1550 to 1900* (Bury St Edmunds, 1908)

Hervey, W. M., *Annals of a Suffolk Village: Being Historical Notes on the Parish of Horringer* (Cambridge, 1930)

Hodgetts, M., 'A Topographical Index of Hiding Places', *Recusant History* 16 (1982), pp. 146–216

Holt, G., *St. Omers and Bruges Colleges, 1593–1773: A Biographical Dictionary* (London, 1979), CRS 69

Holt, G., *The English Jesuits 1650–1829: A Biographical Dictionary* (London, 1984), CRS 70

Hopkins, P., 'Rookwood, Ambrose' in *ODNB* vol. 47, pp. 700–1

Hunter, T., *An English Carmelite. The Life of Catharine Burton* (London, 1876)

Inchbald, E. (ed. B. P. Robertson), *The Diaries of Elizabeth Inchbald* (London, 2007)

Jourdan, E. G. (ed.), *Abstracts of Charles County Maryland Court and Land Records* (Westminster, Maryland, 1994), 2 vols

Jourdan, E. G., *Early Families of Southern Maryland* (Westminster, Maryland, 2007), 10 vols

Kenny, A. (ed.), *The Responsa Scholarum of the English College, Rome: Part I, 1598–1621* (London, 1962), CRS 54

Kenny, A. (ed.), *The Responsa Scholarum of the English College, Rome: Part II, 1622–1685* (London, 1963), CRS 55

Krook, D., *John Sergeant and his Circle: A Study of Three Seventeenth-Century Aristotelians* (Leiden, 1993)

Lemon, R., *Treason by Words: Literature, Law and Rebellion in Shakespeare's England* (Ithaca, NY, 2006)

Lord, E., *The Stuarts' Secret Army* (Harlow, 2004)

Luttrell, N., *A Brief Historical Relation of State Affairs from September 1678 to April 1714* (Oxford, 1857), 6 vols

Marshall, P. and Scott, G. (eds), *Catholic Gentry in English Society: The Throckmortons of Coughton from Reformation to Emancipation* (Farnham, 2009)

Morison, S., *English Prayer Books: An Introduction to the Literature of Christian Public Worship*, 4th edn (Cambridge, 2009)

Murrell, P. E., 'Bury St. Edmunds and the Campaign to Pack Parliament, 1687–8', *Bulletin of the Institute of Historical Research* 54 (1981), pp. 188–206

Newman, H. W., *The Flowering of the Maryland Palatinate* (Washington DC, 1961)

Nicholls, M., 'Rookwood, Ambrose' in *ODNB*, vol. 47, pp. 699–700

Payne, J. O., *Records of the English Catholics of 1715: Compiled Wholly from Original Documents* (London, 1889)

Pickford, J., 'The Rookwood Family of Coldham Hall, Suffolk', *Notes and Queries* 206 (1889), pp. 442–3

Pickford, J., 'Ambrose Rookwood', *Notes and Queries* 267 (1903), pp. 115–16

Questier, M., 'Conformity, Catholicism and the Law' in P. Lake and M. Questier (eds), *Conformity and Orthodoxy in the English Church, c. 1560–1660* (Woodbridge, 2000), pp. 237–61

Rookwood, A., *A True Copy of the Paper Delivered By Brigadier Rookwood, to the Sheriff at Tyburn, the Place of Execution* (London, 1696)

Rookwood, A., *A True Copy of the Paper delivered by Brigadier Rookwood, to the Sheriffs of London and Middlesex, at Tyburn, the Place of Execution, April 29 1696. With Reflections thereupon* (London, 1696)

Rookwood, A., *True Copies of the Papers which Brigadier Rookwood, and Major Lowick, delivered to the Sheriffs of London and Middlesex, at Tyburn, April 29. 1696* (London, 1696)

Rowe, J., 'Suffolk Sectaries and Papists, 1596–1616' in E. S. Leedham-Green (ed.), *Religious Dissent in East Anglia* (Cambridge, 1991), pp. 37–41

Rowe, J., 'The 1767 Census of Papists in the Diocese of Norwich: The Social Composition of the Roman Catholic Community' in D. Chadd (ed.), *Religious Dissent in East Anglia* III (Norwich, 1996), pp. 188–9

Rowe, J., '"The lopped tree": The Re-formation of the Suffolk Catholic Community' in N. Tyacke (ed.), *England's Long Reformation 1500–1800* (Abingdon, 1998), pp. 167–94

Rowe, J., 'Drury Family' in *ODNB* vol. 7, pp. 997–9

Rowse, A. L., *The England of Elizabeth: The Structure of Society* (London, 1950)

Ryan, G. H. and Redstone, L. J., *Timperley of Hintlesham: A Study of a Suffolk Family* (London, 1931)

F. H. S., 'Henry Barrow and Ambrose Rookwood, Conspirators in the Gunpowder Plot', *EANQ* 11 (1906), pp. 145–6

Sánchez Cano, A., 'Entertainment in Madrid for the Prince of Wales: Political Functions of Festivals' in A. Samson (ed.), *The Spanish Match* (Aldershot, 2006), pp. 51–74

Sanderius, A., *Flandria Illustrata* (Hague, 1732), 3 vols

Scarisbrick, E., *The Holy Life of Lady Warner* (London, 1691)

Scott, G., *Gothic Rage Undone: English Monks in the Age of Enlightenment* (Bath, 1992)

Sigl, P., 'The Elizabeth Inchbald Papers', *Notes and Queries* 29 (1982), pp. 220–4

Skinner, V. L., *Abstracts of the Testamentary Proceedings of the Prerogative Court of Maryland* (Baltimore, Maryland, 2006), 6 vols

Spraggon, J., *Puritan Iconoclasm during the English Civil War* (Woodbridge, 2003)

Squiers, G., *Secret Hiding-Places* (London, 1933)

Tesimond, O., (ed. F. Edwards), *The Gunpowder Plot: The Narrative of Oswald Tesimond alias Greenway* (London, 1973)

Thomas, H., 'The Society of Jesus in Wales, c. 1600–1679: Rediscovering the Cwm Jesuit Library at Hereford Cathedral', *Journal of Jesuit Studies* 1 (2014), pp. 572–88

Tomko, M., *British Romanticism and the Catholic Question: Religion, History and National Identity, 1778–1829* (Basingstoke, 2011)

Trappes Lomax, R. (ed.), *Franciscana* (Exeter, 1923), CRS 24

Tymms, S., 'Coldham Hall in Stanningfield', *PSIA* 3 (1863), pp. 299–310

Venn, J., *Biographical History of Gonville and Caius College 1349–1897* (Cambridge, 1897)

Venn, J., *Alumni Cantabrigienses* (Cambridge, 1924)

Whiteman, A. and Clapinson, A. (eds), *The Compton Census of 1676: A Critical*

Edition (London, 1986)

Wodderspoon, J., *Historic Sites, and Other Remarkable and Interesting Places in the County of Suffolk* (London, 1839)

Worrall, E. S. (ed.), *Returns of Papists Volume 2: Dioceses of England and Wales, except Chester* (London, 1989)

Young, F., '"An Horrid Popish Plot": The Failure of Catholic Aspirations in Bury St. Edmunds, 1685–88', *PSIA(H)* 41 (2006), pp. 209–55

Young, F., 'The Shorts of Bury St. Edmunds: Medicine, Catholicism and Politics in the Seventeenth Century', *Journal of Medical Biography* 16 (2008), pp. 188–94

Young, F., 'The Tasburghs of Bodney: Catholicism and Politics in South Norfolk', *Norfolk Archaeology* 46 (2011), pp. 190–8

Young, F., *English Catholics and the Supernatural, 1553–1829* (Farnham, 2013a)

Young, F., 'Elizabeth Inchbald's "Catholic Novel" and its Local Background', *Recusant History* 31 (2013b), pp. 573–92

Young, F., 'The Bishop's Palace at Ely as a Prison for Recusants, 1577–1597', *Recusant History* 32 (2014), pp. 197–220

Young, F., *The Gages of Hengrave and Suffolk Catholicism, 1640–1767* (London, 2015)

WEB RESOURCE

'Who were the Nuns? A Prosopographical Study of the English Convents in Exile 1600–1800', http://wwtn.history.qmul.ac.uk (accessed 10 July 2014)

INDEX OF PEOPLE AND PLACES*

* Authors whose names appear in Documents 30 and 32 are not listed in the index unless they are mentioned in the Introduction.

INDEX OF SUBJECTS

JOHN BLATCHLY, MBE, MA, PhD, Hon Litt D, FSA

The Suffolk Records Society records with deep sorrow the death on 3rd September 2015 of Dr John Blatchly, a member of the Society's Council for nearly forty years and its Chairman from 1988 to 2013, a quarter century which, under his guidance, saw the publication of thirty-five annual volumes. He also edited two of his own volumes for the Society and acted as general editor for two others, the second of which was published earlier in 2015.

Under John Blatchly the Society was fortunate to enjoy for many years the guidance of a scholar of great range and diligence who also brought determined leadership gently applied, unflagging energy and the gift of encouragement to all those around him.

A full tribute by Diarmaid MacCulloch to Dr Blatchly, on his resignation as Chairman, appeared in Volume 58.

THE SUFFOLK RECORDS SOCIETY

For nearly sixty years, the Suffolk Records Society has added to the knowledge of Suffolk's history by issuing an annual volume of previously unpublished manuscripts, each throwing light on some new aspect of the history of the county.

Covering 700 years and embracing letters, diaries, maps, accounts and other archives, many of them previously little known or neglected, these books have together made a major contribution to historical studies.

At the heart of this achievement lie the society's members, all of whom share a passion for Suffolk and its history and whose support, subscriptions and donations make possible the opening up of the landscape of historical research in the area.

In exchange for this tangible support, members receive a new volume each year at a considerable saving on the retail price at which the books are then offered for sale.

Members are also welcomed to the launch of the new volume, held each year in a different and appropriate setting within the county and giving them a chance to meet and listen to some of the leading historians in their fields talking about their latest work.

For anyone with a love of history, a desire to build a library on Suffolk themes at modest cost and a wish to see historical research continue to thrive and bring new sources to the public eye in decades to come, a subscription to the Suffolk Records Society is the ideal way to make a contribution and join the company of those who give Suffolk history a future.

THE CHARTERS SERIES

To supplement the annual volumes and serve the need of medieval historians, the Charters Series was launched in 1979 with the challenge of publishing the transcribed texts of all the surviving monastic charters for the county. Since that date, nineteen volumes have been published as an occasional series, the latest in 2011.

The Charter Series is financed by a separate annual subscription leading to receipt of each volume on publication.

CURRENT PROJECTS

Volumes approved by the Council of the Society for future publication include *William Morris and the Restoration of Blythburgh Church*, edited by Alan Mackley, *The Diary of John Clopton, 1648–50*, edited by John Pelling, *Crown Pleas of the Suffolk Eyre of 1240*, edited by Eric Gallagher, *Household Inventories of Helmingham Hall: 1597, 1626 and 1707/8*, edited by Moira Coleman, and *The Woodbridge Troop of the Suffolk Yeomanry, 1794–1818*, edited by Margaret Thomas; and in the Charters Series, *The Charters of the Priory of St Peter and St Paul, Ipswich*, edited by David Allen, *Bury St Edmunds Town Charters*, edited by Vivien Brown, and *Rumburgh Priory Charters*, edited by Nicholas Karn. The order in which these and other volumes appear in print will depend on the dates of completion of editorial work.

MEMBERSHIP

Membership enquiries should be addressed to Mrs Tanya Christian, 8 Orchid Way, Needham Market, IP6 8JQ; e-mail: membership@suffolkrecordssociety.com.

The Suffolk Records Society is a registered charity, No. 1084279.